Economic Growth and Structure in the Republic of Korea

A Publication of the Economic Growth Center, Yale University

ECONOMIC GROWTH AND STRUCTURE IN THE REPUBLIC OF KOREA

PAUL W. KUZNETS

New Haven and London, Yale University Press, 1977

Designed by Sally Sullivan
and set in Times Roman type.
Printed in the United States of America by
The Alpine Press, Inc., South Braintree, Massachusetts.

Published in Great Britain, Europe, Africa, and
Asia by Yale University Press, Ltd., London.
Distributed in Latin America by Kaiman & Polon,
Inc., New York City; in Australia and New
Zealand by Book & Film Services, Artarmon,
N.S.W., Australia; and in Japan by Harper & Row,
Publishers, Tokyo Office.

Library of Congress Cataloging in Publication Data

Kuznets, Paul W
    Economic growth and structure in the Republic of Korea.

    (A Publication of the Economic Growth Center, Yale
University)
    Bibliography: p.
    Includes index.
    1. Korea—Economic conditions—1945–   2. Korea—
Economic policy. I. Title. II. Series: Yale University.
Economic Growth Center. Publications.
HC467.K87   330.9'519'5043   76-45407
ISBN 0-300-02019-8

Contents

Tables and Charts

CHART

Foreword

This volume is one in a series of studies supported by the Economic Growth Center, an activity of the Yale Department of Economics since 1961. The Center is a research organization with worldwide activities and interests. Its research interests are defined in terms of both method of approach and subject matter. In terms of method, the Center sponsors studies which are designed to test significant general hypotheses concerning the problem of economic growth and which draw on quantitative information from national economic accounts and other sources. In terms of subject matter, the Center's research interests include theoretical analysis of economic structure and growth, quantitative analysis of a national economy as an integral whole, comparative cross-sectional studies using data from a number of countries, and efforts to improve the techniques of national economic measurement. The research program includes field investigation of recent economic growth in twenty-five developing countries of Asia, Africa, and Latin America.

The Center administers, jointly with the Department of Economics, the Yale training program in International and Foreign Economic Administration. It presents a regular series of seminar and workshop meetings and includes among its publications both book-length studies and journal reprints by staff members, the latter circulated as Center Papers.

Hugh Patrick, Director

Preface

The purpose of this study is to describe and explain the economic structure and development of Korea (the Republic of Korea, or South Korea) from 1953 to the present. There is of course another Korea (the Democratic People's Republic of Korea, or North Korea), but it has been a separate political and economic entity since 1945. Very little information is available on the North Korean economy and the subject deserves treatment in its own right, so this work is limited to South Korea, referred to hereafter simply as "Korea."

The current boundaries of Korea were established in 1945 upon liberation from the Japanese, but the country was too unstable during the period of American military government (1945–48), the government too inexperienced during the first years of the republic (1948–50), and the situation too chaotic during the Korean War (1950–53) for gathering data of a scope and quality that would allow comparison with the data available for later years. Also, although reliable information exists for much of the colonial period (1910–45), economic relationships in the southern part of a unified Korea that was itself a component of the Japanese Yen Bloc differed fundamentally from those characteristic of Korea since independence. For these reasons, comparison of the economic situation after the Korean War with that of earlier eras is either impossible or misleading. Discussion is therefore confined to the period beginning in 1953, mainly the years 1953–72.

A 20-year span is relatively short compared to periods of similar homogeneity in other countries, particularly for establishing economic trends, yet a basic change that revolutionized Korea's economic outlook is discernible within this brief period. Growth from 1953 through 1960–62 was unimpressive. There was virtually no increase in per capita income and little in Korea's economic performance to distinguish it from that of other so-called developing (sometimes a euphemism for stagnating) countries. After 1960–62, however, the pace of growth accelerated so that gross domestic product per capita almost doubled by 1970–72 and Korea had achieved one of the world's highest growth rates.

Factors responsible for this acceleration in the pace of growth are of intrinsic importance and are emphasized in the analysis. To the extent that they are policy determined rather than autonomous, such factors may also be of interest in evaluating the economic policies of other less economically developed countries. Nevertheless, the study focuses mainly on economic relationships rather than policy issues and on the characteristics of Korea's accelerated growth rather than on lessons to be learned by other countries from the Korean experience.

The description and analysis are primarily quantitative. Interest lies not only in the fact that manufacturing output grew rapidly from 1960–62 to 1970–72, for instance, but also in answering such questions as: What were the actual growth rates for each of the major manufacturing-industry groups? Why have some industry groups grown more rapidly than others? How have capital intensity, labor intensity, and establishment size changed as output expanded? In what sense has the structure of manufacturing in Korea been typical or "normal" for a country of its size and degree of industrialization? Impressionistic statements that "the structure of Korean manufacturing has been unintegrated" or that "manufacturing has been dominated by output for export" are not nearly so informative as evidence that manufacturing production has been increasingly concentrated in more labor-intensive industries, that manufactures have accounted for a growing share of rapidly expanding exports or, viewed differently, that the fastest growing industry groups have been those producing primarily for export markets.

Many quantitative questions cannot be answered satisfactorily in less economically developed countries, because the necessary data are either not available or too unreliable. This is less of a problem in Korea than might be expected, for the breadth of the statistics is unusually ample and the quality surprisingly good for such a poor country. Good data may, in fact, have been an important ingredient of Korea's rapid growth in recent years because economic policies based on accurate information were more likely to prove effective than those based on ignorance.

However, statistics are not necessarily reliable, consistent, or unbiased, even in the most economically advanced countries with the best statistical information. Nor are they always in a form that is useful for analysis. This is why accuracy is sometimes at issue in the discussion, and why derived measures are often employed. Where possible, problems of accuracy are evaluated, the derivation of measures is explained, and the sources of the data are listed. This should allow the reader to duplicate any measure shown here and to reach his or her own conclusion as to how much analytical weight the data will bear.

Decisions had to be made early in the study on what was to be covered and how to do it. The choice of topics was determined by what seemed to be important and, within broad headings, by the author's own interests. The table of contents provides a guide to the choices made; it may surprise the reader who fails to find a chapter on international trade. There is not a separate chapter on trade, though trade has been significant in Korea's growth, because the topic is covered in practically every chapter where the effects of trade on growth and structure, agriculture, industry, and other subjects— or their effects on trade—are discussed.

The problems of how to treat particular topics were mainly what questions to ask, how to evaluate results, and how to present con- clusions. There is as yet no generally accepted theory of economic development that might serve as a guide to what to ask, but many of the questions posed have received attention in the recent literature on development. For example, Was output growth during the 1960s sufficient to absorb any excess labor supply? Have the benefits of rapid growth been obtained at the cost of increased income inequality? To what extent was domestic saving limited by foreign capital inflows?

Some of these questions reveal the need to compare the situation in Korea with situations elsewhere. Domestic saving was equivalent to 8 percent of GNP in 1963–65, for instance, but this is significant only because such a saving ratio was very low by international standards. Results for Korea are frequently evaluated by comparing them with data on Taiwan, Japan, or the United States. Cross-section surveys, based on samples that included Korea, have been used to estimate the relationships between foreign assistance and growth rates, stage of development and the composition of the money supply, and other economic variables. These are also used here. In each case, irregularity is of particular interest. How does Korean experience differ from that of other countries, if at all? If it differs, what are the reasons?

A survey of Korean history from 1876 to 1953 is given in the first chapter, with special emphasis on economic developments and political or diplomatic events with significant economic consequences. Those familiar with the historic background are advised to begin with chapter 2, Accelerated Growth and Structural Change, in which the main characteristics of economic development since 1953 are outlined in terms of growth rates, sectoral shares, and the major national-accounting aggregates. Causes and consequences of accelerated growth after 1960–62 are examined in chapter 3. The labor-absorption problem, the contribution of agriculture, the rapid growth of manufacturing, money, prices, and monetary policy, and Korea's first three five-year plans are discussed in subsequent chapters.

The goal throughout has been to present the argument in as straightforward a manner as possible. Economic terms are usually defined when first introduced, the methodology used is quite simple, and the more technical points of interest mainly to economists are confined to footnotes. The McCune–Reischauer system of spelling Korean words has been used except for proper names. These are spelled in English as their owners have spelled them.

A version of chapter 2 originally was presented at a conference on population and development in Korea, sponsored by the Joint Committee on Korean Studies of the Social Science Research Council and the American Council of Learned Societies, and the Population and Development Studies Center of Seoul National University, held in Seoul, Korea, on January 7–8, 1975.

I am most grateful for the support and assistance provided by a number of institutions during the course of this study, particularly Yale University's Economic Growth Center, whose support made this work possible. The Bank of Korea and Indiana University have been most generous in rendering assistance. I would also like to thank the University of Washington's Russian and Far Eastern Institute, the Harvard–Yenching Institute, and Harvard's Institute for International Development for providing summer working quarters in recent years.

It is impossible to thank properly all those people who have helped me in my work, especially the many members of the Bank of Korea and its Research Departments who were unstinting in their assistance. I would like, however, to single out Hong Wan Mo, Paik Myung Won, Lee Sang Ho, Kim Dong Soo, Park Chung Jae, Park Sawng Sang, Park Kyung Soon, and Kim Kun for special thanks. My research assistants, Choi Mun Kyu, Lee Seung Yoon, and Lee Tai Young also deserve particular mention. In addition, the study has benefited from discussion and from comments made on earlier drafts. I owe much to Irma Adelman, Frank P. Baldwin, Jr., David C. Cole, John C. H. Fei, Charles R. Frank, Jr., Roger D. Norton, James Palais, Gustav Ranis, an anonymous referee, and, above all, my father—Simon Kuznets—for their valuable contributions. None of the institutions or individuals named here, however, are in any way responsible for the errors to be found or for the opinions expressed in this study.

1

Historical Background

Korea, opened to the modern world by the signing of the Kanghwa Treaty with the Japanese in 1876, had been the "hermit kingdom," a small, reclusive country in the Far East about which relatively little was known. It had a long history marked by periods of major intellectual and cultural achievement, and a sense of national identity fostered by a common language and ethnic homogeneity as well as by historic unity. Though more unified than many of today's newer nations, Korea was unprepared when thrust into the world by outside events, chief among which were the imperial aspirations of Western countries and their recently aroused interest in the Far East, and the Meiji restoration in Japan.

The extent of Korea's backwardness as late as the third quarter of the nineteenth century, or the period immediately before the opening of the country to the West, is documented in letters of French missionaries to Charles Dallet and in the work of Homer B. Hulbert, one of the first American missionaries to Korea (he stayed there from 1886 to 1907).[1]

Both Dallet's missionaries and Hulbert describe a highly centralized form of government during the period just prior to the opening of Korea that became less viable as a series of weak kings and regents allowed power to slip away from the center. Civil and military administration was in the hands of the *yangban*, or nobles (similar to Chinese mandarins), who were divided into four hereditary factions devoted mainly to one another's downfall. In these struggles the palace eunuchs, because they had the king's ear and could intrigue with the royal concubines, formed another locus of power. Offices

---

1. See Dallet, *Traditional Korea,* and Hulbert, *The Passing of Korea.*

1

were sold, "tax farming" was widespread, and although there was in theory a chance for advancement through merit among those who passed a set of public examinations patterned on those of the Chinese, higher offices were held only by nobles, and the highest office—that of prime minister—only by a noble sufficiently wealthy to bribe successfully the palace eunuchs and royal concubines. The system inevitably tended to reduce the king's ability to cope with the problems of his people.

The government followed an exclusionary policy that had adverse effects on the economic situation. Communication was poor partly because Korea is a mountainous country with few navigable streams. The art of road building was undeveloped, and coastwise vessels were unfit for ocean voyages. In fact, the government prohibited sea trade and refused to let foreigners or Koreans pass closely guarded borders; as a result, there was no commerce with foreign countries. The Catholic missionaries were particularly interested in finding ways to enter Korea and to conceal themselves once there. Their difficulties, outlined by Dallet, show that the government's isolation policy was rigorously pursued. Internal commerce was also discouraged by the government and limited by an inadequate monetary system. The only legal tender was a coin of small denomination produced by private foundries on order of the king. There was no gold or silver coinage; the coins were often debased by those who obtained minting privileges; low denominations made transport a real problem. The inadequacies of the system are also indicated by the prevalence of barter, especially in the northern provinces.

Industrial and commercial development were virtually nonexistent. Since everyday necessities were manufactured in the home, there was little specialization and there were no factory operations. When the services of specialized craftsmen (specialized in that they used special tools and served an apprenticeship) were needed, these craftsmen came to the house, for they had no workshops. Even potters and ironsmiths who needed special materials or heavy equipment did not locate permanently but moved from place to place as their raw material supply began to dwindle. During the early Yi dynasty (1392–1910) a number of specialized craftsmen had worked for the court and, in subsequent years, metropolitan merchants lent funds to local craftsmen in a form of wage-labor or putting-out system. These arrangements may be regarded as constituting the origins of an incipient manufacturing stage if not the beginning of a modern factory economy.[2] The principal trading activity took place at fairs, and what business was not conducted at fairs was handled by peddlers. There were few stores.

The political weakness and economic backwardness of Yi dynasty Korea described here are characteristic of an isolated country. With the opening of Japan, a quick end to the isolation that Korea shared with Japan was inevitable. So was the transformation of political and economic institutions in response to foreign influence. This transformation, a precondition to later economic development, was aided by Korea's long history as a single country and by an unusually high degree of ethnic, linguistic, and cultural homogeneity. Unity ended in 1945 with partition of the peninsula into North and South, but subsequent development in each region has undoubtedly been fostered by the Koreans' homogeneous language, culture, and historic background.

Korea's modern history has been a history of tragedy. From the opening of Korea in 1876 to annexation by Japan and loss of identity in 1910, the story is essentially one of Byzantine intrigue among competing domestic factions while the country's fate was being determined by a struggle for power among China, Japan, and Russia. In such company Korea was truly "a shrimp among whales," as a Korean proverb expresses it, and one can understand her earlier policy of isolation. From 1910 until 1945, Korea was part of the Japanese Empire. This was a period in which the economic and other benefits of Japanese rule have to be weighed against the oppression and exploitation that characterize colonial status. When Japan was defeated in World War II, Korea, like Germany, emerged as a divided country, victim of the new cold war. The North became a pawn of Soviet power, the South of American power. The South was run by an American military government from 1945 to 1948, when the first national elections were held and an independent Korean government, the Republic of Korea, was established. The Korean War began in June 1950, less than two years later. Battles raged up and down most of the peninsula until the front stabilized around the 38th parallel in 1951 and a truce was signed in July 1953.

Subsequent chapters of this book are concerned with various aspects of economic structure and development in the Republic of

2. Choi Hochin, "The Process of Industrial Modernization in Korea: The Latter Part of the Chosen Dynasty Through 1960's," pp. 1–4.

Korea during the era after the Korean War (1950–53). This period was chosen primarily because sufficient, continuous statistical series are available for analysis of the major, quantitative economic relationships. It is also a period unified by reconstruction and development, uninterrupted by war or other national catastrophes.

THE OPENING OF KOREA (1876–1910)[3]

Beginning in the eleventh century, Korea was subjected to a series of invasions by Manchurians, Mongols, and the Japanese. Mongols under Ghengis Khan swept over the country in the thirteenth century. The Wāko (Japanese marauders) raided the coastline in the fourteenth and fifteenth centuries. A series of attacks by the Japanese under Hideyoshi devastated the country at the end of the sixteenth century. After the Manchus had overthrown the Ming dynasty in China, they attacked and conquered Korea in the early seventeenth century. These invasions confirmed Korea's weakness and led the government to close frontiers and withdraw as much as possible from contact with other countries. The Japanese were allowed to maintain a trading post near Pusan, and scholars and tribute were sent to Peking and Japan during the Tokugawa period, but any attempts to violate Korea's seclusion policy or to introduce foreign (and potentially dangerous) ideas were forcibly put down. Korea had become the "hermit kingdom."

French priests who tried to enter the country were executed and many Christian converts were massacred. An American ship, the *General Sherman*, was burned and her crew killed near P'yŏngyang in 1866. An American fleet sent in 1871 to obtain a treaty with Korea failed after a battle with the Korean fort at the mouth of the Han River. The Japanese sent a gunboat to the same place in 1875; when it was fired upon by the Koreans, Japan dispatched a fleet. Under pressure from this fleet, a treaty of commerce with Japan was signed in February 1876. Korea, though formerly a vassal of China, was recognized as an independent nation. Similar treaties were signed with

---

3. The discussion here is necessarily brief. Readers interested in more detail, especially about social and economic as well as political conditions, are referred to Takashi Hatada's *A History of Korea*. A description of political relations is given in C. I. Eugene Kim and Han Kyo Kim, *Korea and the Politics of Imperialism, 1876–1910*. Other, more recent works that focus on early periods are Sohn Pow-key, Kim Chul-choon, and Hong Yi-sup's *The History of Korea*, Han Woo-keun's *The History of Korea*, and William E. Henthorn's *A History of Korea*.

the United States, England, and Germany in the 1880s. Korea was no longer the hermit kingdom.

The primary relation between Korea and the outside world had for many centuries been with China. Korea's role was that of a dependent country (*Shu-pang*), very much like the Confucian relationship of a younger to an older brother in which the younger owes allegiance to the older in return for his protection.[4] Chinese dominance continued until 1894, when the Tonghak (or "Eastern learning") Rebellion broke out. This was a movement led by disaffected nobles and Confucianists who wished to drive out foreigners, particularly the Japanese. It became a major force when its leaders assumed command of a peasant rebellion and threatened King Kojong. He called for assistance from China, but when the Chinese sent troops the Japanese took the opportunity to send troops too. Although the king's forces put down the rebellion, neither the Chinese nor the Japanese would leave first. The stalemate was broken when the Japanese seized the palace, reinstalled the king's father (the regent, or Taewŏn'gun) and sank the *Kowshing*, a British steamer bringing Chinese reinforcements. Then came the Sino-Japanese War, which ended in disaster for the Chinese and terminated Korea's Shu-pang relationship with China.

The Japanese moved to reform the Korean government, reduce royal power, and install ministers favorable to their interests even before the Treaty of Shimonoseki (which ended the war with China) was signed in 1895. The Japanese also required the Koreans to cut off their topknots, wear their hair in Western fashion, and modify their dress. When the king, a virtual palace prisoner, escaped to the Russian legation early in 1896, the Japanese lost control to the Russians, who then received major concessions and took over training of the Korean Army. Russia had now replaced China as Japan's chief enemy in Korea.

After 1896, there was a race by the Western powers and Japan for concessions and privileges in the Far East, including Korea. Rivalry was especially strong between the Russians and the Japanese, but the two powers agreed to recognize each other's interests and Korea's sovereignty in the Nishi–Rosen agreement of 1898. Korea was to enjoy independence for the next six years, but these were hardly halcyon days in Korean history. The government became more conservative after the king's progressive advisers were removed in

4. See M. Frederick Nelson, *Korea and the Old Orders in Eastern Asia*, pp. 203–20.

1896, and Confucian patterns of administration were revived. Absolute power prevailed, and the court of the time was described by Horace Allen as a "corrupt cabal."[5]

Both the Japanese and the Russians were attempting to extend their economic and political interests; the Japanese by establishing offices of the Bank of Japan in Chemulpo (Inch'ŏn) and Seoul and by buying up land in strategic port areas, the Russians by securing whaling concessions and building forts to protect lumber concessions in the Yalu River valley. An Anglo–Japanese alliance signed in 1902 was countered by the extension of the Franco–Russian dual alliance of 1895 to cover the Far East as well as the other, formerly designated areas. The two alliances were signs of increasing tension in both Korea and Manchuria (Russia regarded the latter much as Japan viewed Korea) that increased to the breaking point when direct negotiation between the two powers broke down. In early February 1904, Japan severed relations; Russian ships were attacked in Port Arthur and Chemulp'o, and war was formally declared a few days later.

The Japanese attempted to control Korea even before declaring war on Russia by capturing Seoul and surrounding the palace. A protocol was signed in which Korea agreed to adopt Japanese advice on government improvement and make no treaties contrary to the principles of the protocol. In return, Korea's independence and territorial integrity were guaranteed by Japan. The protocol was followed in subsequent months by decrees in which the absolute power of the emperor was renounced, Japanese advisers with veto power were appointed to the Finance and Foreign Affairs departments, Japanese took over police functions, Korean legations abroad were recalled, and indemnity was required for every Japanese killed by Koreans in the previous decade.

After Japan's victory over Russia, the United States and Great Britain as well as Japan and Russia signed a treaty in September 1905 (the Treaty of Portsmouth), which recognized Japan's paramount political, military, and economic interests in Korea. Once the treaty was signed, Japan sought to obtain complete supervision over Korean affairs, especially foreign affairs.

By asserting direct control, the Japanese ended Korean independence. Their next move was to rid Korea of an international identity.

5. Ibid., p. 241.

Marquis Itō (Itō Hirobumi), who became the first Resident General of Korea in 1906, supervised the transfer of power to Japan. The Korean emperor had never signed the treaty validating Japanese control and remained a potential focus for opposition. He managed, in fact, to send a delegation to the Hague Peace Conference in 1907 to protest the failure to invite Korea to the conference and also to protest Japanese violation of Korean sovereignty. The delegation failed to obtain the invitation from the Dutch government needed to attend the conference and was denied a hearing. The Japanese retaliated by calling upon the emperor to abdicate. Under heavy pressure, the emperor abdicated in favor of his son, the feebleminded crown prince. The Japanese then strengthened their position by dropping departmental advisers and taking over the actual functions of government.

During the following years, Japanese repression led to anti-Japanese riots, the beginnings of Korean insurgency, and the increase in police forces and gendarmerie needed to preserve order.[6] In 1909 Itō was assassinated in Harbin and General Terauchi (Terauchi Masatake), a member of the military faction in Japan's governing circles, was appointed Resident General. He is reputed to have felt that Korea must be absorbed or decimated. Shortly after he arrived in Seoul, the native police were placed under his charge, the Korean emperor renounced his sovereignty, and a treaty of annexation was signed on August 22, 1910. This move, virtually a foregone conclusion after Japan eliminated independence in 1905, marked the end of Korea's national identity until 1945, when a fragmented country emerged after the Japanese defeat in World War II.

A basic question raised by the history of this period is What motivated the Japanese to conquer Korea? One possible answer is that reactionary elements in Japan saw Korea as a "dagger pointed at the heart of Japan" and wished to conquer it for strategic reasons. A second possibility, which has received fairly wide support among Japanese historians, is that economic factors predominated; it was a

6. There are two views of the situation during this period: one, that the Japanese acted with skill and moderation in dealing with mutinous Koreans; two, that Koreans had ample cause to rebel against injustice and oppression. See Hilary Conroy, *The Japanese Seizure of Korea,* pp. 344–47; Hulbert, *The Passing of Korea,* pp. 208–20; and Andrew J. Grajdanzev, *Modern Korea,* pp. 34–46. Disagreement is essentially between those impressed with the Japanese role of bringing civilization and reform to Korea, and those concerned with the helplessness of a relatively backward people at the mercy of the Japanese.

search for markets, the need to protect commercial interests, and the desire to develop Korea as a colony in the best imperialist tradition that led to Japan's conquest of the country.[7] The question of motivation, though interesting, has yet to be answered satisfactorily nor is it likely that a definitive answer is forthcoming.

THE COLONIAL PERIOD (1910–1945)

The period before 1910 may be regarded as the transitional stage from a closed economy to development as a colony. Even before 1910 there was evidence of Japanese economic penetration and the beginnings of an economic infrastructure with the establishment of a banking system, railroads, and the Oriental Development Company, this last to be the chief instrument of agricultural reform. Development during the colonial period can perhaps be best understood by viewing Korea's role in the Japanese Empire as determined by the requirements of Japan herself. If this is done, the period can be divided into subperiods, each marked by different and internally consistent policies. The first subperiod covers the years 1910 to the end of World War I or perhaps to 1920—years characterized by emphasis on agricultural development, firm establishment of internal security in Korea after an independence

---

7. Conroy examined this last possibility in some detail and found it unconvincing (*The Japanese Seizure of Korea,* pp. 442–91). He shows that Japanese trade with Korea was unimportant in Japan's total trade and that Japanese ventures there—primarily rail interests and the Oriental Development Company, an agricultural land development enterprise—were not particularly successful prior to annexation. Though the Oriental Development Company tried to attract Japanese farmers, there was little emigration from Japan to Korea. It has been observed that "Japanese do not like to leave home, and they do not like to settle in countries where the climate is cold and harsh, or where the resident population has a standard of living lower than their own" (E. B. Schumpeter, ed., *The Industrialization of Japan and Manchukuo, 1930–1940,* p. 66). In fact, the Japanese comprised less than 3 percent of the total population of Korea even by the late 1930s, and most of them were employed in government service, commerce, and industry. The limited settlement of Japanese in Korea indicates that one possible argument for territorial aggrandizement—more living space was needed by the inhabitants of a densely populated country such as Japan—was disproved by later developments. It does not necessarily follow, however, that the desire for more living space was not among the reasons that lay behind Japan's desire to conquer Korea. Similarly, low levels of trade and the limited success of emergent capitalist (i.e., large-scale industrial and financial) interests in Korea before 1910 do not mean that Japanese entrepreneurs did not hope to benefit from an expanded empire or the type of business created by military adventures. What is at issue here is motivation, not achievement. Limited achievement indicates only that particular reasons for conquest proved wrong, not that they were nonexistent. Conroy has shown that Japan had limited economic success in Korea before 1910; he has failed to demonstrate, however, that economic factors were insignificant in Japan's desire to annex Korea.

movement was crushed in 1919, and rapid industrial growth in Japan. Japan's manufacturers thrived on war-induced demand, and development had reached the point where labor rather than capital was becoming the scarce factor. Partly for this reason, and partly because of Korean opposition, the Corporation Law, designed to limit non-agricultural investment in Korea that might compete with Japanese industry, was abolished in 1920. From this point to the early 1930s, there was a second phase, marked by the growth of consumer goods industries, particularly food and textiles, in response to a rapidly expanding consumer market in Korea. Cheap labor and cheap raw materials were also a source of attraction to industry during these years. With the Great Depression, the subsequent boycott of Japanese goods, and the increasing emphasis on autarky in such circumstances, a third stage can be discerned during the 1930s. This was a decade marked by the Manchurian incident in late 1931, growing government intervention in economic affairs, and preparations for war. Because Korea was strategically located between Japan and Manchuria and possessed abundant minerals and cheap electric power, colonial policies shifted toward the creation of heavy industry. Korea entered a fourth subperiod during World War II, especially from 1942 on. This was a time of economic disruption for which relatively little information is available.

The major economic and institutional changes that occurred in Korea during the colonial period can be evaluated by examining the growth and pattern of trade; size, composition, and tenure arrangements in agriculture; population growth, emigration, and the shifting structure of the labor force; and the development of a modern manufacturing sector. My basic information is largely derived from secondary sources, which, in turn, rely mainly upon official Japanese statistics published by the Government General of Chosen.[8]

Trade

Data for the period before 1910 are spotty and probably subject to severe and fluctuating bias, but the evidence indicates that Korea's trade increased substantially during the three and a half decades between opening and annexation. Available estimates show that trade with Japan (exports plus imports) grew from an annual average of 2.5 million yen in 1879–81 to 36.3 million by 1907–09; annual averages

8. See especially Sang Chul Suh, "Growth and Structural Changes in the Korean Economy Since 1910."

Table 1.1. Volume, Distribution, and Relative Importance of Foreign Trade: 1910–12 to 1939–41

	Volume[a]	Percent distribution[b]						
	(million yen	Exports to			Imports from			Trade
Period	in 1936 prices)	Japan	China[c]	Others	Japan	China[c]	Others	ratios[d]
	(1)	(2)	(3)	(4)	(5)	(6)	(7)	(8)
1910–12	380.1	73.7	16.8	9.5	62.4	10.1	27.5	13.8
1914–16	567.4	79.9	13.0	7.1	67.5	12.9	19.6	17.6
1919–21	961.6	89.9	8.8	1.3	64.4	23.7	11.9	28.7
1924–26	1,593.3	93.1	6.6	.3	68.0	24.3	7.7	39.9
1929–31	2,073.5	91.4	8.2	.4	76.5	15.9	7.6	51.7
1934–36	3,813.6	87.7	11.6	.7	84.8	10.8	4.4	57.2
1939–41	4,174.4	77.4	21.2	.4	88.3	4.8	6.9	53.5

Sources: Distribution and trade ratios; Suh Sang-Chul, "Growth and Structural Changes in the Korean Economy Since 1910," tables II-11 and II-14; Bank of Chosŏn, Economic Review, 1949, table 56 and pp. 426–34.
Note: Foreign trade here includes only commodity exports and imports.
[a] Three-year totals, deflated by the Seoul wholesale price index.
[b] Three-year averages based on current values.
[c] Includes Manchuria and areas in north occupied by the Japanese.
[d] Exports plus imports divided by commodity product plus imports.

for Korea's total trade increased from 16.0 million yen to 55.3 million over this same period. Crude deflation with Japanese wholesale price indices suggests that the real volume of Korea's total commodity trade almost doubled from 1879–81 to 1907–09 while Korean-Japanese trade rose by a factor of eight. The real volume of trade continued to expand rapidly during the colonial era so that by 1939–41, trade had risen more than tenfold since 1910–12 (see the three-year totals shown in table 1.1).[9]

Not only did trade grow rapidly, but it reached levels in Korea that were notably high by international standards. Professor Suh has computed trade ratios (exports plus imports divided by commodity product plus imports) that rise from 14 percent in 1910–12 to more

9. The 1879–81 trade figures are from Conroy, The Japanese Seizure of Korea, p. 457, those for 1907–09 from the Bank of Chosŏn, Economic Review, 1949, table 56. They were deflated with the Asahi Shinbun wholesale price index, given in the Bank of Japan's Hundred-Year Statistics of the Japanese Economy, pp. 76–77. The Seoul wholesale price index was used to deflate the trade data during the colonial era but, as Suh notes, prices of agricultural and mining products (major export items) were generally high relative to the prices of manufactures (Suh, "Growth and Structural Changes," pp. B54–B56). The trade-volume estimates given in table 1.1 (exports plus imports in 1936 prices) are therefore subject to offsetting biases (imports are dominated by manufactures) that may or may not cancel.

than 50 percent during the 1930s (table 1.1). The latter are well over the 1938–39 average of 38 percent for the world's smallest countries, which tend to have the highest ratios.[10] Though Korea's trade ratios are biased upward (Suh notes that the denominator omits services, for which no data are available), they are too high and rise too sharply to be dismissed as artifacts of statistical omission. In fact, these ratios represent an enormous volume of trade which so impressed observers that a number of them have characterized Korea's economic growth during the colonial era as "export-led" growth.[11]

Korean trade, as might be expected, was predominantly with Japan and, to a lesser extent, with other members of the Yen Bloc (table 1.1). Trade with Manchuria and the parts of northern China occupied by Japanese forces, although included here under trade with China, actually constitutes Yen Bloc trade. The distribution of imports and exports by country not only shows the overwhelming importance of Japan in Korea's trade but also reveals that Korea exported proportionately more to Japan than it imported from Japan. This difference is characteristic of an economic satellite, which typically sends most exports to its dominant partner but whose imports are less concentrated and tend to come from a broader range of countries.

The composition of trade, shown in table 1.2, brings out the complementary relationship of the Korean and Japanese economies. Until the late 1930s Korean exports were dominated by crude foods, especially rice. Even as late as 1936–38, rice accounted for 37 percent of the value of exports. The data show, however, that the relative shares of manufactures and of industrial crude materials were increasing in the 1930s. Imports were dominated by finished manufactures despite the fact that the share of finished manufactures declined in the late 1920s and early 1930s as imports of crude food, industrial materials, and semifinished manufactures increased. The rise in food imports during the 1920s (mainly millet and cheap foreign rice) served to offset increasing domestic shortage as population growth accelerated and high-quality Korean rice was exported to Japan. The increase in imports of semifinished manufactures and industrial materials reflects mostly the growth of Korean industry after the abolition of the Corporation Law (see p. 18). Imports of finished manufactures also changed: in early years they were mainly consumer goods, whereas in

10. Simon Kuznets, *Six Lectures on Economic Growth*, p. 96.
11. Suh, "Growth and Structural Changes," pp. II 59–II 61; Schumpeter, *The Industrialization of Japan and Manchukuo*, pp. 288–90; Grajdanzev, *Modern Korea*, p. 226.

Table 1.2. Commodity Composition of Trade, 1915–41
(Percent distribution: from current price data)

| Period | Crude materials | | | Manufactures | | | |
	Food	Other	Total	Food	Semi-finished	Finished	Total
Exports							
1915–19	48.7	20.5	69.2	1.0	7.6	22.2	30.8
1920–24	63.0	11.1	74.1	1.7	11.0	13.2	25.9
1925–29	64.2	8.7	72.9	2.5	12.2	12.4	27.1
1930–34	59.1	15.6	74.7	3.8	15.6	5.9	25.3
1935–39	41.8	15.2	57.0	3.5	21.0	18.5	43.0
1940–41	25.8	14.5	40.3	4.7	26.8	28.2	59.7
Imports							
1915–19	7.0	6.4	13.4	7.1	14.9	64.6	86.6
1920–24	11.6	14.7	26.3	5.9	20.2	47.6	73.7
1925–29	18.3	11.7	30.0	5.8	17.1	47.1	70.0
1930–34	10.3	21.9	32.2	6.7	12.6	48.5	67.8
1935–39	7.2	13.5	20.7	4.6	13.2	61.5	79.3
1940–41	8.1	8.8	16.9	3.6	9.9	69.6	83.1

Source: Suh Sang-Chul, "Growth and Structural Changes in the Korean Economy Since 1910," table II-13. Several of Suh's figures for 1940–41 have been revised here.

the 1930s they were dominated by machinery and the other investment goods needed to expand heavy industry in Korea.

Several aspects of this trade are noteworthy, particularly the simultaneous import and export of food grains, the implications of continued deficit in Korea's commodity accounts, and the shift within finished imports from consumer goods to producer goods. Simultaneous import and export of the same product can be justified in terms of national differences in consumer tastes and transport costs; however, import of cheap food grains and export of costlier and more desirable food grains suggest that Korean agriculture was squeezed for the benefit of the Japanese consumer, particularly since rice—the main food export—was highly prized in the Korean diet. Trade was the vehicle of exploitation here.[12] This conclusion is apparently contradicted by the fact that Korea, unlike Taiwan (then Formosa), ran a sustained deficit in its trade balance, which would seem to indicate that instead of being exploited, Korea enjoyed greater access

12. Differences in income as well as differences in tastes might also justify simultaneous rice export and import of cheaper grains. But then the exploitation issue revolves around the determinants of income rather than the trade process.

to resources within the Yen Bloc than it might have had as an independent country. However, Grajdanzev notes that about 35 percent of the deficit was offset by exports of specie and bullion from Korea. Also, there was considerable "smuggling" of goods from Korea to Shantung and Manchuria (to preserve the appearance of independence in Manchukuo, Japan's puppet state organized in 1932) while remittances from the many Korean emigrants to Japan and Manchuria probably took care of the balance.

Finally, the changing composition of imports reflected Japan's decision to build heavy industry in Korea. This resulted in a shift from consumer-goods imports to producer-goods imports and, toward the end of the 1930s, a corresponding increase in the relative importance of producer goods (mainly industrial raw materials and machinery) in Korea's output and exports.

Agriculture

The overwhelming importance of agriculture can be seen in the first Korean census made under the Japanese, which showed that in 1910, 84 percent of all households were engaged in agriculture and forestry. The occupational distribution at this time was dominated even more by agriculture than Japan's in 1878–80, a period during the middle of Japan's transition to modern economic growth.[13] A second basic characteristic was the low level of agricultural productivity, low not only relative to productivity in other sectors within Korea but low relative to productivity in Japan too.[14]

13. Henry Rosovsky, "Japan's Transition to Modern Economic Growth, 1868–1885," in Henry Rosovsky, ed., *Industrialization in Two Systems*, p. 93. The Japanese figures refer to gainfully employed population, not households. Rosovsky feels they overstate the agricultural population, and he suggests the figure of 79 percent as being more realistic than the published figure of 83 percent.

14. Suh shows annual average commodity product per worker in 1929–31 and 1939–41 by sector. Per worker product in agriculture and forestry averaged 91 percent of the national average during the first period, only 74 percent in the second (this last figure, though, is biased downward by the poor rice crop in 1939). Net product per worker in constant prices was four times as high in manufacturing in 1929–31 and nine times as high during 1939–41 (Suh, "Growth and Structural Changes," p. III 106). Grajdanzev shows that average gross output per capita was about three times as high in Japan as in Korea in 1938 (*Modern Korea*, p. 84). Although some of this difference was due to differences in the occupational structures of the two economies (in Japan a larger proportion of workers was concentrated in manufacturing and other relatively high productivity sectors), calculation of gross value of output per occupied person in agriculture for 1938 indicates that output was two-thirds higher in Japan than in Korea (sources: gross value of production [Grajdanzev p. 84]; occupied population [Schumpeter, *The Industrialization of Japan and Manchukuo*, p. 76; Bank of Chosŏn, *Economic Review, 1949*, p. IV 18]).

Table 1.3. Measures of Agricultural Production:
1910–12 to 1939–41

Annual average	Crops (1)	*Market value current prices (million yen)* Other (2)	Total (3)	*Production indices (1929–31 = 100)*[b] Total output (4)	Rice (5)	*Rice export indices (1929–31 = 100)* (6)
1910–12	288	30	318	65.7	67.4	4.0[c]
1914–16	356	54	410	83.7	82.1	21.6
1919–21	1,034	102	1,136	84.5	85.9	37.7
1924–26	987	147	759	89.3	88.8	76.3
1929–31	618	141	1,759	100.0	100.0	100.0
1934–36	901	179	1,080	104.9	110.8	118.6
1939–41[a]	1,537	330	1,867	125.3	142.8	—

Sources: (1)–(3), Suh Sang-Chul, "Growth and Structural Changes in the Korean Economy Since 1910," Appendix table A-1; (4)–(5), ibid., table III-3; (6), B. F. Johnston, *Japanese Food Management in World War II*, p. 264.
[a] Production indices exclude the year 1939, in which the rice crop was exceptionally poor.
[b] Includes both agriculture and forestry output.
[c] Covers only 1911 and 1912.

A third feature of Korean agriculture was the strong concentration on the production of crops (as opposed to livestock, fertilizers, and silk products), especially food grains and, within food grains, rice. Crops accounted for 91 percent of net agricultural product in 1910–12, and 81 percent as late as 1934–36. Rice production accounted for more than half the value of output of the major crops throughout the colonial period; its share, in fact, rose during the 1930s. Data on crop shares, increase in agricultural output, and the growth of rice production are given in table 1.3.

One last aspect to be noted was the large and increasing proportion of rice output being exported. Rice exports accounted for 16 percent of production in 1910–15, rising to 44 percent in 1930–36. Rice imports from Korea made up over half of Japanese rice imports from 1925–26 through 1937–38 and, with the exception of 1939, probably into the war years as well.

These developments suggest that sources of increase in output be examined and raise the question of how growth in rice exports was achieved. One possible source of increase in output is growth of cultivated area. Figures for cultivated area (both paddy and dry fields) doubled between 1910 and 1938, with practically all the growth from 1910 to 1919. Grajdanzev observes that this earlier period was marked by an extensive cadastral survey undertaken by the Japanese to improve the tax base and establish ownership rights. He suspects that the increase was largely a statistical phenomenon, reflecting better coverage of cultivated land on which farmers had previously failed to pay taxes. If so, other sources must have been responsible for the rising production shown in table 1.3. They might include land improvement (particularly construction of irrigation and drainage facilities), more and better material inputs (such as superior seeds or greater use of fertilizers), increased use of machinery, draft animals, and farm implements, more-labor-intensive methods of cultivation or more intensive use of land (i.e., more double cropping), shifts in the system of land tenure or cost-price relationships that provided greater incentive to increase output, and, finally, possible effects of changes in Japanese policy that encouraged Korean agriculture.

Japanese policy is reflected in the activities of the Oriental Development Company, which, when unsuccessful in bringing Japanese farmers to Korea, assumed a major role in irrigation and agricultural finance during the early colonial period and in the first and second Rice Production Increase Plans of 1920 and 1926. Following the riots of 1918 in Japan induced by rice shortages, the Government General of Korea embarked on the first of these plans to raise output by improved irrigation, land reclamation, use of better seeds, and increased compost application. Neither government nor private targets were met; output rose very little (see table 1.3) and so a second, more ambitious plan was initiated in 1926. The second plan met with somewhat greater success but was discontinued in 1934 after Japanese farmers threatened to boycott Korean rice when domestic rice prices slumped during the economic crisis of the early 1930s. Renewed shortages of rice occurred in the late 1930s after the war with China, however, and led to a further attempt to increase Korean rice production, mainly by methods other than increased irrigation or land improvement.

Improvement and reclamation attempts did not succeed, it has been argued, because rates of return on already cultivated land were so high that landlords were unwilling to make the heavy outlays required for land improvement.[15] Failure also had an adverse affect on land utilization, which is particularly dependent upon irrigation. An average

15. Korea Land Economic Research Center, *A Study of Land Tenure System in Korea,* p. 151.

utilization rate of about 1.34 or 1.35 had been reached by 1938 (i.e., a second crop was gathered on a third of the cultivated land), but Grajdanzev, for one, felt that the irrigated area (and hence the utilization rate) could have been expanded with more attractive rice cost–price relations.

Although agricultural production almost doubled between 1910–12 and 1939–41 (see table 1.3), expansion of cultivated area, increased utilization, and various improvements (irrigation, seeds, fertilization) were insufficient to account for all this growth. Mechanization was insignificant during the period, but the use of draft cattle (the primary form of capital input) doubled while labor inputs rose about 50 percent. Ban has estimated that three-quarters of the growth in agricultural output can be attributed to increased factor inputs, the rest to improved productivity. Since cultivated area was relatively fixed, increases came mainly in capital and labor inputs, and these increases served to raise land productivity substantially. Though capital and labor inputs grew, partial productivities remained positive; Korean agriculture may have been subject to diminishing returns, but output could have probably been expanded with greater inputs of labor and capital.[16]

One of the principal factors behind the increase in agricultural output, and certainly the main impetus for the even more rapid growth of rice exports, was the change in the landownership and tenure systems introduced by the Japanese. The process was initiated by a cadastral survey that began in 1910, lasted eight years, and required a full-time work force of over 3,000. Land belonging to the royal household and uncultivated land was turned over to the government for sale to Japanese land companies and landlords. Peasants who had previously been permitted to cultivate land under hereditary arrangements with the owners lost these rights and became tenant farmers. Concentration in holdings can be seen in the changing distribution of ownership: the proportion of farm households that were pure tenants (as opposed to proprietors or part-owners) rose from 39 percent in 1913–17 to 56 percent by 1938. Of large holdings (over 100 *cheongbo*: one cheongbo

16. Ban Sung-whan, "Growth Rates of Korean Agriculture, 1918–1968," pp. 26–28, 37–39. The partial productivities for land, labor, and capital grew at annual rates of 4.23, 1.09, and 0.80 percent, respectively, from 1918, 1920, and 1921 to 1938, 1940, and 1941 in South Korea—and probably for all Korea as well. Allocation of output growth between increasing inputs and productivity, as Ban notes, is sensitive to choice of factor shares. For this reason, the figures cited in the text provide only a rough approximation of the actual allocation.

equals 2.45 acres), Japanese landlords owned 54 percent in 1921 and 62 percent by 1935. Since the ownership information does not include firms with Korean charters as Japanese even though such firms were owned by Japanese, official data tend to underestimate the extent of Japanese ownership. If government property is included, the Japanese may have controlled more than half the land in Korea.[17]

Land rent was usually collected in kind, generally as a proportion of annual output. Rents averaged half the crop, although in some cases the amount was as high as 90 percent. The distribution of output was investigated in 1932 by the Japanese authorities, who found that rice available per member of landlords' families averaged 11.4 *koku* (one koku equals 5.12 U.S. bushels), for tenants' families, only 0.4 koku per member.[18] This uneven distribution of output, plus a system of land taxes that accounted for over half of total government revenue before 1920, was the means by which Korean rice was channeled into exports to Japan. One result of the system was a decline in the average per capita consumption of rice and food grains as a whole in Korea during the colonial period.[19] Poorer farm families were reduced to eating wild grass during the spring months just before the harvest: "The phrase 'starvation export' was quite commonly applied . . . by Japanese food officials."[20] A second result was that agriculture provided a ready source of labor as industry expanded rapidly during the late 1930s. Because the manufacturing sector did not expand early enough or quickly enough to absorb impoverished tenants and *kadenmin* (roving farmers or squatters), a third development can be seen in emigration statistics. By 1930, half a million Koreans moved to Japan. By 1937, almost a million lived in Manchuria. This was a flow

17. Tenancy estimates are shown in the Korea Land Economic Research Center's *A Study of Land Tenure System*, p. 44. Japanese ownership shares are given in Suh, "Growth and Structural Changes," p. III 79, and Grajdanzev, *Modern Korea*, p. 106.

18. Rents are discussed in Hoon K. Lee, *Land Utilization and Rural Economy in Korea*, p. 163. The Japanese investigation of rice distribution is cited in Grajdanzev, *Modern Korea*, p. 117.

19. Schumpeter, *The Industrialization of Japan and Manchukuo*, p. 292; Johnston, *Japanese Food Management in World War II*, p. 55; Korea Land Economic Research Center, *A Study of Land Tenure System*, p. 53; Suh, "Growth and Structural Changes," p. IV 40. All the calculations shown in these sources suffer from absence of accurate data on inventories and carryover. Suh notes, however, the expansion of warehouse capacity in Korea during the early 1930s and the imposition of controls after 1937 to minimize consumption and increase commodity reserves in preparation for war, both of which suggest a possible decline in consumption levels (ibid., pp. IV 139, IV 141).

20. Johnston, *Japanese Food Management*, p. 54.

of major magnitude, for the population of Korea was then (1936) only 22 million (see Statistical Appendix, table A1).

It is interesting to compare the development of agriculture under the Japanese in Korea and Formosa. In each case, colonial policies were designed to expand output and squeeze out the surplus for the benefit of Japan proper. In Korea, rice production increased at an average annual rate of 2 percent from 1910 to 1935. During roughly the same period (1906–10 to 1936–40), agricultural production in Formosa grew at an annual rate of slightly more than 3 percent.[21] In both countries, land improvement was encouraged by government subsidies, especially to irrigation cooperatives, while agricultural technicians were sent and schools established to improve agricultural practices. As in Korea, there is evidence of substitution of less desirable food (potatoes) for rice and possible long-term decline in per capita food consumption. "Technical progress in Formosa was much more impressive," however, and one reason may lie in the different methods used to expropriate the agricultural surplus.[22]

In Korea, a combination of land taxes, high rents, and extension of Japanese ownership was the means employed to provide rice for export of Japan; in Formosa, it was taxation and the monopsonistic power of large Japanese food processors operating in the colony.[23] Tenure arrangements also differed. In Formosa, absentee owners were required to exchange hereditary rights for interest-bearing bonds; resident owners were guarantee title to land; rents were reduced and set at fixed levels.[24] The contrast could not have been more marked; for the peasant, the incentive to expand production must have been much greater in Formosa than in Korea.

Manufacturing

The development of a modern manufacturing sector in Korea was delayed by the so-called Corporation Law (Chosen Company Regulations), a law giving the Government General authority to approve the establishment of new firms. The law was probably designed to restrict investment in nonagricultural enterprises, to limit capital

---

21. Samuel P. S. Ho, "Agricultural Transformation under Colonialism: The Case of Taiwan," p. 315.
22. Johnston, *Japanese Food Management*, p. 57.
23. Ho, "Agricultural Transformation under Colonialism," pp. 238–40.
24. Ramon H. Myers and Adrienne Ching, "Agricultural Development in Taiwan Under Japanese Colonial Rule."

outflow from Japan, and to prevent the development of domestic (Korean) enterprise. This does not mean that there were no examples of manufacturing activity before the law was repealed, or even before the time of Japanese annexation. Americans had built an electric power station and established a gold mine; the Russians had begun a match factory before the Russo-Japanese War; the Korean government had established a modern cocoonery and industrial training centers; and the Japanese founded soy manufacturing, rice refining, electric power, and lumber mill operations—all before 1910. Nevertheless, the share of manufacturing in total output was low at the beginning of the colonial era: the first census of 1910 shows that fewer than 1 percent of all households were engaged in manufacturing (though 11 percent of Japanese households were), while the share of manufacturing in total commodity product in 1910–12 was less than 7 percent (see table

Table 1.4. Output Growth, Population Increase, and Industrial Structure:
1910–12 to 1939–41

A. Output and population indices (1929–31 = 100)
(net commodity product in 1929–31 market prices)

Period	Agriculture	Forestry, fishing, and mining	Manufacturing	Total	Population[c]
1910–12	67.3	33.7	17.4	54.2[b]	66.0
1914–16	86.5	45.9	31.5	69.6	—
1919–21	88.6	46.2	59.7	76.9	84.5
1924–26	91.2	69.0	97.5	89.6	—
1929–31	100.0	100.0	100.0	100.0	100.0
1934–36	98.7	161.5	194.2	127.1	—
1939–41	117.3[a]	227.6	255.5	165.5 (155.5)	115.2

B. Industrial structure (percent share of net commodity product)[d]

	Agriculture	Forestry	Fishing	Mining	Manufacturing	Total
1910–12	84.6	5.3	1.9	1.5	6.7	100.0
1919–21	78.6	2.7	3.0	1.4	14.3	100.0
1929–31	63.1	6.6	5.8	2.2	22.3	100.0
1939–41	49.6	7.2	6.3	7.9	29.0	100.0

Sources: Suh Sang-Chul, "Growth and Structural Changes in the Korean Economy Since 1910," tables B-5 and II-4; Statistical Appendix, table A1.
[a] Excludes 1939, an exceptionally poor rice year. The index for total output in parentheses includes 1939.
[b] Only 1911 and 1912.
[c] Based on Oct. 1 census counts in 1920, 1930, and 1940.
[d] Based on current values.

1.4). When the Corporation Law was abolished in 1920, both the number of companies and amount of paid-in capital mushroomed. Between 1921 and 1930, the number of companies quadrupled while the amount of the paid-in capital rose three and a half times.

Except for rice mills, manufacturing was dominated in 1920 by handicraft or cottage industries; imports from Japan fulfilled the demand for most modern manufactures. Suh has derived crude estimates which show that handicraft establishments produced half of total manufactures in the early 1920s before their output share declined to about a quarter of the total in 1935–38. Although price data are insufficient to allow construction of output indices for handicraft products, current-value measures and evidence of policies discriminating against household enterprise suggest that there was an absolute as well as a relative decline in the output of handicraft industry after the mid-1920s. This conclusion is supported by examining the structure of factory output. In 1930, three-quarters of factory output originated in light industry (food, textile, ceramic, printing, lumber, and miscellaneous products) while a little less than half of total factory product was food and textiles. The new factory product must have been to some extent competitive with, rather than complementary to, the output of the handicraft industries.

Because output of the manufacturing sector began from a very small base at the time of annexation, growth rates during earlier years were quite high despite the inhibiting effect of the Corporation Law. However, continued rapid growth after 1929–31 was no statistical mirage but rather the result of Japan's decision to substitute imports from within the Yen Bloc for imports formerly obtained elsewhere. Net commodity product of the manufacturing sector almost doubled between 1929–31 and 1934–36 and rose another 30 percent between 1934–36 and 1939–41.[25] The manufacturing sector's share grew to 29 percent of total product during this last period (see table 1.4). Growth in manufacturing output was accompanied by major changes in the structure of manufactures, location of industry, composition of exports and imports (see table 1.2), and corporate ownership.

Not only did the relative (and perhaps absolute) share of handicraft industry decline rapidly in the 1930s, but so did the share of light

---

25. Estimates of the shares of handicraft establishments and composition of factory output are from Suh, "Growth and Structural Changes," III 87 and table A-14. If the output of modern factories were taken separately, growth rates would have been even higher.

industry, from three-quarters of factory product in 1930 to less than half in 1940. Among heavy industries, growth was dominated by chemicals, especially fertilizers, and, later, probably war goods (chemicals composed over a third of factory output by 1940). No direct information is available on capital formation, but if commodity product available for domestic use (domestic production plus imports less exports) is broken down into materials and finished goods, and the latter into producer and consumer goods, the share of producers' goods in total finished goods is found to have quadrupled from 4 percent in the early 1920s to 16 percent in the late 1930s.

Much of the new industry was built in the northern part of Korea. Whereas less than 40 percent of manufactured product originated in the North in 1934 (probably about 30 percent in the 1930s), the North's share was over 50 percent by 1940. More rapid growth of the North is seen in all other sectors except mining, and in accelerated population increase as well. Korea's advantages within the Japanese Empire of cheap labor, strategic location, and abundant power were particularly marked in the North. The economic structures of the northern and southern regions were complementary not only in manufacturing but in agriculture too. In 1936, for example, three-quarters of the cultivated area devoted to raising rice and the summer grains (barley and wheat) was in the South, while 60 percent of the area used to grow beans and 80 percent of that used for cereals (millet, sorghum, corn, buckwheat) was in the North. Within manufacturing, the South produced five times the value of textiles that were produced in the North in 1939–40. Machine tool output was two and a half times that of the North, printing volume over six times as large, and production of manufactured food about 1.8 times greater. The North, on the other hand, dominated the output of metals (by a ratio of 8 to 1), ceramics (2.5 to 1), and chemicals (5 to 1).[26]

Information on ownership and capitalization is particularly treacherous: data on invested capital are available only for corporations; information refers to paid-up or subscribed capital so that debt, often quite large, is excluded; establishment data exclude establishments with fewer than five workers though their output is included in estimates of the gross value of production. Since paid-up or equity capital is probably not too bad a surrogate for borrowing and since many enterprises were incorporated, data showing that Japanese-owned

26. Ibid., tables V-4, V-8, and V-9.

establishments produced three-quarters of the gross value of output in 1938, or that Japanese firms comprised 60 percent of the total number of firms in Korea and commanded 90 percent of paid-in capital, are undoubtedly indicators that reflect, in a not very accurate fashion, the dominance of Japanese in Korea's industry. Even before the wave of industrialization of the 1930s, Japanese and mixed Japanese–Korean firms held the lion's share of ownership and paid-up capital. In the 1930s, the big Japanese financial-industrial firms (*zaibatsu*) became interested in Korea. A number of large enterprises were begun by the Mitsui, Mitsubishi, Yasuda, and Sumitomo complexes, and by some of the younger interests (especially Noguchi) as well.

Figures given by Choi and Suh for the late 1930s indicate that a very large proportion of factory employment and output originated in fewer than 7 percent of the total number of firms in the textile, metal, machine tool, ceramics, and chemical industries.[27] Over 60 percent of total factory product in 1939, in fact, was produced by only 1.2 percent of all factories. The rapid growth of manufacturing, then, was accompanied by increasing concentration of output in large, Japanese-controlled firms.

Net commodity product shown in table 1.4 grew at annual average rate of 4 percent, or 2 percent per capita, during the three decades from 1910–12 to 1939–41. This growth, even after the reduction likely to result from including services, is impressive by contemporary standards. But agricultural output per capita failed to increase while substantial exports limited the domestic supply of rice (see table 1.3). Both developments suggest that growth may not have brought substantial benefits to most Koreans during the colonial era. This inference is reinforced by examination of the detailed trade statistics for the period.

Grajdanzev found that imports consisted mainly of high-value items such as *sake*, beer, canned goods, wool and silk tissues, while exports were predominantly low-value, mass consumption items such as rice, cotton, and hemp tissues, and concluded that imports of consumer goods were destined chiefly for Korea's Japanese and rich Korean inhabitants.[28] Even though the average level of domestically available consumer goods per capita rose quite sharply during the 1930s, both the decline in rice and grain consumption mentioned earlier and the

27. Ibid., table III-11; Choi Ho-chin, "The Process of Industrial Modernization in Korea," p. 17.
28. Grajdanzev, *Modern Korea*, pp. 230–34.

special nature of consumer goods imports noted by Grajdanzev suggest that the aggregate data are likely to be misleading if used to draw conclusions about welfare. Divergence between domestic production and consumption, and systematic differences in income elasticity of demand for exports and imports may mean that the average Korean did not benefit from industrialization and expansion of trade. Evidence in point can be obtained when money wages are deflated by wholesale price indices for the period 1929–31 to 1938–40. The calculation indicates that real wages of urban workers dropped almost 30 percent.

Population, Labor Force, and Education

A population count made in Korea at the time of Japanese annexation showed a population of 13.3 million, including 172,000 Japanese. Total population reached 25.9 million in 1944, a 95 percent increase over 1910. Of the total, 780,000 were foreigners (mostly Japanese). Published vital statistics are too poor to be trusted, but Choe presents figures for crude death rates of 18 to 22 per 1,000, and estimated crude birth rates of between 42 and 48 per 1,000.[29] The picture is one of high fertility, possible combined with the beginnings of the drop in mortality often associated with early stages of economic development, but it is complicated by massive emigration. By 1940, there were 1.2 million Koreans in Japan and 1.5 million in Manchuria. Most of this outflow occurred during the 1930s.

Given such migration levels, the "only possible conclusion is that the rate of natural increase of the Korean population of prewar Korea was between two and two-and-a-half percent per year."[30] This was considerably higher than the Japanese rate and was maintained, despite an average life expectancy only three-quarters that of the Japanese, because the "family and reproductive patterns of the Korean peasant remained relatively untouched by . . . the diffusion of . . . elements of Western culture."[31] Though population growth was accompanied by increasing urbanization (population of *shis*, or cities with a minimum of 50,000 inhabitants, rose from 4.4 percent in 1925 to 11.6 percent of the total in 1940) and changes in the sectoral distribution of the labor force, the increase in rural population was much larger absolutely than the increase in urban population. Korea was still a predominantly rural country at the end of the colonial era. Irene Taeuber noted

29. Choe Ehn-hyun, *Population Distribution and Internal Migration in Korea*, p. 20.
30. Irene B. Taeuber, "The Population Potential of Postwar Korea," p. 298.
31. Ibid., p. 295.

shortly afterward that the Japanese occupation had checked the decline in mortality and had prevented the decline in fertility that usually accompany industrialization and urbanization and concluded that "the possibility of a demographic crisis is ever present."[32]

Labor force data collected during the colonial period suffer from confusion between industrial and occupational categories and, even worse, from noncomparability over time.[33] Also, the "gainful-worker" concept was used to classify the total population (workers and their households) by occupation. Consequently, published estimates do not show the number of persons actually employed by the industrial sector. Although the available data cannot be used with any degree of confidence to describe changes in the structure of the labor force, we know that the rural population increased almost 10 percent during the 1930s while agricultural production rose 17 percent (rice 43 percent) and manufacturing output 260 percent. Was this output growth sufficient to absorb the expanding rural population? Increases in the gap between net commodity product per worker in manufacturing and in agriculture, the drop in real wages of urban workers, and the large-scale emigration of the 1930s all suggest that it was not.

In addition to the information about changes in the structure of trade, agriculture, manufacturing, and labor force—changes that mark the economic growth of Korea as a Japanese colony—there is also information on prices, interest rates, government, education, prisons, and labor conditions that provides insight into the quality of life led by Koreans during the colonial era. This information generally confirms the impression that the Koreans were an oppressed majority, politically and socially as well as economically. The educational

32. Ibid., p. 306. Korea was not unique in this respect, since the same situation, with similar causes, occurred in Taiwan under Japanese domination (see George W. Barclay, *Colonial Development and Population in Taiwan*, chap. 10).

33. Im Tae-bin gives the distribution of gainfully employed workers by sector in 1930 and 1940, and totals for gainful workers by sex in 1944 (*The Korean Labor Force and School Population*, pp. 108–12). Im's figures agree with Suh's for 1930 and 1940; both show that the number of workers declined by half a million between the two dates. Suh's information was obtained from Government General census data, Im's from an article by Park Chai-bin ("A Review of Korean Population Statistics," Economic Planning Board, *Monthly Statistics of Korea*, vol. 4, nos. 1 and 2). Park's data for 1930 and 1940 undoubtedly came from the same source as Suh's. They show that the decline came mainly among women (gainful workers as a proportion of the total female population fell from 33 percent in 1930 to 22 percent in 1940 before rising to 30 percent in 1944). The 1930 census was probably taken in the fall, when a large number of farm women participate in the harvest, whereas the 1940 census came at a time of the year when the labor force and its composition reflected seasonal lows.

system and distribution of jobs between Koreans and Japanese, both of which reflect the colonial situation, deserve particular attention for their adverse impact on Korea's economic future.

Grajdanzev cites Government General statistics which show that the number of registered students in Korea rose from 111,000 in 1910 to more than 1.2 million in 1937. Only one in three children attended a primary school, however, and the proportion of Koreans drops as one moves up the educational ladder until the Japanese outnumber Koreans at Keijo Imperial University, the "crown of the [educational] edifice."[34] Japanese was the language of education (Korean language lessons were abolished entirely toward the end of the colonial period), and separate primary and high schools were maintained for Korean and Japanese children. Expansion of education was confined mostly to primary and technical schools, education was highly differentiated, and the curriculum was designed largely to prepare loyal subjects of the Japanese Empire. The system clearly did not foster the kinds of talent required or provide training for sufficient numbers to enable Koreans to man either the government agencies or private enterprises need for the country's future development.

The extent of educational advantage, or the Japanese monopoly of jobs requiring specialized training and administrative and economic skills is seen in the occupational distribution by nationality. The data are not good, but the differences shown in distributions between Koreans and Japanese are so great as to overwhelm probable errors. The urban–rural makeup of the two groups was different too. Whereas 12 percent of the population lived in the cities by 1940, the figure for the Japanese in Korea was over 70 percent. Estimates for 1938 and 1940 show that 75 percent of Korean families (72 percent of male workers) were employed in agriculture: the corresponding figure for the Japanese in Korea is 5 percent. Depending on the body of data used (household or gainfully employed workers), 17–25 percent of the Japanese were engaged in manufacturing activities, 23 percent in commerce, 25–38 percent in public and professional services, and 6–15 percent in transport and commerce. The proportion of Koreans engaged in these activities was negligible; the proportion of Japanese engaged in other occupations such as mining or fishing was also negligible. The differences between Korean and Japanese occupational structure are even greater if one looks at the different types of jobs

34. Grajdanzev, *Modern Korea*, p. 263.

within each sectoral category. Among the top 58 officials in the Department of Agriculture and Forestry in 1941, for example, there was only one Korean.[35] In industry, most Japanese were overseers, accountants, engineers, and owners, whereas the Koreans were mainly unskilled workers.

These various pieces of evidence reveal a country in which most Koreans were less educated, lived elsewhere, and held different (and lower) types of jobs than most Japanese. The training and work experience of the majority of the population, as in many other less developed countries, were not of the kind needed to meet the manpower requirements of a developing economy.

World War II

As is true for most other countries, information necessary to establish a clearly defined picture of economic developments in Korea is not available for the World War II years. There was also a break in the pattern of development, particularly toward the end of this period, which tends to separate the colonial era from the years after 1945. Yet, the economic structure of the Japanese Empire had been increasingly influenced by military requirements and demands for self-sufficiency since the early 1930s. For Korea and the rest of the empire, then, World War II did not mark an entirely new economic phase but rather a continuation of earlier trends before the final collapse.

After the Manchurian incident in 1931, Japan was unable to borrow abroad. When war broke out with China in July 1937, even short-term commercial credits to Japan were restricted. Because large amounts of raw-material imports were needed to maintain and expand industrial output within the Yen Bloc and because outside credit was unavailable, and partly for military reasons and the prevalent desire for economic self-sufficiency, government control was extended to encourage production of essential (i.e., war oriented) goods, restrict profits and prices, and curb consumption of food and other materials. A Five-Year Plan for expansion of industry in connection with the national defense program was begun in 1936. Large import balances were required in 1937 and 1938 to achieve "a substantial gain in self-sufficiency in heavy industry and other capital goods [*sic*] for which Japan is at present largely dependent upon foreign imports." From this viewpoint

35. Ibid., p. 243.

"military expenditures ... instead of being merely unprofitable expenses, are playing a role as a much-needed stimulant in the development of heavy industry."[36]

In Korea, these policies were seen in the expansion of warehouse capacity and increased pressure to squeeze the agricultural sector for rice to be exported to Japan, emphasis on heavy industry with war potential, and attempts to restrict consumption by appeals to patriotism. Already low levels of consumption were undoubtedly reduced during the last few years of the war. Wartime fertilizer shortages encouraged a shift from rice to rye and other crops, but it is unlikely that the increase in other cereals (almost 50 percent between 1941 and 1944) offset the drop in rice output of almost a third during the period. Both exports and imports fell after 1941, though unusually large imports of semimanufactures in 1943 followed by a two-and-a-half-fold increase in exports of manufactures in 1944 suggest a transfer of activity from Japan to Korea as the war approached the Japanese homeland. After 1941, when gold no longer served as a source of foreign exchange to purchase strategic materials from the United States, mines were stripped of machinery. "What happened to gold mining was in general the fate of Japanese resources throughout the Japanese economy in Korea . . . after mid-1944, scrapping became commonplace as the Japanese tried to cannibalize the economy . . . and fed everything that could possibly be sacrificed to war needs."[37] One observer who arrived in Seoul in January 1946 noted that "metal railings, fire escapes, and metal fixtures of all kinds have been removed from buildings. Even the iron water mains and fire plugs were taken up during the war and concrete pipes substituted."[38] Acute shortages of consumer goods inevitably followed the diversion of the economy to military ends, and these shortages were just as inevitably accompanied by rising prices.

Evidence of inflationary pressure can be found in government finance and in price measures. Government surpluses in 1941–43 fell to zero in 1944 and a large deficit occurred in 1945. Expansion of the money supply, when note issue more than doubled between 1943 and 1944, was followed by a sharp rise in prices and wages. Also, "when the Japanese saw the war was lost, and finally realized they would have to leave Korea, they began to disorganize the finances. . . . All government

36. Kamekichi Takahashi, "Protracted War and the Stability of the Japanese Economy," cited in Institute of Pacific Relations, *Industrial Japan*, p. 22.
37. George M. McCune, *Korea Today*, pp. 36–37.
38. J. Earnest Fisher, "Korea Today," p. 263.

employees, and the employees of Japanese companies were paid a year's salary in advance. All savings bank deposits and life insurance policies were paid out in full."[39] Whether the Japanese acted purely from malice or, more likely, were monetizing their assets in preparation for eventual departure, inflation was rampant. The Seoul wholesale price index rose almost eightfold between April 1945, before the war ended, and September 1945, when the first American forces arrived in Korea. These were official prices: black market prices had risen to 20 or 30 times official prices immediately before the war's end.

MILITARY GOVERNMENT, INDEPENDENCE, AND THE KOREAN WAR (1945–1953)

The question of Korea's future was discussed among the Allied powers before the end of World War II at the Cairo and Yalta conferences. In December 1943, after the Cairo Conference, a declaration was issued that "in due course Korea should become free and independent." At Yalta in February 1945, the Allied powers agreed that Korea might become a multipower trusteeship under the proposed United Nations. On August 8, 1945, the Russians declared war on Japan; Soviet troops entered northern Korea on August 10. Japan surrendered on August 14, but American troops did not reach southern Korea until September 8. Secretary of State Byrnes declared a few months later that "for purposes of military operations the occupation of Korea was divided north and south of latitude 38 into Soviet and American areas."[40] The line was set only to establish areas of responsibility for receiving the Japanese surrender and was considered to be temporary.

American Military Government

The three years from the surrender of Japan in August 1945 to the establishment of an independent republic in August 1948 were marked in South Korea by internal political struggle and by constant friction between the American Military Government (AMG) in the South and the Soviet occupation forces in the North. The political scene was too complex to describe here, but the economic situation and AMG efforts to cope with it are of special interest because South Korea's colonial inheritance and its new status as a dismembered

39. Ibid., p. 265.
40. McCune, *Korea Today*, p. 103.

fragment of a formerly much larger economic system are particularly evident during the AMG period.[41] Also, a number of economic problems seen in subsequent years were first observed in 1945–48. As a colony within the Japanese Empire, Korea was developed to complement the Japanese economy with no regard for self-sufficiency. Even though Korea had a comparative advantage within the Yen Bloc in producing rice, iron ore, mineral oil, and other export products, autarkic considerations had led the Japanese to employ subsidies, tariffs, and other forms of discrimination favoring Korean exports when, as Grajdanzev noted, rice from Indochina and Burma was cheaper than Korean rice, Malayan iron ore better than Korean ore, and American mineral oil much less expensive than Korean mineral oil. After liberation, Korean exports were thrown into world competition, where their former comparative advantage no longer existed.

A unified Korea would have faced problems of excessive dependence on a specialized form of industrial structure that was no longer appropriate when transferred from Yen Bloc to world markets. Such problems were further aggravated by the separation into North and South. Agricultural and industrial development of the two regions under the Japanese, as remarked earlier, was highly complementary so that the territorial division was a second, perhaps even more basic, reason to question the long-run economic viability of each part of Korea. These were not, however, the immediate problems faced by the American Military Government in the fall of 1945. Inflation, food shortages, the collapse of industrial production, scarcity of trained manpower, disposition of Japanese property, and a flood of refugees and repatriates were the main objects of initial concern.

Excessive Japanese currency issue was responsible for rampant inflation in 1945, but the drop in output following repatriation of Japanese managers combined with shortages of basic necessities to continue inflation during the next few years. The price of rice rose from 220 *won* per *mal* in August 1945 to 500 won in May 1946, 1,000 won in May 1947, and 1,500 won in January 1948.[42] The national urban retail price index for all commodities increased from 55.9 in 1946

41. Among the works that deal with Korea's internal and external political situation during the AMG period are: Richard C. Allen, *Korea's Syngman Rhee*; Soon Sung Cho, *Korea in World Politics*; Richard E. Lauterbach, "Hodge's Korea"; McCune, *Korea Today*, and "Korea: The First Year of Liberation"; E. Grant Meade, *American Military Government in Korea*; W. D. Reeve, *The Republic of Korea*; and Bertram D. Sarafan, "Military Government: Korea."

42. McCune, *Korea Today*, p. 338. One mal equals 4.76 gallons.

to 100.0 in 1947 and 158.3 in 1948. Inflation was symptomatic of the shortages created by worn-out physical plant, economic dislocation, and AMG policy blunders.

The AMG instituted a "free-market economy" upon arrival in Korea since there were not enough Americans to enforce rationing and the newly liberated Koreans were not in the mood to accept controls. This led to hoarding, speculation, and rapid price increases. After this inauspicious beginning, compulsory collection of rice and summer grains was started in the spring of 1946 to prevent widespread starvation. Grains collected were to be rationed at set prices. Since grains were major consumption items, the collection program had the threefold purpose of providing a more equitable distribution of food, preventing starvation (particularly in urban areas), and holding down prices. The program was marked by food riots in the spring of 1946, when collection proved insufficient (1946 and 1947 were years of flood and drought) and by reduced rations in mid-1947 as more and more refugees from the North entered the South. The anti-inflationary impact of the program was questionable; 15–20 percent of the national budget was used until mid-1947 to subsidize grain purchases at a time when large government deficits were financed by overdrafts on the Central Bank.[43]

The food problem was aggravated by low agricultural productivity, tenure uncertainties, the deterioration of Korea's fishing fleet, and, perhaps most important, a rapid increase in the number of mouths to feed. Diversion of nitrates and sulfates from fertilizer production and the switch to rye and other poor land crops during the war caused poor harvests in 1944. Output and yields were low in 1945 and 1946 too because no facilities existed for producing chemical fertilizer in the South. Fertilizer was first imported from the United States in time for the 1947 crop, however, and this plus subsequent fertilizer imports raised output and yields substantially. There was also an obvious need to increase average farm size, reduce tenancy, and limit landlord exploitation. Land formerly held by the Oriental Development Company and individual Japanese landlords was turned over to the government-run New Korea Company. In late 1945, annual rents were reduced to a maximum of one-third the value of

43. Overdrafts were necessary because the tax system was woefully inadequate. It was inadequate pratly because the Japanese had derived revenues from government monopoly enterprise and public utilities whose output had been too expensive to be used by most Koreans, and partly because collection procedures were poor.

the crops, but the effect of this measure was partly offset by a swift increase in rural population. When the conservative, landlord-dominated Interim Assembly refused to act on land reform, the AMG began distributing government holdings to tenants in the spring of 1948. More than 90 percent of the land formerly owned by Japanese was distributed among almost a quarter of South Korea's farm population.

Fish, another major component of the Korean diet, was also in short supply. Wartime deterioration of the fleets and Japanese removal of better ships at the end of the war substantially decreased the annual fish catch. Any drop in food grains output, the fish catch, or other agricultural production was to some extent offset by the cessation of food exports to Japan, but the population of South Korea rose 27 percent between 1944 and 1949. During this period, about 1.7 million Koreans entered the country. This large-scale, rapid increase in population would have strained any country's food-supply capabilities. In South Korea, the AMG estimated that the average daily calorie intake fell from a little over 2,000 in 1932–36 (for all Korea) to a little under 1,500 in May 1946–April 1947 in the South. The situation clearly called for emergency relief, so over $400 million worth of economic aid (listed under the heading GARIOA, or Government and Relief in Occupied Areas) was sent by the United States to South Korea in 1945–48. Ninety percent was in the form of food, fertilizer, clothing, fuel, and other commodities. Despite massive food and fertilizer shortages, supply conditions improved so much by the late 1940s that agricultural self-sufficiency was predicted for the 1950s.[44]

In the industrial sector, the occupying authorities were faced with the question of how best to dispose of Japanese property and the problems of deterioration, inappropriate structure, and low output. The first job was to register and administer Japanese assets. Then, in the spring of 1947, a policy was initiated of selling the vested property. Since there were few qualified buyers and the economic outlook discouraged investment, the custodians had to choose between retaining inefficient public management or virtually giving away assets to those who had not developed them. Most of the vested

44. Calorie intake estimates are given in McCune, *Korea Today*, p. 121; aid figures are taken from the Bank of Korea, *Annual Economic Review, 1955*, table 135; the prediction of self-sufficiency was made in a joint ECA–State Department *Semi-Annual Report on Korea* (Jan.–June 1949), quoted in McCune, *Korea Today*, p. 115.

firms remained under government control; even after the Rhee government was inaugurated, there was little disposition of the government's vested interests.

Heavy industry that had been producing military goods was dismantled by American ordance teams immediately after the war. Also, deterioration of plant accelerated after the Japanese surrender so that only about half the factories that had operated in 1944 were estimated to be operating in 1946, and they were producing at only 20 percent of capacity.[45] Because of previous reliance on Japan and North Korea for supplies, there were parts, materials, and power shortages. An immediate problem was coal. Large stockpiles were available in the northeast but there were no rail connections to other points in the South. The coal could be hauled by sea to Pusan, but the railroads were in such poor shape that further distribution was limited. Electricity was generated largely in hydroplants located in the North, so when the supply was cut off in May 1948, emergency power barges had to be brought in from the United States. Even then, total supply was only 80 percent of already low precutoff levels.

Coal and power shortages were acute but the situation was generally poor. Output of tungsten and graphite (major export items) was below prewar levels. Construction materials, especially cement and lumber, were in short supply. Even the textile industry, which employed almost 30 percent of the industrial labor force in 1946, was unable to meet domestic requirements. Urban streetcar systems and railroads were dilapidated. Railroad rolling stock was so inadequate that the 101 locomotives the United States sent in 1947 represented 40 percent of all locomotives in Korea. Reconstruction requirements were reflected in the Korean program of the Economic Cooperation Administration (ECA) for fiscal 1950. Of the $150 million budget, 80 percent was to be spent on materials and replacement items and only 20 percent on expansion of capacity.

Industrial output was also limited by lack of trained manpower. A 1946 survey of the industrial labor force found that 40 percent of laborers had no formal education and over 50 percent had attended only primary school. Only one third of "technicians" had gone

---

45. McCune, p. 141. Estimates are based on calculations by the U.S. Army Military Government in Korea (USAMGIK) from a 1944 Japanese census of manufactures and a South Korean Interim Government (SKIG) survey of operating plants in November 1946. The number of workers as well as the number of factories in the South also dropped by one-half from 1944 to 1946 (see J. L. Kaukonen, "The South Korean Wage Earner Since Liberation").

beyond primary school. "Lack of technical education, as much as lack of supplies and machinery, has made development of an industrial economy in South Korea difficult."[46] The AMG recognized this and concentrated on improving education so that reconstruction of the educational system became "one of the most noteworthy achievements of the American occupation authorities."

The labor situation, especially that of urban workers, was especially depressed. In May 1949 almost 900,000 persons were listed as unemployed (from a population of 20.2 million); the actual number was undoubtedly higher. Union activity had been suspended under the Japanese; the AMG issued decrees requiring compulsory arbitration of strikes and did little to encourage labor union activity. Later the republic, under Syngman Rhee (Yi Sŭngman), extended government influence over unions so that any meaningful labor activity became impossible.

Data on income and expenditure during the occupation period are too poor to derive reliable conclusions about living standards. Fragmentary information on wages and prices suggests that the inflation, particularly between mid-1945 and the spring of 1946, served to reduce real wages substantially. Absence of data on expenditure patterns and the lack of statistics on output and consumption of incentive and distribution goods (which were sold at controlled levels, in some cases as low as 20 percent of market prices) make such a conclusion hazardous. One survey in 1948 showed that the main activities of heads of households engaged in wage and salaried jobs covered less than 30 percent of households' monthly expenditure (the rest came mostly from loans and the sale of household possessions). Another in early 1949 found that workers were better off than at any time since liberation but that their living standards were still well below prewar levels.[47]

Although a small number of people may have been able to benefit from the postliberation chaos to improve their economic status, the bulk of the population included peasants subject to compulsory rice collection and increased competition from a rapidly expanding rural population; the rest were primarily urban workers especially

46. Kaukonen, p. 402.

47. According to Kaukonen, the unusual 1948 survey findings were caused by "illegal bonuses in kind, which were known to be paid frequently in the consumer goods industries" and because "profits from black-market operations were reported as proceeds of loans and sale of possessions" (ibid., p. 404). The 1949 survey results were cited in McCune, *Korea Today*, p. 169.

vulnerable to inflation. For most people, then, liberation brought a decline in already low living standards.

The New Republic

Between August 15, 1948, and June 25, 1950, the Republic of Korea enjoyed an externally peaceful if somewhat brief and turbulent development as a newly independent country. President Rhee pursued a domestic policy of stamping out opposition with the aid of the National Security Law, ostensibly designed to cope with the communist menace, and a foreign policy of Korean reunification (on his terms), unswerving hostility to communism, and the extraction of the maximum amount of American aid with a minimum of donor interference. The economic situation was better in 1949, the last preinvasion year, than it had been at any time since liberation. The chief problem was now one of security.

At the time of independence, there was a 26,000-man constabulary, several rightist paramilitary youth groups, and American military assistance sufficient to supply 50,000 troops. By June 1950 the Republic of Korea (ROK) Army had grown to 98,000 but was poorly equipped, poorly trained, and busy with antiguerrilla activity. The Yŏsu Rebellion had raised the specter of internal subversion (or at least violent reaction against an unpopular government), while the North was known to have a well-equipped, well-trained army of 125,000–150,000 that was possibly the superior of the two forces.

Domestic politics in the republic centered on the clash between the Rhee government, aided by a constitution giving the president wide powers, and the National Assembly, which, although possessing only limited power, made the most of it. Rhee was criticized for failing to use the best talents available in forming his cabinet; his nominee for the premiership was successfully opposed by the assembly; a land-reform act very popular with the electorate (but not Rhee's land-owning backers) was passed over the president's veto in June 1949.[48]

48. Land reform was undertaken first in the North and was more extensive there than in the South. Lack of reform became a major source of rural discontent and opposition to the Rhee government during the early days of the republic. What was not known at the time was the sharp difference between the form and substance of North Korea's land reform. One observer who later interviewed peasants in the vicinity of Hamhung (North Korea) and refugees from the North found that the peasants were victimized by unfair assessments and requests for "voluntary" extra contributions of food and services. He also found that many of those who had fled to the South were embittered peasants. See J. M. Spey, "The Peasants of Korea"; see also T.O. Engebretson, "Agriculture and Land Reform in Korea."

Rhee struck back by using the National Security Law to arrest opposition members of the assembly and to close down newspapers critical of his regime. When Kim Ku (an opposition leader and Rhee's principal rival) was assassinated the same month, there were rumors of administration complicity.

After the government announced its intention to delay the assembly elections scheduled for May 1950, American threats to review the aid program forced the elections to be held. Despite the arrest of many opposition candidates and their supporters for violating the National Security Law, Rhee's following in the assembly dropped from 56 to 12 of the 210 members. This was a major blow to the government; another came after the new assembly convened and reintroduced a measure to make the cabinet responsible to the assembly. Rhee was saved by the outbreak of war six days later.

When the Rhee government took over from the AMG, tenancy problems had been somewhat alleviated by land reform. However, reform served to fragment holdings and thus impede agricultural recovery. Industrial management was another formidable problem. About 90 percent of industrial plant was vested property taken over by the government. This property posed difficulties for both the AMG and the new Rhee government. There were few managers; production was inefficient because market discipline was lacking; product pricing was subject to political pressure, and overemployment was chronic. In spite of these problems industrial production, which had been abnormally depressed in 1947 and 1948, rose substantially in 1949. Agricultural output was also above previous levels in 1948 and 1949 due to particularly favorable rice crops in 1948 and summer grain harvests in 1949. Though Korea managed to export a small amount of rice, shortages of important commodities such as cotton textiles persisted as did the large current-account trade deficit.

In 1949, for the first time, the United States Army imports with GARIOA funds were supplemented by deliveries under a new aid agreement between the United States and the Republic of Korea. The agreement, to be administrated by the ECA, marked a shift in American policy away from relief toward longer-term development aid. A three-year program costing $350 million started with $150 million in fiscal 1950, $110 million of which was to cover the cost of importing fertilizer, food, and industrial raw materials. The rest was for a three-stage capital development program aimed at increasing coal production first, then electric power capacity, and finally fertilizer output.[49] Safeguards to ensure that funds were used properly included an agreement that the ROK would attempt to balance its budget, control currency issue and bank credit, regulate foreign-exchange transactions, facilitate foreign private investment, develop export industries, either dispose of former Japanese property or administer it more effectively, and establish a counterpart fund (equal to the won equivalent of the dollar cost of grant aid) to be used in ways agreed upon by both parties.

These terms were regarded unfavorably by the Korean government, which felt that it knew its own needs best and did not welcome the sort of interference in domestic policies called for by the agreement. Nor was Congress enthusiastic about the proposed program. The House proved especially reluctant to provide the funds requested, partly as a maneuver to continue aid to Nationalist China but also to avoid increasing the prize if the communists took over the South. After an initial defeat, a bill was passed that provided $110 million of the $150 million asked for fiscal 1950, with the proviso that aid would be terminated if any government should be formed in the Republic of Korea that included one or more members of the Communist party. The Koreans were understandably disturbed by the inconsistency of an American policy that first assisted the creation of a democratic government in Korea and then proved reluctant to give it economic support. On the other hand, a number of Americans felt that the ROK government had been lax in promoting economic recovery; they were also unhappy about the government' disregard for civil rights. Providing aid for Korea would obviously be difficult, but the issues associated with the program soon had to be put aside when war broke out.[50]

The War

The Korean War began on June 25, 1950, and ended with a military armistice rather than a peace treaty on July 27, 1953. These years

49. William Adams Brown, Jr., and Redvers Opie, *American Foreign Assistance*, pp. 375–76.
50. Brown and Opie note that the chief grounds of criticism were "uncontrolled Government spending (especially for hunting down opponents to the Government), inadequate tax collection, and the failure to absorb ECA supplies" (ibid., p. 378). Reeve mentions that the budget deficit for the ROK fiscal year ending in March 1950 was two-and-a-half times the expected amount (*The Republic of Korea*, p. 108). Also, inflation seemed to be getting out of hand (the Seoul retail price index for all commodities more than doubled between March 1948 and March 1950).

constitute the one period during which Korea received worldwide attention. The history of the war, as a result, has been dealt with by many authors and is therefore not discussed here.[51]

Two basic difficulties arise in trying to assess the economic impact of the war on South Korea: there are no quantitative or monetary correlates of the death and misery that are the essence of war, and a number of other important costs cannot be measured adequately. Nevertheless, the war had a major effect on individual well-being, political development, and institutional structure that cannot be ignored. Though necessarily imprecise, an estimate of the magnitude of lossess and the extent of the subsequent recovery should prove helpful in evaluating later events.

Civilian war casualties have been estimated at almost a million in South Korea, including 166,000 killed, 98,000 "slaughtered" (i.e., executed), 169,000 wounded, 78,000 abducted, and 253,000 missing. Casualties among the United Nations forces totaled 420,000 including 48,000 killed, 186,000 wounded, 119,000 missing, and 67,000 prisoners. Almost three-quarters of these United Nations forces casualties were Korean.[52] With the population of 20.2 million at the May 1949 census, and 21.5 million by the September 1955 census, the average annual (compound) population growth rate during the interim was 1 percent. It was almost 3 percent per year from the 1955 census to the December 1, 1960 census. If population had grown at the same rate between 1949 and 1955 as it did between 1955 and 1960, the 1955 population would have been 24.1 million, not 21.5 million. Almost a million of the 2.6-million difference between these two figures is accounted for by military and civilian war casualties. The rest (1.6 million) is a crude estimate of the loss in population that would have been born during the interval that includes the Korean War or would not have died from war-associated diseases if there had been no war.[53]

Actual physical loss in the South, including damage to buildings, equipment, and other movables, was estimated at over 400 billion

---

51. See, for example, Samuel L. A. Marshall, *The River and the Gauntlet*; Carl Berger, *The Korea Knot*; T. R. Fehrenbach, *This Kind of War*; Robert Leckie, *Conflict: The History of the Korean War*; Ely J. Kahn, Jr., *The Peculiar War*; and Isidor F. Stone, *The Hidden History of the Korean War*.

52. Bank of Korea, *Annual Economic Review, 1955*, tables 9 and 10.

53. The estimate of potential population loss is probably conservative since no account is taken of the net immigration from the North, which may have been quite large. John P. Lewis, *Reconstruction and Development in South Korea*, says that "casualties were more than offset by new refugees from the North" (p. 16).

hwan in July 1953 prices, a sum only slightly less than the current value of 1953 GNP. Agricultural production fell sharply in 1951 and 1952 but had recovered by 1953. Output series for cotton yarn and sheeting, paper, rubber shoes, cement, light bulbs, and other major products show mostly a decline in 1950 or 1951, then recovery to prewar levels by 1952 or 1953.[54] These declines were large: output of cotton yarn and sheeting in 1951 was less than half the 1949 levels; production of rubber shoes in 1950 was less than 20 percent of that in 1949; 1951 cement output was only a third of the output in 1949. Imports fell sharply too. Foreign aid received in 1950 was about half the 1949 level, which was, in turn, substantially below 1947–48 aid levels. These earlier peaks were not reached again until 1953, when UNKRA (United Nations Korean Reconstruction Agency) supplies arrived to supplement large-scale imports under the American CRIK (Civil Relief in Korea) program.

Damage to productive facilities and the interruption of domestic production and imports touched off wild inflation and a decline in already low standards of living. The national urban retail price index was 197.8 in 1949 (1947 = 100). It more than doubled between June and September of 1950 (the 1950 annual average was 531.5), and then shot up to 2,128.5 in 1951, 5,243.6 in 1952, and 7,618.8 in 1953. Furthermore, inflation did not end with the armistice in 1953; the same index averaged 10,319.5 in 1954 and even passed 20,000 in August and September 1955. In addition to inflation, the first rough estimates of Korean GNP made by Robert Nathan Associates for UNKRA show a sharp decline in wartime GNP and an even sharper drop in per capita consumption. GNP in 1949–50 was 1.8 billion, measured in 1952–53 U.S. dollars. It fell to 1.4 billion in 1952–53 and then increased to 1.7 billion in 1953–54. Per capita consumption dropped from $71 in 1949–50 to $50 in 1952–53 before recovering to $60 in 1953–54. The recovery in consumption at first appears to have been greater since net imports (less direct military imports) quadrupled between 1949–50 and 1953–54 so that total available resources per capita rose over the period; the increase, however, was more than offset by growth in national security expenditures.[55]

54. Damage estimates and output figures are from the Bank of Korea, *Annual Economic Review, 1955*, tables 8, 75, and 90.

55. United Nations, Korean Reconstruction Agency, *An Economic Programme for Korean Reconstruction*, Appendix tables 1 and 2. Years given are ROK fiscal years that at the time began on April 1 and ended on March 31.

The shift in final demand from consumption to national security expenditure indicates one failure of the measures given here to show the magnitude of the war's effects. They do not reflect the cost of raising the size of the ROK Army from 100,000 men in 1950 to as many as 650,000 in 1951. Also, they do not show the wasteful use of the current output during wartime or the cost of war and postwar dislocation. "At the peak ... in 1951 probably half of all South Koreans fell into some refugee or relief category."[56] The war also resulted in institutional and political changes that influenced Korea's later economic growth. "War and American support for the Korean military ... had made the army pre-eminent."[57] Rhee was aware of the potential threat to his government of the well-trained army after 1953 and developed the policy of moving high-ranking commanders at regular intervals. Although the army was not responsible for Rhee's downfall, it overthrew his succussor, Dr. John M. Chang (Chang Myŏn) in May 1961. It is hard to imagine such a coup taking place before the Korean War.

When opened to modern influences in the 1870s, Korea presented an unusual combination of economic backwardness, dynastic survival, and xenophobic isolationism. A policy of isolation had not only preserved the country's identity and territorial integrity but also had cut off Koreans from the flow of ideas and technological development that penetrated much of the rest of the world. An extremely centralized autocracy, freed from external pressure and foreign influences for several centuries, had become weak and corrupt. The result was inept response to new demands upon the government that arose as foreign powers entered into relations with Korea. Perhaps this weakness was a long-term asset, for there were no established forces of sufficient strength to resist the sort of social and political adaptation needed to convert an autocratic society into a modern nation. Furthermore, a long common history and Korea's ethnic, linguistic, and cultural unity might all have been expected to foster such adaptation. The process was interrupted, however, as Japan obtained hegemony over Korea after the Russo-Japanese War and formally annexed the country in 1910.

During the years when Korea was a colony within the Japanese

56. Lewis, *Reconstruction and Development in South Korea*, p. 16.
57. Gregory Henderson, *Korea: The Politics of the Vortex*, p. 186.

Empire, the country was subjected to typical colonial exploitation. Nationalistic aspirations were crushed; Koreans were demoted to second-class citizens in their own country; even linguistic and cultural identity were threatened by Japanese policies. Economic development was frankly exploitative and the peasants, who comprised the bulk of the population, were probably no better off at the end of the colonial era than at the beginning. Industrial growth, on the other hand, was atypical. Korea was more heavily industrialized than most colonies and much more dependent upon trade with the imperial center, Japan. This was a result of Japanese attempts to achieve self-sufficiency within the Yen Bloc and in later years was due to Japan's preparation for war.

The unusually high degree of economic dependence on Japan that distorted Korea's colonial growth proved a burden after liberation at the end of World War II; Korea's division into North and South was even more of an economic tragedy because it split two essentially complementary regions into separate countries. The division, based on military expediency and, fundamentally, inability to foresee the nature of the problems that would arise in a postwar world divided into Eastern and Western blocs, became a source of tension and ultimately war. The American military government that ran the South for three years until South Korea achieved independence in 1948 was unprepared for the difficulties facing it and, more basically, was ineffective because Korea's importance to America's national interest had never been defined. On the other hand, although occupation authorities faced virtually insurmountable difficulties, they succeeded in land reform and relief operations and left a heritage of "westernized democratic mannerisms and procedures, if not the institutional substance to make them effective."[58]

The new republic enjoyed less than two years of peace before the Korean War began in the spring of 1950, but even this was a difficult, turbulent period in which the country's energies were focused on the struggle for power between President Rhee and the opposition parties in the National Assembly, on civil disturbances, and on the increasing threat, accompanied by border skirmishes, from the North. The economic inheritance from the Japanese and American occupations was sufficiently meager to require full-time attention, but political and security problems were paramount—with the consequence that

58. Lewis, *Reconstruction and Development in South Korea*, p. 12.

the country's economic situation was neglected. Fortunately, there were good harvests in 1948 and 1949 and the United States, despite initial reluctance to underwrite the cost of economic and military assistance for Korea, had started aid deliveries under a long-term program. Although the country's economic performance was considerably better than it had been at the time of liberation from the Japanese, large government budget deficits and continuing rapid inflation were signs that Korea was not yet prepared to adopt the policies needed to stimulate economic growth.

The new government's economic failings became immaterial after the outbreak of war with the North in June 1950. With the exception of a few small areas, the whole peninsula was ravaged by war. In terms of lost lives, physical damage, and human suffering, the war was a disaster. After the first year the fighting became localized in the vicinity of the 38th parallel; the next two years proved an exercise in futility as casualties mounted and negotiations dragged on. The end brought armistice, not peace, and the spectacle of Panmunjom. Panmunjom, the site of armistice talks for over two decades, symbolizes the inconclusiveness of the Korean War, the economic burden of persistent military requirements, and the forlorn hope for peaceful reunification.

The war had profound consequences for the economy in later years. Extensive physical damage and institutional disarray made reform and reconstruction essential. Much of the economic growth from 1953 to 1958 or 1959 represented reconstruction and the replacement of previous productive capacity rather than expansion beyond previously achieved output levels. War-engendered inflation led to a variety of barter techniques, a degree of government corruption much greater than was traditional in Korea, and the breakdown of many ordinary business arrangements. The side effects of inflation served to bind enterprise with controls, distort incentives, intensify the inflexibility and dislocation of the economy, and hamper reconstruction efforts. On the other hand, substantial recovery had been achieved by 1953–54.

Syngman Rhee continued to govern Korea from the armistice in 1953 until April 1960, when the government was overthrown by a student revolution. Economic developments during this period are examined in the chapters that follow, but more emphasis is placed on the accelerated growth that occurred in later years. The radical shift from slow growth in the 1950s to the rapid development of the 1960s and early 1970s and the improvement in the quality of life, the impressive growth rate, and the more optimistic outlook that characterized the later period cannot be explained simply by the overthrow of Rhee's government. Much of the subsequent discussion is therefore devoted to describing and analyzing the more recent changes that have transformed Korea into one of the world's most rapidly growing economies.

2

Accelerated Growth and Structural Change

Continuous, resonably reliable economic data for Korea are available only back to 1953. Discussion is therefore limited to the two decades that have now passed since the end of the Korean War. The marked shift in the pace of economic growth that took place during this period was accompanied by such broad changes in economic structure that the Korean economy of the early 1970s was very unlike that of the mid-1950s. Here I am primarily concerned with establishing what happened. Causes of the acceleration in the growth rate are also considered here, but the topic is covered more thoroughly in chapter 3 before examining the implications of past growth for future development.

Gross national product, measured in constant 1970 prices, rose 3.6-fold from 1953 through 1972. One of the main features of this growth was its unevenness. National product grew at an annual average (compound) rate of 4.1 percent from 1953–55 to 1960–62; the rate more than doubled to 9.1 percent from 1960–62 to 1970–72. The 1953–72 period can be divided in a number of ways, but the years 1953–55 to 1960–62 and 1960–62 to 1970–72 are distinguished here to simplify the exposition and because the underlying forces responsible for economic growth differ more between than within these two subperiods.

Measures for real domestic product, population, per capita output, and other basic aggregates are given in table 2.1. These measures reveal the acceleration in growth of GDP (and GNP [the two are practically identical for Korea]) after the first subperiod, and a second subperiod growth rate that was one of the world's highest. Population rose 50 percent from 1953–55 to 1970–72 at gradually declining rates. This population growth restricted the annual increase in per

Table 2.1. Growth of Aggregate and Per Capita Product:
1953–55 to 1970–72

A. Gross domestic product (measured at 1970 factor costs)

	Average level during period			Average annual growth rate			
Period	GDP (billion won) (1)	Population (million) (2)	Per capita (thousand won) (3)	Interval (years) (4)	GDP (5)	Population (6)	Per capita GDP (7)
1. 1953–55	836	20.6	40.7	—	—	—	—
2. 1956–59	961	22.8	42.1	3.5	4.1	3.1	1.0
3. 1960–62	1,091	25.3	43.1	3.5	3.7	3.0	0.7
4. 1963–69	1,603	29.0	55.3	5.0	8.0	2.8	5.1
5. 1970–72	2,525	31.9	79.1	5.0	9.5	1.9	7.4
6. 1953–55 to 1960–62	—	—	—	7.0	3.9	3.0	0.8
7. 1960–62 to 1970–72	—	—	—	10.0	8.8	2.3	6.3

B. Other aggregates

	Average (annual) level[c]			Average annual growth rate	
	1953–55 (1)	1960–62 (2)	1970–72 (3)	1953–55 to 1960–62 (4)	1960–62 to 1970–72 (5)
8. Total[a] current resources	978	1,293	3,553	4.1	10.6
9. GNP	891	1,178	2,813	4.1	9.1
10. Commodity[b] product	510	680	1,633	4.2	9.2
11. Private consumpt.	714	970	2,063	4.5	7.8
Per capita					
12. Line 8	48.1	51.4	111.3	1.0	8.0
13. Line 11	34.8	38.3	64.7	1.4	5.4

Sources: Tables A1 and A2.
[a] GDP plus imports.
[b] Agriculture, forestry, fisheries; manufacturing; mining; construction; electric, water, sanitary services; transport, storage, and communications.
[c] Totals in billion won, per capita in thousands.

capita GDP to 0.8 percent during the first subperiod; per capita GDP increased to 6.3 percent in the second. All values in table 2.1 are adjusted to remove the effects of price increases, which averaged 16.5 percent a year during the first subperiod and 16.4 percent in the second. This first average, in particular, conceals wide year-to-year changes in rates of inflation and it may be significant that accelerated output growth coincided with greater price stability during the second subperiod.

Other major aggregates such as total current resources, commodity product, and private consumption are shown in rows 8–11 of table 2.1. Growth rates averaged around 4 percent a year for these measures in 1953–55 to 1960–62 and then rose to 8–10 percent from 1960–62 to 1970–72. Total current resources, which includes gross domestic product plus imports, is intended to measure all the resources available to the economy. Resources grew faster than the other aggregates during the second subperiod because, unlike the others, resources include imports, which rose more rapidly than other components of gross domestic product except for exports. Such above-average increase provided the means for expanding consumption, investment, and exports. Commodity product, which includes the output of goods-producing sectors plus other activities associated with goods production such as transportation, behaved much like GDP. Output of the service sector (government, trade, and other services) increased at about the same rate as aggregate output.

Estimates given for total and per capita private consumption indicate that the average Korean was much better off in 1970–72 than in 1953–55 and that most of the improvement came during the second subperiod. Private consumption rose substantially less than the other measures, however, so that investment and the remaining expenditure categories must have grown more. Comparison of per capita resources and consumption (rows 12 and 13), which reveals a widening gap by the end of the second subperiod that confirms this, also shows that more than 40 percent of total current resources were used for investment, exports, and government expenditures.

The output and expenditure aggregates given in table 2.1 conceal substantial variation among their component categories. However, panel B reveals greater dispersion of growth rates during the second subperiod than in the first. Variation or dispersion of growth rates is a sign of the structural change that has accompanied accelerated growth in Korea. Acceleration and substantial structural change are

Table 2.2. Comparison of Output, Per Capita Output, and Population
Growth Rates for Korea and Other East and Southeast Asian
Countries: 1953–55 to 1960–62, 1960–62 to 1968–70

	Gross domestic product[a]		Per capita product		Population	
	I[b]	II[c]	I	II	I	II
	(1)	(2)	(3)	(4)	(5)	(6)
Korea	4.5	9.6	1.6	6.8	3.0	2.4
Taiwan	7.0	10.2[d]	3.3	7.0[d]	3.5	2.9
Japan	9.4	10.9	8.2	9.8	1.0	1.1
Thailand	5.1	8.3[d]	2.1	5.1[d]	3.0	3.1
Philippines	5.4	4.9	2.2	1.5	3.1	3.0

Sources: United Nations, *Yearbooks of National Accounts Statistics*, *1970*, (vol. 2, table 7), *1971* (vol. 3, table 7); United Nations, *Demographic Yearbooks*, *1970* and *1971*; Organization for Economic Cooperation and Development, *National Accounts of Less Developed Countries* (July 1968), table C.
[a] At constant (1965) factor costs.
[b] 1953–55 to 1960–62.
[c] 1960–62 to 1968–70.
[d] Rates calculated for the period 1960–62 to 1968–69.

the two main characteristics that distinguish Korea's economic development during the years 1960–62 through 1970–72 from development in earlier periods. Causes of acceleration are discussed in the next section; shifts in sectoral shares and in employment distribution, and growth of output per worker are then examined in order to evaluate structural changes.

Causes of Acceleration

Growth rates of countries whose location, size, trade ties, or other similarities permit reasonable comparison with Korea should show whether the acceleration in Korea's growth rate was in some way exceptional. Output, per capita output, and population-growth estimates for comparable periods in Korea, Taiwan, Japan, Thailand, and the Philippines are given in table 2.2. Growth rates for Korea are different from those presented in table 2.1 (mainly because 1970 price weights are used in table 2.1, 1965 weights in table 2.2) but it is clear that Korea had the lowest rates of increase in GDP and per capita GDP during the first subperiod, and that these rates jumped in subsequent years almost to the Japanese and Taiwanese levels and well above rates for Thailand and the Philippines. Though output in other countries also increased more rapidly after 1960–62 than before, acceleration was greatest in Korea. Moreover, the marked drop in population growth rates for Korea and Taiwan, which is a sign of modernization, is not seen in either Thailand or the Philippines. The sort of increase in per capita product found in Korea during the first subperiod might ordinarily be considered adequate if it had not come immediately after a war, when the combination of recovery and normal expansion should have produced particularly rapid growth. Taiwan's per capita product grew twice as fast as Korea's during these years and at roughly the same rate subsequently. If per capita product could increase at an annual 6.8 percent rate in Korea from 1960–62 to 1970–72, why was growth so much less in earlier years? Some obstacle or set of obstacles must have been restraining development during the first subperiod.

One obstacle to growth may have been the long time lag between institutional or other changes and their effects on the pace of economic development. Approximately three-quarters of the population was illiterate in 1945, for instance. Although a literacy campaign after the Korean War greatly reduced this proportion by 1960, most of the benefits of increased literacy would not have occurred before the second subperiod. Similarly, school enrollments rose rapidly, but given the limited occupational distribution of Koreans when Korea was a Japanese colony and the small stock of educated manpower at the time of liberation, a shortage of managerial and technical skills was inevitable during the next 15 or 20 years.

Another obstacle to growth was a food shortage, which was responsible for inadequate nutrition and probably lowered labor productivity as well. Calorie intake and other characteristics of the typical diet in the late 1950s were near or below minimum requirements before diets improved in the 1960s.[1] Korea's agricultural heritage was unfavorable, certainly less promising than Taiwan's. Also, postindependence production began from below-average levels, and increases went largely to feeding the country's rapidly expanding population.[2] A series of land reforms initiated in 1948 and completed a decade later eliminated tenancy and improved farmers' incentives, but reform without expanded credit, better marketing, and increased physical inputs

1. A strong, statistically significant relationship has been found between calories per head and labor quality (see W. Galenson and G. Pyatt, *The Quality of Labour and Economic Development in Certain Countries*). Estimates for nutritional levels in Korea are given in Kwon E Hyock et al., *A Study in Urban Slum Population*, pp. 31, 62, and *Korea Times*, 4 July 1972.
2. See Yujiro Hayami, "Green Revolution in Historical Perspective: The Experience of Japan, Taiwan and Korea," p. 28.

(especially irrigation and fertilizer) is unlikely to stimulate production. Since none of these were forthcoming, the reform had few immediate output benefits.

Although industrial production grew rapidly from 1953–55 to 1960–62, the industrial sector was too small to have much influence on the overall growth rate (see table 2.3). Production centered in manufacturing, where it was concentrated, in turn, in materials-producing and consumer-goods industries. Postwar reconstruction needs, consumer demand, and development of import substitutes supported manufacturing until the late 1950s, when a combination of poor harvests, termination of UNKRA relief, reduction in U.S. aid, and monetary and fiscal restrictions reduced aggregate demand and slowed growth.

Slow growth was not due solely to external forces, however, but also to a government that showed little interest in economic goals or ability to achieve them. This was manifest in a number of ways. Power shortages, poor management, and inadequate markets left factories idle. Such idleness, a sign of misallocation, occurred because a new business elite profited from subsidized credit and access to cheap foreign exchange rather than from increasing production, the bureaucracy benefited from payments received for benefits granted to the new elite, and the government had no overall economic plan and seemed mostly interested in maximizing foreign aid.

No development plan was formulated by the Rhee government until 1959, possibly because it was preoccupied with political problems and because any national plan would have been inconsistent with hopes for reunification; moreover, reconstruction strategy called for maximizing foreign aid and more aid could be obtained by demonstrating need than by submitting to the discipline of a plan.[3] Whatever the reason, the first subperiod was an era of overvalued exchange rates and heavy trade deficits, low bank interest rates and insignificant private saving, and government budget deficits financed by borrowing from the Bank of Korea (BOK). Government policies, in short, were at least partly responsible for poor economic performance. Planning is significant in this context not because a plan necessarily improves economic performance but because it indicates that high priority is attached to development goals and there was no sign of this before 1959.

3. This argument is given in David C. Cole and Princeton N. Lyman, *Korean Development*, pp. 79, 164–66.

Political turmoil marked the close of the first subperiod as the Rhee government fell victim to a student revolution in April 1960 and the successor Chang government was overthrown by a military coup in May 1961. An ill-conceived currency reform in the spring and a disastrous harvest in the fall of 1962 combined with revolution and coup to transform slow growth to virtual stagnation at the close of the first subperiod. The economic outlook was bleak in the early 1960s, but with the benefit of hindsight one can see that a number of factors already existed that were to permit rapid growth during the second subperiod.

Increased literacy, land reform, industrial recovery, and a whole range of institutional changes initiated after independence had continued long enough, despite interruption during the Korean War, to begin influencing the pace of development by the start of the second subperiod. The country also had a government no longer bound by economic policies that had inhibited growth in earlier years. In addition, the new military regime was strong enough to implement programs, however unpopular, that might promote development. A case in point was the normalization treaty with Japan that was signed in 1965, despite public opposition, and that promised to provide economic support at a time when American aid was diminishing. Finally, there was only one important public issue: how to improve the economic situation. The new government, which needed to establish its legitimacy, realized this and adopted a political strategy that made economic development its main goal.[4] The stabilization program of the mid-1960s and Korea's three five-year plans were perhaps the principal economic policies adopted to implement this political strategy.

Passage of time, change of government, and the increased importance of economic goals are credited here with responsibility for the accelerated growth observed in Korea during the second subperiod, but it is unclear whether these conditions were necessary or simply sufficient. Nor do such noneconomic factors explain why the specific set of economic policies adopted was chosen instead of some other set or why Korean development has displayed certain features and not others. Yet is seems reasonable to expect some relationship between

---

4. For example, President Park said, during a campaign to revise the constitution in order to allow him to serve a third term, "I proposed the referendum because I thought that retaining the present system ... will contribute to economic development.... I wanted to ... add the finishing touch to the vast enterprises of construction I started" (*Korea Times*, 11 Oct. 1969).

economic and noneconomic factors, and between earlier and later economic events. The export-promotion program and swift export expansion of the second subperiod could be implemented only by a strong government, for example. The same program and results would be inconceivable in one of Myrdal's "soft states" of South Asia.[5] Similarly, excess demand for loans and inadequate saving caused by artificially low interest rates during the first subperiod made interest-rate reform and the raising of rates a logical policy action during the second.

CHANGES IN SECTORAL SHARES

The structure of the Korean economy changed radically from the beginning of the first subperiod to the end of the second. Agriculture's share of total domestic product dropped from 50 percent in 1953–55 to 30 percent by 1970–72 and domestic product originating in the service sector declined somewhat, while the industrial sector's share increased from 11 to 35 percent (see table 2.3). This growth in the relative significance of industrial product was equivalent to that which had occurred previously in Japan (from 1878–82 to 1923–27) or Sweden (1861–65 to 1901–05), but whereas the process lasted 40 to 45 years in these countries, it took only 20 years in Korea.[6]

Industry expanded at least twice as fast as the service sector and four to five times more rapidly than agriculture during each subperiod. Subcategories for the industrial sector (mining and manufacturing, construction, and utilities) and services (trade, other services) in table 2.3 show that growth rates and, consequently, shares of these sectors are averages of activities that behaved quite differently during the two subperiods. Perhaps the leading example here is the service sector, where product originating in trade, the largest single category, has increased much more rapidly than output of other services, a hetero-geneous grouping of educational, other professional, government, and domestic services.

Differences in sectoral growth rates can be explained in a number of ways. One source of difference is the change in the structure of foreign and domestic demand as per capita incomes rise and goods

5. Countries are "soft states" when "policies decided on are often not enforced, if they are enacted at all, and in that the authorities, even when framing policies, are reluctant to place obligations on people" (Gunnar Myrdal, *An Approach to the Asian Drama*, p. 64).
6. Simon Kuznets, *Modern Economic Growth*, table 3.1.

Table 2.3. Changes in Output Structure: 1953–55 to 1970–72
(Gross domestic product at 1970 factor costs)

| | Average level (billion won) | | | Distribution (% share) | | | Average annual growth (%) | |
	1953–55 (1)	1960–62 (2)	1970–72 (3)	1953–55 (4)	1960–62 (5)	1970–72 (6)	(1) to (2) (7)	(2) to (3) (8)
1. Total GDP	836	1,091	2,525	100.0	100.0	100.0	3.9	8.8
2. Agriculture	421	493	744	50.4	45.2	29.5	2.3	4.2
3. Industry	89	187	889	10.6	17.1	35.2	11.2	16.9
a. Mining, manufacturing	57	120	555	6.8	11.0	22.0	11.2	16.5
b. Construction	16	29	148	1.9	2.6	5.8	8.9	17.7
c. Utilities	16	38	186	1.9	3.5	7.4	13.2	17.2
4. Services	326	411	892	39.0	37.7	35.3	3.4	8.1
a. Trade	84	142	408	10.0	13.0	16.1	7.8	11.1
b. Other	242	269	484	29.0	24.7	19.2	1.5	6.0

Source: BOK, Economic Statistics Yearbook, 1973.

and services with high income elasticities of demand become more important in final consumption. There is also a supply explanation. Differences in growth rates arise from uneven expansion of factor inputs among sectors and unequal increase in productivity as new processes and techniques are adopted, at different rates, among sectors that differ in relative technological backwardness. In addition, a historical reason can be offered for observed differences, namely, that activities lost through liberation, division, or war should grow fastest. This last is essentially a demand explanation that assumes some overall structure of demand to be served. Finally, sectors that receive priority in the government's economic plans are likely to grow faster than those that do not.

Evidence to support the income-elasticity explanation for changes in sectoral shares can be found in the declining proportion of food in total private consumption. Food outlays dropped from two-thirds to less than half of total consumption as average per capita outlays almost doubled from 1953–55 to 1970–72. This meant that a larger share of a rising total was available for expenditure on other consumer goods and on services. Similarly, employment and investment data can be used to evaluate the supply explanation. Agricultural employment rose only 10 percent during the second subperiod while industrial employment more than doubled. A large and increasing share of total investment during these years was also allocated to the industrial sector. Since new techniques are typically embodied in new capital, a combination of above-average increase in factor inputs and improved technology provided the mechanism for spectacular growth of the industrial sector.

Historical reasons for structural change are difficult to document because South Korea was formerly part of larger economic units so that without input–output data (there are none for any year before 1960) one cannot locate sources of goods and services that were consumed in what is now the republic but were produced elsewhere. Also, independence should create new demand that did not exist when the present economy formed the southern half of a unified Korea that was, in turn, a colony within the Japanese Empire. In addition, replacement of former sources of supply from 1945 to 1953 is not covered by our data but undoubtedly affected growth and structure after 1953. Nevertheless, southern Korea was once a major rice exporter and source of textiles and other light manufactures within the Yen Bloc. Replacement might therefore be expected to concentrate in nonagricultural activities, particularly electric power and chemical fertilizer, which had formerly been produced chiefly in northern Korea, and the other inputs lost with liberation and partition.

Such expectations have been justified, in part, by government policies that favored industrialization. The major goals of the first two five-year plans (1962–66 and 1967–71) were to "build an industrial base" and to "promote modernization of the industrial structure."[7] This was first done largely by encouraging import substitution and later by promoting exports. One result was that exports rose from $30 million a year in 1953–55 to $43 million in 1960–62 before a phenomenal increase to $1.6 billion by 1972 (these are current dollar estimates). Less than one-sixth of total exports were manufactures in the late 1950s, but by 1972 the share of manufactures had increased to over four-fifths. Much of the accelerated growth during the second subperiod occurred in the industrial sector, the industrial sector was dominated by manufacturing, and the expansion of manufacturing has been led by output for export. Structural changes that have given more weight to the industrial sector, then, can be traced to export growth.

EMPLOYMENT DISTRIBUTION AND OUTPUT PER WORKER

One correlate of the change in sectoral shares is a shift in the labor force from work where output per worker is low to work where it is high or, historically, from agriculture and other primary industries to manufacturing and other secondary activity and, in some cases, to the service, or tertiary, sector. Growth of output per worker has been substantial, especially during the second subperiod, and can be divided into two parts: one, intersectoral, owing to changes in the distribution of employment as workers shift to sectors where output per worker is high; the other, intrasectoral, owing to increasing output per worker in any given sector. Estimates for employment, its distribution, and output per worker in agricultural and nonagricultural activities for each subperiod and for selected subsectors during the second subperiod are given in table 2.4. These estimates can be used to evaluate the components of growth in output per worker.

Average output per worker rose from 136,000 won in 1953–55 to

7. Republic of Korea, *Summary of the First Five-Year Economic Plan*, p. 24; Government of the Republic of Korea, *The Second Five-Year Economic Development Plan*, p. 33.

Table 2.4. Employment Shares and Output per Worker
(GDP at 1970 factor costs)

A. Agricultural and nonagricultural employment and output per worker: 1953–55 to 1970–72

	Employment share (%)			GDP per worker (thousand won)			Average annual growth rate (%)	
	1953–55[a] (1)	1960–62[b] (2)	1970–72 (3)	1953–55 (4)	1960–62 (5)	1970–72 (6)	(4) to (5) (7)	(5) to (6) (8)
1. Total (thousands)	6,170	7,236	10,123	135.5	150.8	249.4	1.5	5.2
Percent Distribution (%)								
2. Agriculture	67.0	63.1	49.9	101.8	108.0	147.4	0.8	3.2
3. Nonagriculture	33.0	36.9	50.1	204.0	224.0	350.8	1.3	4.6

B. Sectoral employment and output per worker: 1960–62 to 1970–72

	Employment share (%)		GDP per worker (thousand won)		Av. ann. grth. rate (%)	Productivity relatives[d]	
	1960–62[b] (1)	1970–72 (2)	1960–62 (3)	1970–72 (4)	(3) to (4) (5)	1960–62 (6)	1970–72 (7)
1. Total (thousands)	7,236	10,123	150.8	249.4	5.2	—	—
	100.0	100.0	(142.0)	(238.3)	(5.3)	1.00	1.00
2. Agriculture[c]	63.1	49.9	108.0	147.4	3.2	0.76	0.62
3. Industry	13.0	21.1	198.4	415.5	7.7	1.40	1.74
a. Mining, manufacturing	8.7	14.2	190.1	384.9	7.3	1.34	1.62
b. Other	4.3	6.9	215.1	478.5	8.3	1.51	2.01
4. Services	23.9	29.0	201.3	265.3	2.8	1.42	1.11
a. Trade	9.9	12.7	198.3	317.8	4.8	1.40	1.33
b. Other	14.0	16.3	203.4	224.6	1.0	1.43	0.94

Sources: GDP, table 2.3 above; employment, EPB, *Annual Reports on the Economically Active Population.*

[a] Figures for 1953–55 and 1960–62 are estimates based on the ratio of employment to population in subsequent years (approximately 0.3). The distribution between agricultural and nonagricultural workers in 1953–55 was derived from the proportion of rural to total population in 1955, adjusted for gradual decrease in more recent years of the ratio agricultural employment/total employment ÷ rural population/total population.

[b] Categories for 1960–62 are based on the 1963 distribution. Figures for 1970–72 are, in some cases, estimates since detailed employment breakdowns have not been published for the years after 1970.

[c] Total GDP per worker shown in parentheses, the category for "other services," and the productivity relatives all exclude GDP originating in banking, insurance, real estate, and ownership of dwellings.

[d] Output per worker is given as a proportion of the average for all workers (expressed as 1.0).

151,000 in 1960–62 and reached 249,000 won in 1970–72. Panel A reveals that this average is composed of low levels of output per worker in agriculture and high levels in nonagricultural employment, and that the distribution of employment shifted substantially as the proportion of workers engaged in nonagricultural jobs grew from one-third at the beginning of the first subperiod to one-half by the end of the second. Output per worker was twice as high in other activities as in agriculture, and the disparity has grown.

Employment shares and output per worker are shown in more detail for the second subperiod in panel B of table 2.4. As agriculture's employment share declined, shares of both the industrial and service sectors increased, with most of the increase occurring in industry. Output per worker varies substantially between and within sectors and variance has been increasing so that by 1970–72, output was more than three times as high in other industry (construction, utilities, transport–storage–communications) as in agriculture. Except for particularly low growth in the other services category, output per worker increased at annual rates of 3 percent or more per year during the second subperiod. The effects of differential growth rates can best be seen in columns 6 and 7 of panel B, where output per worker in each category has been expressed as a proportion of average output for all workers.[8] These output relatives reveal more clearly than the absolute levels of columns 3 and 4 the decline in relative output per worker in other services and the growing differentiation among sectors in output per worker.

Growing differentiation may result from unequal increase among sectors in inputs of capital and other factors, particularly since output per worker reflects the contribution of all inputs, not just labor, and the second subperiod was marked by a sharp rise in industrial-sector capital formation (see table 2.8). Or sectoral differences in quality of labor may widen with increasing age–sex differentials or growing differences in education and training. Other possibilities are that specific product or factor markets are imperfect or that opportunities

8. Growth in output per worker shown for other services is likely to be biased downward because one-quarter of the workers in this category are government employees, and no allowance is made for increasing output per worker in calculating gross domestic product originating in the public administration and defense sector. Average output used in deriving the output relatives is based on gross domestic product less product originating in banking, insurance, real estate, and ownership of dwellings. Product derived from these categories is excluded on the grounds that it derives primarily from capital rather than from labor.

for factor substitution differ among sectors. Fixed factor proportions or differences in educational requirements may also be responsible for the existence of noncompeting factor markets that should, in turn, generate differences in output per worker. Whatever the reasons, the presence of large and increasing sectoral differentials in output per worker indicates that factor-price and marginal-product equalization conditions did not hold in Korea during the second subperiod. Given the rapidity of structural change, it would be surprising if they did. Such differentials are important because they are necessary if intersectoral shifts in employment distribution are to contribute to output growth.

One clue that suggests this possibility is an apparent anomaly found in panel A of table 2.4, namely, that the growth of aggregate output per worker has been greater than growth in either its agricultural or nonagricultural components. This can occur only if the employment distribution shifts toward activities where output per worker is above average. Estimates of the contribution of intrasectoral and intersectoral portions of the aggregate increase in output per worker are sensitive to sectoral detail and are therefore approximate, but such estimates indicate that the intersectoral portion was significant during both subperiods. Roughly three-fifths of the overall increase in output per worker during the first subperiod and three-quarters during the second can be attributed to rising output per worker or intrasectoral change. The contribution of intersectoral changes or shifting employment was thus two-fifths and one-quarter, respectively, during the two subperiods.[9]

Uses of National Product

Estimates for the main expenditure categories of gross national product, their percentage shares, and growth rates during each subperiod are presented in panel A of table 2.5. National product is used rather than domestic product, as in previous tables, because it includes net factor income from the rest of the world that is spent in

---

9. The contribution of intrasectoral increase to aggregate output growth was calculated as the sum of the increases in output per worker in each sector, weighted by the sector's employment share during the period (an average of 1960–62 and 1970–72 values). The contribution of intersectoral shifts was estimated as the sum of changes in employment shares (taken with regard for sign) weighted by the absolute deviation in sectoral output per worker from the all-sector average (an average of 1960–62 and 1970–72 values).

Table 2.5. GNP: Expenditures: Uses and Sources
(1970 Market prices)

A. *Expenditures (annual averages in billion won)*

	1953–55 (1)	1960–62 (2)	1970–72 (3)	% Share[a] 1953–55 (4)	% Share[a] 1960–62 (5)	% Share[a] 1970–72 (6)	Growth rate (1) to (2) (7)	Growth rate (2) to (3) (8)
1. Private consumption	714	970	2,064	80.2	82.3	73.4	4.5	7.8
2. Government consumption	150	165	306	17.0	14.0	10.9	1.3	6.4
3. Gross domestic capital formation	100	113	707	11.2	10.3	24.4	1.7	20.2
4. Exports	13	36	495	1.4	3.1	17.6	15.3	29.9
5. Less imports	97	122	739	10.9	10.4	26.3	3.2	19.8
6. Trade balance (4−5)	(−84)	(−86)	(−244)	(9.5)	(7.3)	(8.7)	—	—
7. Statistical discrepancy	—	8	−19	—	—	—	—	—
8. GDP	880	1,170	2,814	98.9	99.3	100.0	4.1	9.2
9. Net income from rest of world	10	8	−1	1.1	0.7	0	—	—
10. GNP	890	1,178	2,813	100.0	100.0	100.0	4.1	9.1

B. *Uses and Sources (% share)*

Period	Uses Private consumption (1)	Uses Govt. consumption (2)	Uses GDCF (3)	Sources Exports (4)	Sources GDP (5)	Sources Imports (6)	Imports−exports as % of Sources (7)
11. 1953–55	73.1	15.4	10.2	1.3	90.1	9.9	8.6
12. 1960–62	75.5	12.9	8.8	2.8	90.6	9.4	6.7
13. 1970–72	57.8	8.5	19.8	13.9	79.2	20.8	6.9

Source: BOK. *National Income Statistics Yearbook*, various years.
[a] The statistical discrepancy is included with gross domestic capital formation in 1960–62 and 1970–72.

Korea though originating elsewhere. The estimates show substantial acceleration in the growth of all types of expenditure from the first to the second subperiod and unusually high growth rates during the second subperiod for investment (gross domestic capital formation), exports, and imports. Differences in growth rates have altered expenditure shares so that the shares of both private and government consumption declined as a growing portion of the national product was allocated to investment and exports. Exports expanded more rapidly but were still substantially smaller than imports in both subperiods. The trade balance (exports less imports: see row 6) has consequently been a large, negative quantity. Such balances must be financed through aid, running down of foreign-exchange reserves, or foreign borrowing and represent the foreign saving that has been available to the Korean economy.

Private and government consumption, investment, and exports are combined in panel B of table 2.5 to represent total uses of national product. This combination serves to emphasize the drop in consumption shares and the sharp, offsetting rise in investment and export shares. Also, gross domestic product is added to imports in panel B to group all resources available for use. (Net factor income from the rest of the world should be included here but was judged too small to merit inclusion.) This grouping reveals that the import share rose from less than 10 to more than 20 percent of total resources during the second subperiod. However, import growth was matched by export expansion so that the proportion of total resources supplied by unrequieted imports (see col. 7 of panel B) remained a stable 7–9 percent during both subperiods.

These measures of sources and uses of national product show changes that can be described only as radical changes, particularly because they occurred during the brief span of the second subperiod. Dependence on imports increased while a larger share of domestic product was exported. Foreign trade was therefore much more important for the Korean economy by the early 1970s than it had been as recently as the early 1960s. The chief finding is a major shift in expenditures from consumption to investment as the growth of domestic product accelerated. Consumption, both private and government, rose absolutely but considerably less than it might have. This left an increasing share of a rapidly growing total for investing in new capacity or otherwise available to generate greater future consumption.

Table 2.6. Private Consumption
(1970 Market prices)

A. Expenditures in billion won (annual averages)

Period	Food (1)	Beverages and tobacco (2)	Clothing[b] (3)	Housing[c] (4)	Services[d] (5)	Total (6)
1. 1953–55[a]	448.1	32.4	62.0	87.6	84.3	714.4
2. 1960–62	553.3	55.4	104.5	122.8	134.3	970.3
3. 1970–72	982.5	189.8	251.4	250.9	388.9	2,063.5

B. Distribution (% share)

Period	Food	Beverages and tobacco	Clothing	Housing	Services	Total
4. 1953–55	62.7	57.0	8.7	12.3	11.8	100.0
5. 1960–62	57.0	5.7	10.8	12.7	13.8	100.0
6. 1970–72	47.6	9.2	12.2	12.2	18.8	100.0

C. Per capita expenditure in thousand won (annual averages)

Period	Food	Beverages and tobacco	Clothing	Housing	Services	Total
7. 1953–55	21.8	1.6	3.0	4.3	4.1	34.8
8. 1960–62	21.9	2.2	4.1	4.8	5.3	38.3
9. 1970–72	30.8	5.9	7.9	7.9	12.2	64.7

Source: BOK, *Economic Statistics Yearbook, 1973.*
[a] The statistical discrepancy, included with consumption in 1953–55, was distributed proportionally among categories.
[b] Includes personal effects.
[c] Includes published categories for rent and water charges; fuel and light; furniture, furnishings, and household equipment; and household operations.
[d] Personal care and health expenses, transport and communication, recreation and entertainment, and miscellaneous services.

Private Consumption

Most of the post-Korean War growth in consumption occurred during the second subperiod (see table 2.6). Average per capita consumption rose from 35,000 won in 1953–55 to 38,000 in 1960–62 and then to 65,000 won during 1970–72 (all values are in 1970 prices). If any single indicator can measure the contribution of accelerated growth to the welfare of individual Koreans, it is this jump in average consumption from the early 1960s to the early 1970s. Both the shifts in consumption patterns that accompanied this jump and the implications of such changes are of special interest here.

Private consumption distributed by major type of expenditure is given in panel B of table 2.6. Food accounted for almost two-thirds of the total during 1953–55, but less than half by 1970–72. The declining share of outlays for food is consistent with Engel's law and with survey data that show particularly low income elasticity of demand for food grains, which have been major components of the typical diet.[10] Fifteen percent of consumption, allocated for food in 1953–55, was released for other consumption by 1970–72, when the total had almost tripled. Housing expenditure rose proportionately with total consumption so that much of the increase in consumer outlays, both absolute and relative, went for beverages and tobacco, clothing, and services.

Food and other basic necessities still make up a larger fraction of consumer expenditures in Korea than in wealthier countries. The share of outlays for food and beverages in the early 1960s, for example, was more than twice the share of these items in the United States. Though Korean consumption patterns may be converging with those found in richer countries, some of the shift reflects inflation and urbanization as well as rising income. Urban transport costs and school fees rose more than other consumer prices from 1965 to 1972, for instance, and so did their consumption shares. Urban families spend relatively more for housing and transport than farm families; the extra expenditure is undoubtedly due to added costs of urban living as well as to the greater outlays associated with higher incomes.[11]

One basis for evaluating private consumption is to compare outlays in Korea for housing, food, or other standard categories with expenditures on these categories elsewhere. This is not entirely valid, because relative prices differ and because the contents of standard categories also differ. Most services in Korea are relatively inexpensive by international standards: thus, the real equivalent of the 389 billion won spent on services in 1970–72 would constitute more than 19 percent of the total consumer expenditures listed in table 2.6 if Korean goods and services were valued according to American prices. Similarly,

10. Outlays for food grains (including the imputed value of grains produced for own consumption) accounted for over half of total food outlays in the early 1960s. The estimated income elasticity of demand for grains, based on expenditure surveys in 1962–64, was around 0.34 (see U.S. Operations Mission to Korea, *Revised Food Grain Production and Consumption for 1962–64, and Projections to 1971*, p. 32).

11. Expenditures of urban families are shown in the Economic Planning Board's (EPB's) *Annual Reports on the Family Income and Expenditure Surveys,* those for rural families in the Ministry of Agriculture and Forestry's (MAF's) *Reports on the Results of Farm Household Economy Surveys and Production Cost Surveys of Agricultural Products.* Urban consumer price indices and indices of prices paid by farmers for household goods and services are given in the National Agricultural Cooperative Federation's (NACF's) *Agricultural Yearbooks.*

Korean housing differs from housing in many other countries and is therefore not really a comparable category. The median size of private dwellings was 5–7 *pyeong* (1 pyeong = 35.6 square feet) in 1970, for instance, and the average household that occupied it contained 5.7 persons.

Another difficulty here is posed by the necessity for using average-per-capita-consumption estimates when such averages are likely to conceal wide variation. Estimates for private expenditure by income-size class do not exist; in fact, there is no regularly published information on how income is distributed among Korea's various income groups. The increase in per capita consumption during the second subperiod can therefore have different welfare implications depending upon how this increase was distributed. If the experience of developing countries should parallel that of today's developed countries, income inequality and hence variation in consumption levels is likely to increase during early phases of industrialization such as Korea's second subperiod. On the other hand, Korea has been listed among a group of poor countries whose income-size shares in recent years were least unequal.[12] Income distribution and changes in income distribution are clearly important for understanding private consumption behavior, but the income-size data needed for this purpose are not yet available.

Government Consumption

Government consumption grew least among the expenditure categories shown in table 2.5 but still accelerated during the second subperiod so that it was double the 1950–53 level by 1970–72. Consumption and other components of government expenditure are shown in panel A of table 2.7. The share of consumption (which includes employee compensation, purchase of goods and services for current operations, plus imputed rents and imputed banking services, less sales of goods and services) in total government expenditure has declined, and the

12. See Simon Kuznets, *Economic Growth and Structure*, pp. 282–83; Montek S. Ahluwalia, "Income Inequality: Some Dimensions of the Problem," p. 4. Ahluwalia shows 1970 estimates for Korea that are based on the EPB family income and the MAF household surveys (see n. 11) and listed in Shail Jain and Arthur E. Tiemann, *Size Distribution of Income*. Small sample size, stratification based on an out-of-date census, and use of coverage never intended to replicate the income-earning population make it unlikely that Ahluwalia's estimates provide an accurate measure of income-size distribution for Korea (see also pp. 96–99).

Table 2.7. Government Consumption
(1970 Market prices)

A. *Consumption and other expenditures (annual averages in billion won)*

Period	Consumption (1)	Other current expenditures[a] (2)	Cap. form.[b] (3)	Net lend.[c] (4)	Transfers, deprec.[d] (5)	Total expend. $(6) = (1)$ through $(4) - (5)$
1. 1953–55	150.3	13.9	12.8	2.8	9.3	170.5
2. %	88.2	8.1	7.5	1.6	5.4	100.0
3. 1960–62	165.0	21.3	46.3	16.3	21.0	227.9
4. %	72.4	9.3	20.3	7.2	9.2	100.0
5. 1970–72	306.4	48.9	180.6	4.9	17.1	523.7
6. %	58.5	9.3	34.5	0.9	3.2	100.0

B. *Consumption by economic-functional category (%)*

	1954	1961[h]	1971[i]
7. Consumer	9.2	19.7	22.8
a. Research, education	5.0	12.6	16.5
b. Health, welfare	4.2	7.1	6.3
8. Economic	39.8	48.1	42.7
a. Gen. admin., police, justice	21.7	15.1	11.5
b. Other economic[e]	18.1	33.0	31.2
(community services)[f]	—	(2.8)	(4.9)
9. Other[g]	3.2	5.2	12.0
10. Defense	47.8	27.0	22.5
11. Total	100.0	100.0	100.0

Sources: Panel A: BOK, *Economic Statistics Yearbook, 1973,* and *National Income Statistics Yearbook, 1972*; panel B: BOK, *Annual Economic Review, 1956,* and *Economic Statistics Yearbooks, 1963* and *1973.*

[a] Mainly current transfers to households. Other current expenditures were deflated by the implicit price index for government consumption expenditure, while the other categories shown were deflated by the implicit price index for gross domestic fixed capital formation.

[b] Includes finance of capital formation in the noncorporate public sector plus capital transfers to the private sector.

[c] (4) = Government saving (current revenue–current expenditure) plus transfers and depreciation (5) less capital formation (3).

[d] Noncorporate public sector depreciation plus capital transfers from households, corporations, and nonprofit institutions.

[e] Outlays for agricultural and nonmineral resources; fuel and power; mining, manufacturing, and construction; transport, storage, and communications.

[f] Expenditure on roads, waterways, fire protection, water supply, and sanitation.

[g] Mainly unallocated transfers to local government.

[h] Includes local government expenditures not covered by transfers from the central government.

[i] Central government expenditures only.

decline has been offset by a rise in the share of government capital formation. Consumption by economic-functional category is given in panel B of table 2.7 for selected years. The panel shows that consumer expenditures on research, education, health, and welfare have grown in relative importance, that economic expenditures are the largest category, and that the defense share of total consumption was halved between 1954 and 1971.

The estimates shown in tables 2.5 and 2.7 raise the question of why there was so little increase in government consumption from the mid-1950s to the early 1970s. One reason is that the Korean War left the country saddled with a swollen army and bureaucracy that were more than large enough to meet Korea's needs for many years. Evidence of this is seen in the published figures for domestic product originating in public administration and defense, most of which is included in government consumption. Product was no higher in 1967 than in 1953 and actually declined during much of the interval between. Another reason is that Korea's tax performance was comparatively poor before 1966, deficit financing had its limits, and so government consumption could not expand much.[13] The main issue here is not one of explaining limited growth, however, but of establishing the dimensions of what actually happened. Omission, exclusion, and accounting convention combine to bias downward the official estimates for government consumption and, possibly, to increase this downward bias over time.

Accounts of government and quasi-government corporations, unlike the practice elsewhere, are included with the private sector rather than with the public sector in Korea. The tobacco monopoly, enterprises such as the Korean National Railway, or government-invested firms such as the commercial banks and the Korea Electric Company are excluded from the government sector even though the government covers losses of such enterprises while monopoly profits are turned over to the general account and appear as tax revenues. Similarly, a large share of government capital expenditure is channeled through the KDB (Korea Development Bank) to these firms. Total government expenditure, and possibly consumption too, is understated by 5–10 percent as a result of this exclusion.

13. Jorgen R. Lotz and Elliott R. Morss, "Measuring 'Tax Effort' in Developing Countries."

United States military assistance has been omitted from the national accounts, balance of payments, and government budgets. Assistance, consisting of equipment and supplies, is denominated in dollars and includes excess stocks that have been valued differently at different times so that the real equivalent of the dollar values is not always the same. Annual amounts from 1956 to 1970, when converted to won, have been as large or larger than published defense expenditures during most of this period.[14]

National accounting convention allows for no increase in productivity of government employees. Most of the valued added in public administration and defense consists of salaries, but any increase in salaries is eliminated in estimating the real product that originates in this sector. Real product is thus largely a function of employment levels and employment has not risen much. This means that the public administration and defense components of government consumption are increasingly understated. If output per worker in public administration and defense rose as much as the average for all nonagricultural workers, understatement would have been increasing by 4.6 percent a year during the second subperiod.

The net effect of excluding government and quasi-government enterprise, omitting U.S. military assistance, and failing to adjust for productivity increase of government workers cannot be specified, but the drop in downward bias as military-assistance levels have been reduced in recent years has probably been more than offset by growing understatement as output per worker rises in the public sector. However, it is clear that inclusion of the omitted military assistance would double the amount of defense consumption shown in panel B of table 2.7 and would reduce the shares of consumer and economic expenditures accordingly. Little is known of the relation between government consumption and economic growth, and accounting definitions are not very helpful here. Nevertheless, outlays on economic goods and services should contribute directly to growth, expenditures for consumer services and administration ought to contribute indirectly, and even defense outlays may provide incidental economic benefits. Health, welfare, and other consumer or social expenditure

14. Information on the value of American military assistance is shown in the Agency for International Development's annual reports. Totals include grants from excess stocks that were first valued at acquisition costs, then at "utility value," and later at "legal value" (one-third of acquisition costs).

Table 2.8 Gross Domestic Fixed Capital Formation
(1970 Market prices)

A. By type (annual average value in billion won, % share)

	Period	Dwellings	Nonres. Bldg.	Other construction	Transport equip.	Machinery, other equip.	Total GDFCF
1.	1953–55	14.8	18.2	12.0	6.1	12.2	63.3
2.	%	23.4	28.7	18.9	9.7	19.3	100.0
3.	1960–62	19.9	23.7	30.7	11.2	26.1	111.6
4.	%	17.8	21.3	27.5	10.0	23.4	100.0
5.	1970–72	91.1	131.0	181.4	111.1	148.7	663.3
6.	%	13.7	19.8	27.3	16.8	22.4	100.0

B. By sector (annual average value, % share)

		Agriculture	Industry	(Manufacturing)	(Transport, storage, commun.)	Services	Total GDFCF
7.	1953–55	6.1	27.1	(12.9)	(11.0)	30.1	63.3
8.	%	9.6	42.8	(20.3)	(17.4)	47.5	100.0
9.	1960–62	12.2	58.9	(12.9)	(23.9)	40.5	111.6
10.	%	10.9	52.8	(20.5)	(21.5)	36.3	100.0
11.	1970–72	60.0	381.2	(129.9)	(180.6)	222.1	663.3
12.	%	9.0	57.5	(19.6)	(27.2)	33.5	100.0

Source: BOK, Economic Statistics Yearbook, 1973.

has been comparatively low in Korea. Since social expenditures tend to be highly income elastic, their share should continue to rise as per capita income increases.[15]

Investment

Gross domestic capital formation grew slowly and its share in GNP actually dropped during the first subperiod. Capital formation soared during the second, however, so that its share in gross product more than doubled. By 1970–72, one-quarter of the national product was going to capital formation, a proportion that was not only high relative to previous levels but also high by international standards.[16] This increase in investment with its multiplier effects, capacity creation, employment, and productivity consequences was perhaps the most important proximate cause of Korea's accelerated growth during the second subperiod. Although the tenfold growth of fixed capital formation from 1953–55 to 1970–72 overwhelms any change in its distribution by type or sector, such changes are sufficiently significant to merit attention and are shown in table 2.8.

Shares of residential construction (dwellings) and of nonresidential building in total fixed capital formation declined throughout both subperiods and were offset by above-average growth of other construction (a category that includes transport and harbor facilities, telephone and power line construction, and land reclamation and irrigation projects) and by investment in transport equipment, machinery, and other equipment (see panel A). The share of dwellings dropped enough so that it was well below such shares in many other countries.[17] This is significant because investment in housing, unlike

15. The problem of relating government consumption to economic growth has been noted by Donald R. Snodgrass, *Ceylon*, pp. 196–97. Salaries of planning officials (general administration), for example, are just as much development expenditures as funds budgeted for operating dams (economic services). Public outlays for social purposes in Korea and other Far Eastern countries are compared in Economic Commission for Asia and the Far East (ECAFE), *The Planning and Financing of Social Development in the ECAFE Region*. Social security expenditure, and possibly total social expenditure as well, has been found to be highly correlated with per capita income (see Richard S. Thorn, "Per Capita Income as a Measure of Economic Development," p. 209).

16. Capital formation as a proportion of GDP (in current market prices) during 1969–71 ranged between 16.8 and 18.0 percent in the United States, 20 and 21 percent in the Philippines, 25.6 and 30.2 percent in Korea, and 36.3 to 39.4 percent in Japan (see United Nations, *Monthly Statistical Bulletin*, June 1973).

17. For instance, investment in dwellings as a proportion of total fixed capital formation in 1967 was 20.7 percent in Japan, 19.4 percent in the United States, 11.2 percent in Taiwan, and 9.0 percent in Korea (United Nations, *Yearbook of National Accounts Statistics, 1968*, vol. 1).

other types of investment, channels resources directly to final consumption rather than to expansion of productive capacity.

Part of the rapidly growing outlay for machinery and equipment was spent on the output of newly opened domestic auto assembly plants and the electric machinery industry, but a large share went for capital-goods imports. Government policies encouraged domestic producers to import machinery in order to reach First and Second Plan output targets, and the influence of these policies can be detected in the pattern of commodity imports. Manufactures accounted for between 55 and 65 percent of commodity imports in recent years; the share of investment goods (transport equipment and machinery), in turn, tripled from 13 percent of manufactured imports in 1956–58 to reach 40 percent by the early 1970s.

Grouping investment by sector (panel B of table 2.8) reveals that the industrial sector has received a large and increasing share of total fixed capital formation. There was a corresponding decline in service sector investment, while agriculture's share has been a small and relatively constant 10 percent of the total. Comparison of product (table 2.3) and investment (table 2.8) provides an interesting contrast between sectoral shares. The industrial sector's investment share was at least triple its output share in 1953–55 and 1960–62, and still much larger in 1970–72. The service sector's investment share has fallen below its output share, reflecting the diminishing role of investment in dwellings, but the major difference is found in agriculture, where output shares have been three to five times investment shares.

Relatively low investment in agriculture may result from downward bias in the estimates. The value of nonmonetized land improvement is important in total agricultural capital formation and is likely to have grown over time, but it is particularly difficult to value and therefore tends to be neglected in the national accounts. Agriculture's small investment share may also reflect the top priority given to industrial investment in Korea's first two five-year plans. It is not a result of particularly low investment–output relationships, however, since the capital coefficient for agriculture is roughly the same as that for manufacturing and not much below the all-sector average. A sector's investment share does not, of course, have to match its output share, but a discrepancy of the sort found here is prima facie evidence that agricultural investment has been neglected.[18]

18. The parallel with mainland China in the 1950s is noteworthy. Eckstein found that "agriculture received the smallest share of investment relative to its size. . . . [This is] not intended to suggest that the pattern of investment allocation in an underdeveloped

Whether agricultural investment has in fact been neglected can be assessed more directly by comparing farmers' investment requirements and the credit available to them with investment needs and credit availability for others (see p. 142). The issue here is part of a larger question of allocative efficiency, namely, whether the distribution of resources between agricultural and nonagricultural activities has been appropriate or not. This question could be answered with reference to marginal returns on investment by sector if such returns were known, but they are not. Though the issue of allocative efficiency cannot be handled, efficiency can be evaluated in comparative terms. The question then is whether investment has been more efficient in Korea than investment elsewhere.

Detailed examination by Norton and Lee of the same industries in Korea (during the mid-1960s) and the United States (1957) shows that the American capital coefficients averaged 24 percent higher than the Korean coefficients. Much of the difference was attributed to lower construction costs instead of to lower materials costs or less elaborate design of industrial structures, the other alternatives considered. American construction costs were found to be 75 percent higher than Korean costs.[19] Such differences in capital coefficients are genuine economic phenomena which indicate that low-cost construction gives Korea considerable comparative advantage in the formation of new capital. The consequence of these differences, at least in comparison with the United States, is that more output has been obtained per unit of capital input. In this limited sense, Korean investment has been relatively efficient.

Exports and Imports

Korea's foreign trade expanded during the second subperiod so that the economy was much more closely tied to international markets by the early 1970s than in earlier years. Involvement has been substantial; trade ratios (exports plus imports/GNP) rose from 12 percent in 1953–55 to 13 percent in 1960–62 before reaching 44 percent in 1970–72. Because imports have been much greater than exports, the imbalance, combined with positive net transfers from the rest of the world, has

country should be governed by the prevailing composition of its national product....
Nevertheless ... neglect of agricultural investment ... is sooner or later bound to cause serious disruptions of the development process" (Alexander Eckstein, *Communist China's Economic Growth and Foreign Trade,* p. 44).

19. See Roger D. Norton and Lee Kee Jung, "The Korean Input-Output Planning Model."

Table 2.9. Commodity Composition of Exports and Imports
(Percentage share)

Period SITC[a]	Food 0	Bev., tobac. 1	Crude mater. 2	Miner., fuels 3	Oils, fats 4	Chem. 5	Manufact. 6	Mach. 7	Misc. manufact. 8	NEC 9	Total
A. Exports											
1. 1955	6.1	—	81.6	2.8	—	0.6	5.0	1.1	2.8	—	100.0 (18.0)
2. 1960–62	31.6	0.6	43.7	4.8	0.2	1.5	11.0	1.9	2.2	2.5	100.0 (42.8)
3. 1970–72	6.9	1.2	8.9	1.1	—	1.8	30.2	9.1	40.8	—	100.0 (1,175.6)
B. Imports											
4. 1955	5.1	1.7	8.5	12.6	0.8	17.5	16.0	16.7	2.4	18.6[b]	100.0 (341.4)
5. 1960–62	11.1	—	20.5	7.5	1.0	21.4	14.8	14.1	2.0	7.6	100.0 (360.5)
6. 1970–72	15.6	0.2	19.2	7.9	0.8	8.5	15.5	29.5	2.8	—	100.0 (2,300.1)

Source: BOK, Economic Statistics Yearbook, various years.
Note: Figures shown are based on annual averages of current values (those in parentheses are the annual averages, denominated in millions of U.S. dollars).

[a] SITC (Standard International Trade Classification) categories: 0, food and live animals; 1, beverages and tobacco; 2, crude materials, inedible, except fuels; 3, mineral fuels, lubricants and related materials; 4, animal and vegetable oils and fats; 5, chemicals; 6, manufactured goods classified by materials; 7, machinery and transport equipment; 8, miscellaneous manufactured articles; 9, not elsewhere classified.
[b] "Includes government imports through simplified customs clearance by aid funds" (BOK, Economic Statistics Yearbook, 1963, p. 217). Such imports were not listed separately by commodity group.

made available resources that permitted investment and consumption to exceed domestic product by 6–10 percent a year during most of the post-1953 era.

Deficits on commodity trade averaged more than a billion dollars a year in the early 1970s but were reduced by surpluses from invisibles. Most of these surpluses, which appear in the balance of payments as "government military transactions, not included elsewhere," were derived from sales to the United Nations forces (largely U.S. Army units stationed in Korea) but also include service receipts from Vietnam. Although such receipts are not listed separately, approximately 10–20 percent of current-account receipts from 1966 through 1971 were derived from sales to Vietnam. However, Korea benefited much less from the Vietnam War than did Japan from the Korean War; the factors responsible for rapid export expansion must therefore lie elsewhere.[20]

The composition of Korea's trade by commodity category and country is given in tables 2.9 and 2.10. Imports immediately after the Korean War consisted principally of food, fuels, chemical fertilizer, and other aid goods used to meet relief and reconstruction needs. Government credit allocation policies and tariff adjustments were employed to encourage import substitution in subsequent years so that Korea was largely self-sufficient in production of cement, flat glass, newsprint, gasoline, and other intermediate goods by the mid-1960s. Plants were also built to replace large-scale imports of chemical fertilizer. The results of import substitution appear in table 2.9 as a long-term decline in the relative significance fuels and chemicals in total imports and, more generally, as a shift in the composition of imports away from manufactured materials toward crude materials, machinery, and other investment goods. Table 2.9 also reveals a marked rise in the proportion of food imports. Such changes in shares have been important, but they were overwhelmed by the striking increase in total imports during the second subperiod. Despite extensive substitution for imported materials, much of the increase has consisted

20. In 1969, for example, military procurement by United Nations forces (which includes service receipts from Vietnam) plus commodity exports to Vietnam reached a peak of $169 million. Export receipts totaled $1.15 billion. Part of the U.N. military procurement went to cover the costs of U.S. forces stationed in Korea, but then the costs of these forces plus unlisted U.S. military assistance may be considered payment for Korea's military services in Vietnam (see James Stentzel, "Seoul's Second Bonanza"). Credits under the "government, n.i.e. military" category in Japan's balance of payments rose from $49 million in 1949 to $803 million by 1953.

Table 2.10. Composition of Trade by Country
(Percentage share)

A. Exports

	Period	Asia	(Japan)	Western Europe	North America	(United States)	Rest of world	Total
1.	1955	51.7	(40.6)	7.2	41.1	(41.1)	—	100.0
2.	1960–62	68.5	(49.1)	10.7	17.9	(17.4)	2.9	100.0
3.	1970–72	36.3	(25.6)	9.3	51.4	(47.8)	3.0	100.0

B. Imports

	Period	Asia	(Japan)	Western Europe	North America	(United States)	Rest of world	Total
4.	1958[a]	20.9	(13.2)	19.3	57.2	(55.3)	2.6	100.0
5.	1960–62	30.6	(23.0)	15.8	48.4	(46.0)	5.2	100.0
6.	1970–72	57.4	(40.5)	11.0	29.2	(27.7)	2.4	100.0

Source: BOK, Economic Statistics Yearbook, various years.
Note: Percentage shares are based on annual averages of current values denominated in U.S. dollars.
[a]The year 1958 was chosen instead of 1955 because a large fraction of imports was not allocated by country before 1958.

of materials. Because the import content of exports has been high (50 percent or more in recent years) and exports have grown even more rapidly than imports, the increase in imports can be traced in large part to export expansion.

Exports were negligible in the mid-1950s and consisted mainly of tungsten ore and other nonmanufactures. An export-promotion program begun in 1962, major devaluation of the won in June 1964, and relaxation of import restrictions (so that local entrepreneurs could obtain the materials and machinery needed to produce for export) provided the stimulus for export expansion during the second subperiod. Tax exemption, access to low-cost credit, subsidies, foreign-loan guarantees, and import licensing have been used by the government to stimulate exports. Because these measures favored manufacturing activity, export shares of agricultural products and crude materials fell as shares of plywood, finished textiles, electronic equipment, wigs, and other miscellaneous manufactures rose (see table 2.9). Increasing concentration in such relatively labor-intensive manufactures has characterized export growth and is consistent both with Korea's comparative advantage and with greater efficiency of resource allocation.[21]

Almost 70 percent of Korea's imports have come from Japan and the United States, whereas two-thirds or more of Korea's exports are shipped to these two countries (see table 2.10). Japan's importance in Korea's trade derives from the proximity of the two countries, Japan's emergence as a major capital-goods exporter, and, possibly, a political situation that has prevented trade between Korea and other nearby countries (North Korea and mainland China). The table also shows a jump in imports from Japan during the second subperiod that was spurred by the signing in 1965 of a normalization treaty between the two countries.

The large United States share in Korean trade is due to Korea's status as one of the chief recipients of American aid and the U.S. role as a major capital-goods exporter. Since aid is usually tied to purchases in the donor country, as grant levels diminished in recent years, so

21. Norton compared capital coefficients for manufacturing sectors in 1965 with export/import values in 1960 and 1968 taken from the BOK's input–output tables. Without exception, he found that ratios declined for sectors with capital coefficients of 0.3 or more while sectors with coefficients of less than 0.3 (finished textiles, lumber and plywood, miscellaneous manufactures, and other items) had rising ratios. See Roger D. Norton, "The South Korean Economy in the 1960s."

did the American share in Korea's imports. Reasons for the increase
in the U.S. share of Korea's exports found in table 2.10 are not so
obvious, however. This increase may result from Japan's notoriously
restrictive commercial policies, new restrictions limiting trade with
Western Europe after the formation of the European Common
Market, or Korea's small initial share in the comparatively open
American market. Whatever the reasons, table 2.10 reveals a clear
reversal of Japanese and American positions in Korea's trade during
the second subperiod as Korea sold relatively more to the United
States and bought more from Japan.

Imports substitution, export expansion, and a trade deficit of more
than a billion dollars a year in the early 1970s generated substantial
costs and benefits for the Korean economy. Import substitution has
been concentrated in relatively capital-intensive activities and is thus
inconsistent with Korea's relative factor endowments. Import substitution also has drawbacks as a development strategy because it
tends to create uneconomically small units that require tariff protection,
generate monopoly costs, and threaten export competitiveness where
exports incorporate expensive import substitutes. Examples of such
drawbacks have been evident in Korea but are not so serious as they
might otherwise be. Several major First Plan import-substitution
projects have been postponed, and export competitiveness has been
maintained because "exporters were permitted to import intermediate
goods even if comparable goods were available domestically."[22]

Export promotion costs have included the cost of subsidy and
below-normal profits on production for export. The relatively high
import content of Korea's exports has also reduced net foreign
exchanged earned by exporting. In 1968, for example, subsidies cost
an estimated 51 won for each dollar's worth of exports when the
prevailing exchange rate was 277 won per dollar. Forgone profits
added to subsidies raised the estimated cost of exports to 344 won
per dollar. Given an average import content of 50 percent or more,
at least $2 worth of exports had to be sold to earn $1 (net) of foreign
exchange. The won cost of each dollar's worth of foreign exchange
was thus approximately 1.5 times the official exchange rate.[23]

Large trade deficits contributed to a rising foreign debt that had
reached $3 billion by the end of 1972. Interest and amortization on
loans with original maturities of three years or more rose from $60

22. Cole and Lyman, *Korean Development*, p. 161.
23. "The dollar earnings rate [on exports] in 1966 was 60 percent, but the figure
decreased to 50 percent last year [1969]" (*Korea Times*, 31 March 1970).

million in 1968 to $347 million by 1972, or 16 percent of current-account earnings in 1972. If repayment on short-term loans (original maturities of less than three years) is included, the cost of debt servicing doubles. The growing inflow of foreign capital, increased interest charges, and rising repayment obligations led the government to restrict foreign commercial borrowing after 1970.

Benefits of import substitution include greater domestic production capacity, increased employment, improved availability of materials, and the foreign exchange saved by replacing foreign with domestic processing. Export expansion has probably generated even greater benefits. They include the creation of industrial capacity and increased employment and, in addition, foreign exchange earnings that can be used to purchase goods and services not available domestically. It has been suggested, for example, that "50 percent of the increment in Korean manufacturing employment [from 1963 to 1969] was a direct result of export expansion."[24] Other less measurable but potentially important benefits are the learning effects, increased exposure to competition, and the greater access to borrowed technology that have been associated with export production.

Korea's trade deficits, as noted earlier, provided benefits in the form of additional resources so that consumption and investment could exceed domestic output by significant amounts during both sub-periods. Some of these resources have gone to expanding industrial capacity to produce the exports needed to maintain or repay foreign debt. Costs and benefits of import substitution, export expansion, and trade deficits cannot always be measured and, in addition, are some-times incommensurable; there is no way, for example, to weigh the employment benefits against the subsidy costs of exporting. This means that a balance cannot be struck between costs and benefits. Nevertheless, import substitution, export expansion, and trade deficits have been vital in Korea's development. Rapid export expansion, in particular, was responsible to a significant degree for accelerated growth during the second subperiod.

SAVING

Trade deficits and net transfers from the rest of the world have provided resources for domestic use in Korea that would otherwise have been unavailable. These resources, or "foreign saving," plus domestic saving

---

24. Susumu Watanabe, "Exports and Employment: The Case of the Republic of Korea," p. 515.

Table 2.11. Sources of Saving
(% Share, 1970 market prices in billion won)

	Period	Adj. GDCF[a] (1)	For. saving[b] (2)	Dom. saving (3)=(1)-(2)	Govt. saving[c] (4)	Pvt. saving (5)=(3)-(4)	Change in agric. stocks (6)	Adj pvt. saving (7)=(5)-(6)
1.	1953–55	100.3	45.0	55.3	−15.1	70.4	26.3	44.1
2.	%	100.0	44.8	55.2	−15.0	70.2	26.2	44.0
3.	1960–62	107.0	85.9	21.1	−15.9	37.0	−2.5	39.5
4.	%	100.0	80.3	19.7	−14.9	34.6	−2.3	36.9
5.	1970–72	694.9	252.2	442.7	145.3	297.4	19.7[d]	277.7
6.	%	100.0	36.3	63.7	20.9	42.8	2.8	40.0

Sources: BOK, Economic Statistics Yearbook, various years, and National Income Statistics Yearbook, various years.
Note: Annual averages, deflated by implicit deflator for gross domestic capital formation.
[a] Gross domestic capital formation less statistical discrepancy in 1960–62 and 1970–72.
[b] Net borrowing and net transfers from the rest of the world.
[c] General government budget balance (current revenue less current expenditure) plus provision for fixed capital consumption (of general government and government enterprises) less net current transfers from the rest of the world.
[d] Annual average for 1970–71 only.

are equal by definition to gross domestic capital formation. Domestic saving, in turn, can be divided between private and government saving. Interest in each case lies in the source of saving rather than in the intermediaries who transfer resources from savers to investors.[25] Since saving equals investment, and investment accelerated during the second subperiod, a necessary condition for such acceleration was that saving increase at the same pace. This underlines the importance of savings growth and focuses attention on the determinants of saving, which differ according to whether the source is foreign or domestic and, within domestic, private savers or the government.

Foreign saving, calculated as the sum of net borrowing and transfers from abroad, is financed by foreign grants and loans. Such grants and loans have been major components of total saving; they comprised almost half the total in 1953–55 and rose to four-fifths by 1960–62 before dropping to 36 percent in 1970–72 (see table 2.11). At least half the annual trade deficit was covered by official grants and loans before 1966, mostly in the form of United States and UNKRA aid. Aid, including receipts from PL 480 (U.S. Public Law 480) imports, totaled over $5 billion between 1953 and 1972. As American aid levels began to decline, grants and loans under the Japanese PAC (property and claims) program increased. However, the largest offsetting inflow consisted of private loans. Two billion dollars in commercial loans and direct investment were received between 1962 and 1972, primarily after 1965, and this inflow more than offset the decline in aid.

United States aid has been concentrated among relatively few of the world's developing countries, one of which is Korea. A number of different and sometimes contradictory criteria have been advanced by the Agency for International Development to explain the allocation of aid, such as need, efforts at self-help, potential for economic success, and external threats to security. The large share of supporting assistance (an economic aid category justified in terms of national security) and military assistance in Korea's aid totals indicates that strategic considerations, and possibly external threats to Korea's security, have been responsible for Korea's inclusion among the select few.

Private loans replaced aid as the main form of foreign saving because

---

25. For this reason, published measures that show financing of gross domestic capital formation cannot be used to derive the saving estimates. For example, government saving (the current-account balance plus government enterprise and general government depreciation allowances) totaled 206 billion won in 1970, but this included 26 billion won in net transfers from the rest of the world that was saved by foreigners.

the normalization treaty made Korean loans more attractive to Japanese lenders and because demand for credit to finance equipment and materials purchases expanded with export production. Also, the Bank of Korea began issuing repayment guarantees (this function was eventually assumed by the Korea Exchange Bank [KXB]) that served to protect foreign creditors. Foreign credit was relatively cheap, and so much of domestic borrowing was financed by foreign lenders. This is seen in customers' liabilities for acceptances and guarantees of commercial banks, which rose from 4 billion won at the end of 1963 to 319 billion by the end of 1972, or from 16 to 72 percent of total loans and discounts outstanding. Short-term suppliers' credits, the major form of foreign loans backed by these guarantees, totaled $1.5 billion in 1967–69 alone.

Domestic saving was low before the mid-1960s, equivalent to less than 2 percent of GNP in 1960–62 and well below savings levels in many other developing countries.[26] One reason, evident in table 2.11, was the negative government saving in 1953–55 and 1960–62, which later shifted to substantial positive saving by 1970–72. Because government saving is primarily a residual (current revenues less current expenditures), the shift can result either from restraint on expenditures or from increased revenues. Expenditure ratios (current expenditure/ GNP) fell from 18 percent in 1953–55 to 13 percent by 1970–72 since government consumption and other current expenditures rose less than the all-sector average (see table 2.5). Revenue ratios (current revenues/GNP) increased from 11 percent to 19 percent during the same period. These ratios indicate that both expenditure restraint and increased revenue were responsible for transformation of the government from a net borrower to a net lender (saver), and that the increase in revenues was the more important of the two factors.

Korea has the usual array of direct and indirect taxes, customs duties, monopoly profits, and nontax revenues such as profits from government enterprises. In addition, transfers from abroad (i.e., aid) accounted for one-third of current government receipts during the first subperiod. A sharp decline in aid levels after 1958 put heavy pressure on government budgets. Although pressure eased temporarily

26. United Nations, ECAFE, *Economic Survey of Asia and the Far East, 1966*, pp. 11–12; Hollis B. Chenery and Alan M. Strout, "Foreign Assistance and Economic Development," pp. 706–07. Domestic saving in 1963–65 was equivalent to 12 percent of GNP in Ceylon, 19 percent in Taiwan, 17 percent in Greece, and 21 percent in Malaysia. The figure for Korea was 8 percent.

with devaluation in 1961 (each aid dollar generated more won), it continued and was met by deficit financing through overdrafts with the BOK. Inflation in 1960–62 was largely due to these deficits; when it became apparent that continued deficits threatened development goals, reform began with sharp cuts in 1964 outlays so that both nominal and real expenditures were less than in 1963. "Stabilization" was the new guide to fiscal policy as deficits were to be replaced by budget balance or surplus. The next step was to raise revenues.

Since there was "an extensive and sophisticated set of tax statutes . . . the main task [was] to narrow the gap between tax law and practice."[27] The gap resulted from weak administration, marked by low assessments and poor collection. The task of closing the gap was handled by establishing an Office of National Taxation in 1966 and giving priority to improved administration. Tax effort, which had ranked very low by international standards before 1966, began to improve afterward but was still below Second Plan targets; in fact, fiscal performance has been one of the few areas in which actual results failed to meet plan goals.[28] Given plan shortfalls and the substantial military assistance that has been received but not listed in published budgets, it seems evident that in Korea "the government has been a relatively ineffective mobilizer of resources through the normal channels of taxation."[29]

The private saving listed in table 2.11 is presented with and without adjustment for changes in agricultural stocks because this is a residual category that includes inventory change, and changes in agricultural inventories depend upon harvests rather than upon private saving habits. Private saving was negligible during the first subperiod, but rose sevenfold in real terms from 1960–62 to 1970–72, reached 10 percent of GNP, and displaced foreign saving as the largest saving category.

This startling turnabout began with the interest-rate reform of September 1965, when banks first offered depositors rates of 20 percent or more on savings accounts. Prices had risen at an average annual rate of 19 percent from 1960 to 1965, deposit rates were only 12 percent, loan rates averaged 3–5 percent a *month* in unorganized

27. Richard A. Musgrave, "Revenue Policy for Korea's Economic Development," p. 10.
28. P. W. Kuznets, "Korea's Five-Year Plans," in Irma Adelman, ed., *Practical Approaches to Development Planning*, pp. 50–51, 73.
29. Cole and Lyman, *Korean Development*, p. 172.

money markets, and so banks were unable to compete effectively for private savings. Savers who placed funds with banks before September 1965 were, in effect, being asked to subsidize borrowers. The average annual rate of inflation dropped to less than 14 percent in 1965–72 and time and savings deposits of commercial banks soared. They rose from 9 billion won in September 1965 to 50 billion by the end of 1966 and reached 617 billion by the end of 1972. Part of the immediate growth in deposits undoubtedly represented a shift to the commercial banks of saving formerly concealed in unorganized money markets, but much of the subsequent expansion must have consisted of new saving. New saving, together with the increase in government saving, raised the real money balances needed to finance capital formation.[30] The expansion of domestic saving also reduced reliance on foreign saving.

When the post-Korean War era is divided into subperiods, one from 1953–55 to 1960–62 and the other from 1960–62 to 1970–72, we can distinguish between an initial period of relatively slow growth and a subsequent period of very rapid growth. Comparison with growth rates in other Asian countries reveals a general pattern of accelerated growth during these years, but Korea is unique in the magnitude of its acceleration. Domestic product, total current resources, commodity product, and other aggregates were examined for these two subperiods. They all show the same acceleration from one subperiod to the next; moreover, the greater variation among aggregate growth rates after 1960–62 suggests that accelerated growth was marked by changes in Korea's economic structure. Such changes appear as shifts in shares of domestic product originating in the major sectors (see table 2.3), particularly a sharp drop in agriculture's share and an offsetting increase in the share of product originating in the industrial sector.

A large increase in employment, major shifts in labor-force composition, and substantial growth in output per worker were associated with the structural change that occurred during the second subperiod (see table 2.4). Employment rose by 2.9 million, or 38 percent, from

30. To the extent that growth was previously restricted by scarcity of the real money balances needed to finance investment in physical capital, or what has been termed "financial repression," Korea's experience during the mid-1960s provides a classic example of the complementarity of saving (accumulation of real money balances) and capital formation (see Ronald I. McKinnon, *Money and Capital in Economic Development*, pp. 68–69, 105–11).

1963 to 1972. Since output growth was relatively large, even though the labor-absorption rate of income growth was no higher than elsewhere, labor absorption was less of a problem in Korea than in most other East and Southeast Asian countries during the 1960s (see chap. 4). Average output per worker grew by two-thirds, but this is an average of very different sectoral rates and bases. Output per worker was already much higher in the industrial sectors than in agriculture by 1960–62, and the disparity widened even as the proportion of the labor force engaged in industrial activities increased. Most of the increase in output per worker was due to intrasectoral increases, but a significant portion can be traced to intersectoral shifts as employment rose most in industrial sectors with above-average output per worker.

All major components of national product (and imports), except for government consumption, more than doubled during the second subperiod while annual growth rates were much higher than in the first. (Relatively slow growth of government consumption was a result of weak tax performance and an already large army and bureaucracy inherited from the Korean War.) Real per capita private consumption rose two-thirds from 1960–62 to 1970–72 after increasing less than 10 percent from 1953–55 to 1960–62. Accelerated growth during the second subperiod also contributed more to living standards than the modest growth of earlier years, as can also be seen in a shift in consumption patterns away from food toward clothing, services, and other items with higher income elasticities of demand.

Despite rapid growth after 1960–62, individual consumption levels were still much below those in developed countries by 1970–72, and possibly below what they might have been. Consumption increased less rapidly than total current resources, GNP, or GDP, which implies that it could have risen more if fewer resources had been allocated to competitive uses (investment, exports, capital-goods, or materials imports). But then fewer resources might have been available since greater consumption would have reduced investment and the output growth that follows from increased investment. Nonetheless, the choice between more now and more later was evidently settled in favor of more later.

Investment (gross domestic fixed capital formation) soared during the second subperiod. Less than 10 percent of national product had been allocated to investment before 1962; a quarter of a much larger total was being invested after 1968. One reason for this was the un-anticipated increase in demand for transport, electricity, and other overhead services in the late 1960s that resulted from unexpectedly rapid output expansion. Heavy investment in new capacity was required to keep infrastructure bottlenecks from choking rapid growth. Another reason was the sharp increase in saving. Government deficits were replaced by surpluses, private saving expanded under the stimulus of an interest-rate reform, and declining foreign assistance was more than offset by rising inflows of private foreign capital during the second subperiod.

Trade played a much larger role in the Korean economy during the second than in the first subperiod as both exports and imports expanded manyfold after the early 1960s. Before then, exports were negligible and imports averaged $300–400 million a year. By 1972, exports had reached $1.6 billion, imports $2.5 billion. Export growth resulted mainly from strenuous government export-promotion efforts and from Korea's comparative advantage in producing labor-intensive manufactures. The increase in imports was partly due to growing demand for food that could not be wholly met by domestic agriculture but was primarily a consequence of industrial expansion and export growth. Industrialization created new demand for machinery and equipment that could not be supplied locally, while export growth increased import demand since Korea's exports have had a high import content.

The importance of trade deserves emphasis, as does the contribution of exports to accelerated growth. Export expansion was a means of acquiring the foreign exchange needed to equip new industries and a major source of additional employment. Much of the increase in output after 1960–62 originated in the industrial sector, the industrial sector was dominated by manufacturing, and, within manufacturing, the leading industries were those oriented toward export production. Korea's growth was thus export-led growth.

One overriding fact that ought not to be obscured by preoccupation with the characteristics of accelerated economic growth is that Korean growth rates from 1960–62 to 1970–72 were among the world's highest. No one in the early 1960s could have anticipated the rapid growth that was to transform a backward economy with distinctly unpromising prospects into one of the few success stories among the world's less economically developed countries. The causes of this unexpected success merit further consideration. Also, rapid growth and structural change have consequences for the economic welfare of individual Koreans and implications for future development that have not yet been examined. In addition, information now available for 1973–74 permits us to update the picture in order to see the initial effects of worldwide recession, oil embargoes and international market upheavals on Korea's growth pattern. These topics are examined in the next chapter.

3

Causes and Consequences of Accelerated Growth

Evidence of accelerated growth and its characteristics were discussed in chapter 2 within a national-accounting framework. The focus of this framework is necessarily limited so that a number of questions about the Korean economy remain unanswered. For example, Korea was considered to be a typical labor surplus economy in the late 1950s. Was rapid development in subsequent years sufficient to absorb this surplus? What explains the relatively slow growth of agriculture, the rapid growth of manufacturing? The high rates of inflation that prevailed during the 1950s and 1960s must have influenced saving and growth in Korea. To what extent were the monetary authorities able to control the money supply and inflation, or to encourage saving? Have Korea's three five-year plans, which date back to 1962, been influential in shaping development? If so, have targets been met and in what ways do new plan goals reflect previous successes and failures?

Such questions, of particular interest in the Korean context, are examined in chapters 4–8. More general issues involving the causes and consequences of acceleration have not yet been considered and are discussed in this chapter. The discussion summarizes and adds to the discussion in chapters 1 and 2. Contemporary developments and the institutional changes that occurred after liberation were viewed in chapter 2 as causes of acceleration in the early 1960s. But the timing of acceleration cannot be explained without reference to the inherited constraints that prevented rapid growth before the 1960s; these were examined in chapter 1, and we return to them in the next section of this chapter.

Welfare consequences of Korea's accelerated growth are also of interest. Consumer expenditure estimates that were presented in table 2.6 reveal a marked second-period increase in real per capita consumption, suggesting that the average person was significantly better off by 1970–72 than a decade earlier. However, a rising average says nothing about distribution or whether the benefits of rapid development were concentrated among a few or widely dispersed.

In addition, certain internal and external aspects of development are particularly likely to influence Korea's future growth. World output and trade grew more quickly after World War II than before, and this growth, especially in the United States and Japan (Korea's main trading partners), has helped Korea's own trade and growth. However, imports were financed with American aid until the early 1960s, and since then Korea has become increasingly dependent upon Japanese financing. Such dependence, characteristic of Korea's earlier satellite role within the Yen Bloc, has already affected commercial policy and should also shape future international economic relations.

Confrontation with the North, actual as well as potential, has been another pervasive characteristic of life in Korea that has had major internal economic implications. Confrontation not only diverted to military ends resources that might have otherwise been used for development purposes but also shifted the locus of political power and with it the nature of domestic economic policies. The Korean War enhanced the size and power of the army; this development, combined with the weakness of the Chang government, led to the military coup of 1961 and subsequent rule by an authoritarian regime controlled by the military. Because this regime has been authoritarian and has no economic-interest base, it could hold down wages and consumption, largely ignore rural interests, and concentrate on rapid development through industrialization. Rapid development, in turn, fostered sectoral and geographic imbalance, and possibly growing income inequality.

To the extent that balance is inconsistent with accelerated growth and inequality creates social or political stress, future development should depend upon the regime's flexibility in meeting economic and sociopolitical demands. Involved is a conflict between redirection of policies to achieve better balance, but at the cost of slower growth, or continuation of past high-growth policies that are increasingly likely to generate political instability or even the chaos that disrupts economic growth.

The world economic scene, after the close of the second subperiod in 1972, was marked by an oil embargo, raw materials shortages, and international economic recession, all of which influenced the Korean economy. Additional information now available will allow us to discern the course of Korea's growth after the second subperiod, examine the pattern of development during the first half of the 1970s, and bring the record more up to date. The pattern is too brief and unstable to permit extrapolation into the future, but it reveals the short-term variation and the immediate impact of particular economic events that have heretofore been masked by the use of eight- and ten-year subperiods designed to emphasize the trend shift of the early 1960s.

Long- and Short-term Factors in the Acceleration of the 1960s

Economic development after the Korean War was generally unimpressive. Despite reconstruction demand, GNP increased at an annual rate of only 4.1 percent from 1953–55 to 1960–62 (the first subperiod). Annual average growth rates of both per capita consumption and gross domestic capital formation were below 2 percent and exports were inconsequential (less than $40 million a year), while substantial imports ($300–400 million a year) were financed mainly by American aid. The economy was still predominantly agricultural (over 60 percent of the labor force worked on farms, 45–50 percent of output originated in agriculture), there was little change in structure, and not much growth in output per worker (see tables 2.3 and 2.4).

The pace of development from 1960–62 to 1970–72 (the second subperiod) was strikingly different. These years, like the 1953–55 to 1960–62 period, began from a low base, but the GNP growth rate of 9.1 percent was one of the world's highest. Consumption almost doubled for the average person and government consumption increased substantially too. There was a phenomenal expansion of exports, led by labor-intensive manufactures. Imports rose as well, largely in response to increased demand for export materials and new capital equipment. Domestic saving rose sharply, spurred by a fiscal reform that ended government deficits and by an interest-rate reform that encouraged private saving. Foreign saving also increased after 1965, when the signing of a normalization treaty with Japan was followed by growing inflows of commercial loans that replaced declining aid receipts. The increase in foreign and domestic saving permitted significant expansion of investment so that one-quarter of GNP was allocated to capital formation by the early 1970s.

Accelerated growth after 1960–62 was characterized in Korea by radical structural change. Domestic product originating in agriculture dropped from 45 percent of total product in 1960–62 to less than 30 percent in 1970–72 as the industrial sector's share doubled from 17 to 35 percent. There was a corresponding shift in labor-force composition. Agricultural employment fell from 63 to 50 percent of total employment while industrial and service employment increased in importance.

Change of such consequence can be explained by short-term factors that limited development before the early 1960s and other factors that speeded growth afterward. A minimum of institutional change, reconstruction, and economic coherence was necessary, however, before rapid growth could occur. The change from the first to the second subperiod can therefore be explained in terms of loosening institutional or other historic constraints, most of which were a part of Korea's colonial legacy. Rapid growth was possible after the early 1960s only because these constraints had already been loosened. In short, both long-term and short-term elements were responsible for the acceleration in the rate of economic growth that distinguishes the first subperiod from the second. The long-term factors are considered first and then the short-term factors in examining the reasons for the acceleration of the 1960s.

South Korea's pattern of development as part of the unified Korea that was, in turn, a Japanese colony was determined largely by Japan's needs. These included mainly crude food (rice) until the 1930s, when increased demand for manufactures and industrial crude materials is reflected in the changing composition of Korea's exports. Trade ratios (exports plus imports/commodity product plus imports) were very high by international standards, and trade was mostly with Japan. The large size and concentration of trade are probably as good indicators as any of Korea's satellite role in the Yen Bloc before 1945, and of a development pattern in which self-sufficiency had no place. Education or training for modern economic skills was also excluded from the colonial development pattern because they were supplied by the Japanese themselves. Similarly, rural institutions and infrastructure were developed primarily to expand and appropriate agricultural output rather than to provide employment and food for the colony's growing population, especially since dispossessed peasants provided a cheap source of labor that could be used in Japan, Manchuria, and other Yen Bloc territories.

Agriculture dominated the Korean economy at the time of annexation by Japan and productivity was low. Output almost doubled by World War II, and much of this increase consisted of rice exported to Japan. Rising output and growing exports were associated with shifts in landownership and tenure arrangements so that Japanese owned half or more of the land in Korea by the mid-1930s and an increasing proportion of peasant proprietors were reduced to tenancy.

Industrial expansion in Korea was restricted before 1920 in order to limit competition with Japanese enterprise. After the restriction was lifted and the Japanese government decided to substitute Yen Bloc production for imports formerly obtained elsewhere, the zaibatsu groups became interested in Korea and manufacturing output grew rapidly. This growth was marked by shifts in emphasis from handicraft to factory operations, from light industry to heavy industry, and by increasing concentration in large Japanese-controlled firms. Most of them were established in the North, which offered particularly abundant power, cheap labor, and a good location between the homeland and Manchuria.

One can speculate about the nature of Korea's development if the country had been spared 35 years of existence as a colony. Agricultural productivity would undoubtedly have been lower without the import of new seed strains and improved methods from Japan and without the chemical fertilizer industry that was established on the peninsula. Manufacturing, transport, power, and the other elements of industrial infrastructure were unusually advanced for a poor country, especially one that was a colony. However, development was designed to meet Japan's needs, not Korea's, there was no reason to prepare the economy for eventual independence, and, in typical colonial fashion, the Koreans were an oppressed majority.

Oppression can be observed in access to education, occupational distribution, and the economy's capacity to absorb a growing population. Schooling was available to relatively few Koreans and, when available, was designed to create loyal subjects rather than to provide career skills. Higher education was restricted mainly to the Japanese. This educational structure is reflected in the sorts of jobs held by each group. Public and professional, administrative and managerial, engineering and skilled occupations were dominated by the Japanese.

On the other hand, most Koreans were farmers and unskilled industrial workers.

Domestic output (net commodity product) grew rapidly during the colonial era, but so did the population since premodern reproductive patterns were combined with a decline in mortality following annexation by the Japanese. Even when measured in per capita terms, output growth is a misleading indicator of welfare because substantial and growing exports (so-called starvation exports) caused divergence between production and consumption. Aggregates are also potentially misleading welfare indicators when, as in colonial Korea, income is distributed between two nationally and economically distinct groups. Available data for food consumption and real urban wages indicate that the average Korean was probably no better off at the end of the colonial era than at the beginning.

Exploitation, although hardly surprising in a colonial setting, was one of a number of factors that combined to reduce the colony's capacity for absorbing a growing population. Low real incomes, increased tenancy, high rates of population increase, and a small industrial sector (Korea was still predominantly agricultural and rural at the time of liberation) all limited economic opportunity and led to large-scale emigration, particularly during the 1930s. By the end of World War II, more than one of every ten Koreans was living abroad.

These emigrants, most of whom were repatriated after 1945, returned to a divided Korea that was ill-prepared to receive them. Industrial plant and equipment had been run down during the war and agricultural output reduced by fertilizer shortages. Departure of the Japanese left a population without the education or training for the administrative, professional, managerial, and technical skills needed to run the government and the economy. Korea's former specialized role within the Yen Bloc also proved a handicap. Japanese markets for Korean goods no longer existed and the structure of comparative advantage did not hold up in world markets. Specialization within Korea added to the handicap since division of the peninsula separated complementary regions: the South, where agriculture and light industry were concentrated, and the North, which had most of the heavy industry and power supplies.

South Korea's economic and political problems were inherited by the AMG during the brief period from 1945 to 1948. American economic interests in the country were never clearly established and so there was no purposeful development of the economic fragment that was Korea.[1] The AMG role was mainly limited to meeting the immediate problems created by postwar dislocation and the needs of a flood of refugees returning from other areas of the former Japanese Empire.

The Republic of Korea was founded in 1948 under Syngman Rhee but had been in existence less than two years when the Korean War began in June 1950. Most of the peninsula was ravaged, casualties were heavy in the South, and the country's meager stock of industrial capital and high-level manpower was decimated. Reconstruction began even before the war ended with an armistice in mid-1953, but much of the economic growth from 1953 to 1959 or 1960 represented recovery and not advance over prewar levels of development.

The Rhee government was primarily concerned with political rather than economic problems after 1953, there was no overall economic strategy, and the economy was hampered by inflation, overvalued exchange rates, heavy trade deficits, unrealistically low bank interest rates, and inadequate tax collection (in short, the characteristic symptoms of weak administration and inept policies found in many less developed countries). Poor performance during the mid-1950s was followed by virtual economic stagnation from 1959 to 1962. Although aid levels dropped during the late 1950s, it was political turmoil, marked by the student revolt that overthrew the Rhee government in 1960 and the military coup of 1961 that deposed the successor Chang government, that was largely responsible for stagnation at the close of the first subperiod.

---

1. There is an opposing view of American interests that sees a consistent U.S. policy in which Korea is to remain a Japanese satellite. Bix argues, for example, that basic American strategy since the late 1940s "has turned on making industrialized Japan dependent on the United States and economically backward Korea dependent, ultimately, on Japan" (Herbert P. Bix, "Regional Integration: Japan and South Korea in America's Asian Policy," in Frank Baldwin, ed., *Without Parallel: The American-Korean Relationship Since 1945*, p. 179). Other than noting that it has psychological roots in a traditional "Japanese-American ruling class attitude of contempt for the Koreans" (ibid., p. 179), the only reason Bix gives for this policy is that a backward Korea provides an outlet for surplus American manufactures and agricultural products. As evidence, he notes that before 1965 (when Japan took over the task), "the United States . . . had been responsible for thwarting balanced industrialization in South Korea by . . . nurturing the premature development of monopolies in the R.O.K. export sector" (ibid., p. 214). Why export monopoly should prevent industrial balance is not explained, no evidence is provided that such monopolies either existed or were "premature" nor, given well-established data on the nature of trade between the United States and less developed countries such as Korea, does it follow that more American surplus could be dumped on a backward, than on an industrially balanced, Korea.

Similarly, the economic acceleration of the early 1960s can be ascribed to policy change. The 1961 military coup brought to power the Park government, for which economic development was of primary importance because the economy's performance was now a major public issue and economic progress was seen as a means by which the military junta could acquire political legitimacy.

Political change may have been necessary for better economic performance, but it was certainly not sufficient. The new government inaugurated a stabilization program with the fiscal reform of 1963–64 and placed heavy emphasis on export expansion. The program reduced distortions caused by previous policies, freed imports of heavy restrictions, and, more generally, provided a restructuring in which more liberal policy measures were adopted to encourage the market forces that would stimulate economic performance. Because the program and its benefits are readily identifiable, Korea's accelerated growth in the 1960s has typically been attributed to restructuring or the adoption of new policies.[2]

New programs and other short-term consequences of short-term influences are only part of the reason for the acceleration in the growth rate that occurred during the second subperiod. The removal or loosening of long-term constraints also played a part, but this part tends to be obscured by the long time lags associated with the process. For example, widespread illiteracy and food shortages undoubtedly slowed growth following liberation in 1945, after which literacy campaigns, a new educational structure, and a series of land reforms stimulated agricultural production and provided the labor skills needed for rapid development. Similarly, Yen Bloc specialization, partition of the peninsula, and the Korean War left a shattered country that not only had to be rebuilt but also made into a viable whole. Though the actual duration of the lag between additional input and new output is difficult to specify in each case, such lags were undoubtedly substantial.

Economic performance may have been unimpressive during the years immediately after the Korean War (the first subperiod, 1953–55 to 1960–62), but during this time a number of Korea's inherited constraints were loosened. Reconstruction and import substitution restored and added new industry so that the country had a reasonably

2. For example, "the change in overall performance of the economy before [1958–62] and after [1962–68] the second restructuring has been little short of spectacular" (Benjamin I. Cohen and Gustav Ranis, "The Second Postwar Restructuring," in Gustav Ranis, ed., *Government and Economic Development*, p. 459).

coherent economic structure by the early 1960s. Land reform and the disruption of output that tends to follow reform were completed by 1958. Also, the new generation entering the labor force had more education and better job training than its predecessors.

When the Park government began to replace the inept economic policies of former administrations with a stabilization program in the mid-1960s, the response was a notable acceleration in the rate of economic activity followed by high growth rates throughout the rest of the second subperiod. Such new policies or restructuring may have been sufficient to launch the acceleration of the 1960s but only because the restrictive effects of Korea's inheritance had largely been dissipated by then.

Growth, Welfare, and Equality

Long-term restrictions or inherited constraints were emphasized in discussing the causes of Korea's relatively slow growth after the Korean War and the rapid growth of subsequent years. Relations between acceleration in the growth rate and its causes cannot be specified quantitatively, but there is ample quantitative evidence that the rate of increase in consumption rose along with acceleration in the growth of total resources and domestic product. Real per capita consumption increased 69 percent during the decade 1960–62 to 1970–72, or at an annual rate of 5.4 percent, well above the 1.4 percent annual rate of the first subperiod (see table 2.1). By 1972, average consumption was equivalent to $220 at the prevailing won–dollar exchange rate, up from $130 in 1960–62.

The rise in consumption was significant for its welfare consequences and, when taken from a low base as in Korea, should have contributed to output expansion as well. If there is any single indicator that can show how people benefited from the acceleration in Korea's rate of economic growth, it was this increase in per capita consumption. The average person was better fed, better housed, and better clothed by the end of the second subperiod than at the beginning of the first, and most of the improvement came during the second subperiod. Such improvement followed an era when many people were either illiterate or poorly schooled, inadequately fed, and when poor health combined with short life expectancy.

A series of literacy campaigns after liberation reduced the number of illiterates from 78 percent of the population in 1945 to 28 percent by 1960. School enrollments, particularly at the primary level, rose sharply after 1945 and continued to rise both absolutely and relative to the number of persons in corresponding school-age groups. From 1953 to the mid-1960s, for example, primary-school enrollments increased from two-thirds to over 90 percent of children aged 6–11. No tuition and entrance fees have been charged for public primary schooling, but such fees were collected at other levels and parents have also been expected to cover costs of textbooks, uniforms, supplies, and building-expansion programs as well as tutoring, transport, and the other nonschool expenses of education. By the mid-1960s, 7–8 percent of GNP was being allocated to education, of which two-thirds or more was private expenditure.[3]

Private costs of schooling can be seen in household-expenditure surveys, which show that both the size and relative importance of educational costs in family budgets are larger at higher income levels. Affluent families allocate above-average expenditure shares to education in order to provide post-primary schooling for their children. This high income elasticity of demand for education combined with rising incomes and public efforts to expand educational opportunities so that Korea's educational system was already exceptionally advanced for a country of its per capita income or stage of development by the late 1950s.[4]

Surveys of diet made in 1946–47 showed an average caloric intake of less than 1,500 per day. This intake increased to almost 2,500 by the late 1950s and to 2,700 by 1970–71. The first figure reflects post-liberation dislocation and, if accurate, was sufficiently below generally recognized minimum standards that inadequate diet undoubtedly limited energy and stamina and reduced resistance to disease. Insufficient caloric intake was no longer a problem for most people at the end of the first subperiod, although slum diets were still below minimum standards during the mid-1960s.[5]

Morbidity and mortality statistics are too unreliable to provide an

3. Estimates for private expenditure on education by expenditure category in 1964 are shown in the Korea Federation of Education Association's *Korean Educational Yearbook, 1965*, p. 95.

4. "Human resource development" rather than education was the variable actually related to economic development, but many of the indicators used to represent human resource development, such as school-enrollment ratios, numbers of scientists, physicians, and other high-level manpower categories, are education-related variables (see Frederick Harbison and Charles A. Myers. *Education, Manpower and Economic Growth*, p. 102).

5. See George McCune, *Korea Today*, p. 121; Kwon E. Hyock et al., *A Study in Urban Slum Population*, p. 162; *Korea Times*, 4 July 1972.

accurate picture of the health situation in Korea or the effects of disease on longevity, but tuberculosis and intestinal parasitism were still endemic by the early 1970s and most people did not have access to a sanitary water supply. Nevertheless, all the available data show increases in average life expectancy and declines in infant mortality that suggest health conditions had improved. This improvement can be attributed to a decline in population/physician ratios, better access to medical facilities, greater use of chemotherapeutic drugs, and enlarged public health efforts. Roughly 2–3 percent of rising private consumption totals has been allocated to medical care. Though the private share of total medical-health outlays is indeterminate, improved health and increased longevity can also be attributed to growing expenditure for medical care permitted by the increase in per capita consumption.

Such consumption includes an expenditure or investment element that adds to "human" capital as well as pure consumption outlays, particularly when starting from very low consumption levels as in Korea. Thus, the conventional distinction between investment and consumption loses some of its significance since both serve to increase productive capacity and expand future output.[6] Growing expenditure for education, food, and medical care not only contributed to individual welfare after the Korean War but also served to improve labor quality and thus raise output per worker. This indicates that low consumption levels were one of the inherited constraints that had to be overcome before rapid growth was possible, that the rise in consumption was a cause as well as a consequence of output expansion, and that increasing consumption should share the credit for acceleration in Korea's growth rate.

Evidence of rising per capita consumption and the welfare benefits associated with such a rise is based on averages. However, any increase in per capita income, consumption, or individual welfare is not neces-sarily distributed evenly among the population, so that an average may conceal growing disparity rather than measure typical or common experience. This problem of measurement raises the issue of whether the benefits of rapid growth were evenly distributed in Korea. or whether inequality increased so that some groups did not fully share

6. For example, Galenson and Pyatt found a positive relationship between a set of health indicators and output per worker that was especially significant among low-income countries (see W. Galenson and G. Pyatt, *The Quality of Labour and Economic Develop-ment in Certain Countries*).

in the benefits. There is reason to believe that the averages used here are deceptive and that inequality probably increased. It increased because incomes were distributed in an unusually even fashion before the early 1960s and because the rapid growth of subsequent years was accompanied by structural change and disequilibrium that should have increased income inequality.

Liberation in 1945 was followed by confiscation of Japanese property, land reform, increased access to education, and the destruction of income-earning assets during the Korean War. Also, further land reform in the late 1950s and confiscation of "illegally accumulated wealth" after the student revolution of 1961 served to redistribute assets in a more equal fashion. Evidence of this can be found in a series of monetary reforms or currency-conversion schemes that revealed a relatively even distribution of cash holdings.[7] However, the circumstances that fostered equality in postliberation Korea were abnormal and could not be expected to continue once political and economic order had been reestablished in the early 1960s.

The main structural change during the second subperiod was the sharp drop in agriculture's output and employment shares that was offset by the doubling of the industrial sector's output share and the growing relative importance of industrial and service-sector employment. Industrial activity was also increasingly concentrated in urban areas (see p. 172). As output growth accelerated, urbanization increased. The population of Seoul, the country's leading metropolis, rose from 2.4 million in 1960 to more than 6 million by 1972. Not only did Seoul and the other urban areas grow, but the 1966 and 1970 censuses also show an absolute decline in rural population after 1966.

Industrialization, when combined with urbanization and growing output-per-worker differentials, resulted in widening regional income disparities. Output per worker was almost twice as high in industry as in agriculture in 1960–62; the figure for industry was almost three times as large by 1970–72 (see table 2.4). For example, output per worker was more than three times as great in Seoul and Pusan as in Chŏnnam (a predominantly rural and agricultural province) by 1968, and gross per capita income was almost three times as large.[8] Though the relationships here are indirect, they indicate that the industrializa-

7. Choo Hakchung, "*Some Sources of Relative Equity in Korean Income Distribution,*" pp. 27–32.
8. Bertrand S. Renaud, "Conflicts between National Growth and Regional Income Equality in a Rapidly Growing Economy: The Case of Korea," pp. 430, 444, and table 1.

tion and urbanization characteristic of Korea's changing economic structure have been responsible for increasing sectoral and regional income inequality.

This sort of association between economic growth and increasing income inequality is consistent with both historical and contemporary experience elsewhere. Income inequality tended first to increase, then decrease in economically developed countries. Cross-section differences in income inequality yield a U-shaped relationship between per capita GNP levels and income shares of the lowest income groups that indicates today's less developed countries may be following the same pattern. Such evidence says nothing about the relationship between income growth rates and changing shares, however. Cross-section data on this point reveal no "marked relationship between income growth and [overall] changes in income shares," so that Korea's rapid growth during the second subperiod may or may not have contributed to rising income inequality.[9]

A series of income-distribution measures has been constructed for Korea that shows levels of inequality and permits comparison with distributions for other countries.[10] The measures were either derived from household-income surveys constructed specifically for this purpose, from tax data for income earners, or from a combination of the regularly published farm and urban income and expenditure surveys. Such measures, either in the form of decile distributions or Gini coefficients (concentration ratios), have been compared with the same measures for other counties to show that incomes in Korea have been distributed relatively evenly. The measures have also been used to demonstrate that income inequality did not increase as income growth accelerated during the second subperiod.

For example, "available data can be used . . . to construct estimates of the size-distribution [of income] in 1964 and 1970. By 1964, the distribution of income in Korea was among the best in the developing

9. See Hollis Chenery et al., *Redistribution with Growth*, p. 13. The predicted income share of the lowest 40 percent of the population declines to per capita GNP levels of $400, flattens, and then rises above $1,200 while the share of the upper 20 percent moves in a parallel but offsetting fashion (ibid., p. 17). However, Adelman has suggested that Korea was already in the upturn of the U, or moving toward greater equality by 1970 (ibid., p. 285).

10 For example: Harry T. Oshima, "Income Inequality and Economic Growth: The Postwar Experience of Asian Countries"; Bertrand Renaud, *Economic Growth and Income Inequality in Korea.* Estimates for Korea shown in Chenery et al., *Redistribution with Growth*, are based on a paper by Christian Morrison, "Income Distribution in Korea," prepared for the International Bank for Reconstruction and Development (1972).

world, and remained so in 1970 ... since the relative distribution of income changed little during during the rapid growth phase of the Korean economy."[11] Or, "income inequality in Korea ... appears to be much less [than in developed countries]. ... We tried ... to show that inequalities during this period of rapid growth became more pronounced but ... found [that] major indicators within sectors were ... moving in the direction of more equality ... [and] that no serious deterioration has taken place on a nation wide basis."[12]

These arguments contradict the view that income inequality should have increased in Korea during the second subperiod but this view, nevertheless, still appears to be correct. It appears to be correct because an abnormally even income distribution could only be expected to deteriorate when influenced by subsequent growth and structural change. Also, the findings cited above are based on flawed data, but even if the data were accurate, the argument for maintained equality still involves illegitimate comparisons.

The income-size estimates for Korea are derived from surveys that exclude wealthy households, single-person households, nonfarm households in rural areas, and small farmers, which "results in a bias toward overrepresentation of those nearer the mean of the size distribution of income."[13] Also, it has been estimated that urban expenditure (and income) data were as much as 50 percent too low in 1964–66, and 20–30 percent too low in later years.[14] This downward bias produces suspect results (average urban income below average rural income, for example) and, together with bias toward the mean, should affect measures of income distribution so that they appear to be more equal than they actually are.

Decile distributions, Gini coefficients, and other income-distribution measures reveal relative income variation where income size has a welfare equivalent. Households with higher incomes are supposed to be better off than those lower on the scale. Rapid growth and structural change are likely to alter this equivalence so that these measures may prove misleading indicators of the actual welfare distribution.

Growth and change in Korea during the 1960s and early 1970s were

11. Chenery et al., *Redistribution with Growth*, pp. 284–85.

12. Renaud, *Economic Growth and Income Inequality in Korea*, p. 44.

13. Choo Hakchung, "Review of Income Distribution Studies, Data Availability, and Associated Problems for Korea, the Philippines, and Taiwan," pp. 18–19.

14. Renaud, *Economic Growth and Income Inequality in Korea*, p. 21. Renaud checked the survey estimates by deriving urban expenditure for 1964–71 as the residual when farm consumption is subtracted from total private consumption shown in the national accounts (ibid., tables 5 and 7).

characterized by industrialization, changing attachment to the labor force and different working conditions, and urbanization. This was a period of upheaval for many people as they found new kinds of work, marked by different and more demanding terms of employment, in urban rather than in rural areas. Although most people benefited on balance from these changes (why else would they have moved to the cities and found different jobs?), new life styles were so different from the old that comparison is difficult because it involves different sets of costs and benefits.

These difficulties can be seen in the kinds of adjustment that should be made when comparing incomes of rural and urban households in order to make valid welfare statements. Since rural families are larger on average than urban families, an adjustment is needed for family size. Though working conditions are different for the two groups, the welfare implications of such differences can be ignored here; income rather than work is at issue. Differences between rural and urban consumption patterns cannot be ignored, however, particularly when a given type of consumption is a work-related cost rather than a benefit of higher income.

In 1972, for example, the average urban household consisted of 5.31 persons and spent roughly 1.5 times as much on consumption as the typical rural household with 5.71 members. (These are survey figures, and as noted earlier, reported urban consumption was probably 20–30 percent below the actual level.) The urban household spent more than five times as much on housing as its rural counterpart and more than three times as much on tranaportation and communications. Much of the difference was undoubtedly work related, in that urban workers had to pay more for housing and transport as a condition of working in an urban area. Urban incomes should thus be deflated for higher costs. The urban family certainly did not receive five times as much house as its rural equivalent when it spent five times as much on housing.

Income-distribution estimates for Korea were not adjusted to compensate for these rural–urban consumption differences and therefore do not necessarily reflect actual welfare distributions. Some households with lower incomes may thus be better off than others with higher incomes because consumption differences have altered the welfare equivalence of their incomes. Also, changes in actual income inequality may or may not be captured by changes in the estimated distributions. Miscalculation of change is especially likely during the second subperiod because rapid growth and structural change should have increased the discrepancies between actual and estimated distributions. It follows that existing estimates ought not to be employed in drawing welfare conclusions or inferences about equality or changes in the equality of Korea's income distribution. The distribution was evidently abnormally equal at the start of the 1960s, reasons for abnormality no longer obtained in later years, and so there was probably some increase in income inequality during the second subperiod.

THE FIRST HALF OF THE 1970s

In the last section the question of whether Korea's income distribution became more or less equal as the economy grew rapidly during the second subperiod raised a conflict between logic and evidence. Here, the quality of evidence is not at issue but, instead, what can be inferred from a relatively brief chronology. The shift in focus from the subperiod to the year poses a problem of perspective because the foreground is occupied by short-term changes that are important primarily for their long-term implications, yet the period covered is too short and unstable to permit extrapolation. Instability itself is of interest, however, since it has dominated short-term economic policy-making and since it reflects a long-term consequence of economic dependence. In short, the Korean economy has been unstable because it is dependent upon international markets that are themselves unstable.

Problems of overheating in the late 1960s were met in early 1970 by a set of restrictive monetary and fiscal policies and measures to reduce foreign-capital inflows. Evidence of overheating was the 46 percent expansion in the money supply during 1969 and a jump in current-account deficits in the 1968–69 balance of payments as import prices and interest costs increased. Domestic product had risen more than 15 percent in 1969, but the financial pinch reduced investment and output growth in early 1970 before the rate of price increase slackened and restrictive measures were relaxed to stimulate growth during the second half of the year. Domestic product rose 8.6 percent in 1970 (see table 3.1).

Rapid growth during late 1970 lasted through the first half of 1971 before deterioration in the U.S. balance of payment led to de facto dollar devaluation in August and the ensuing upheaval in international trading arrangements reduced demand for Korea's exports. Devalua-

Table 3.1. Leading Economic Indicators: 1969–74

	1969	1970	1971	1972	1973	1974
1. GDP (% change)	15.2	8.6	9.8	7.3	16.5[e]	8.2[e]
2. Prices (% change)[a]	13.2	15.3	11.5	14.5	9.6	18.0
3. Exports (million dollars)[b]	658	882	1,132	1,676	3,270	4,515
4. Imports (million dollars)[b]	1,650	1,804	2,178	2,250	3,837	6,452
5. Balance-of-payments: current acct. (million dollars)[c]	549	623	848	371	309	1,839
6. Money supply (% change)[d]	45.5	40.6	17.7	41.2	40.6	29.5

Sources: EPB, *Korea Statistical Yearbook*, various years; BOK, *Monthly Economic Statistics*, various years; table 7.1 below.
[a] Implicit GNP deflator.
[b] Merchandise only, from balance-of payments statements.
[c] Balance of goods, service, and transfer payments.
[d] Currency in circulation plus demand deposits (adjusted).
[e] GNP, not GDP.

tion of the won in June had already increased the debt service burdens of foreign-financed Korean firms, raised import costs, and pushed up domestic prices. One result was a rise in the balance-of-payments deficit (current account) from $623 million in 1970 to $848 million; another was a drop in output growth during the second half of 1971. However, output (GDP) increased 9.8 percent for the year, up from 1970.

Recession during the second half of 1971 continued during the first half of 1972. This period was marked by the discovery that a number of firms suffered from unsound financial structures (i.e., they were overextended and unable to meet debt-repayment obligations). The recession, combined with inflation, led the government to impose a commodity price freeze in March, gradually devalue the won another 7 percent from December 1971 through June 1972, and issue the Third of August Emergency Decree. This was a set of expansionary measures designed to ease the credit shortage and, incidentally, to wipe out unorganized money markets. Expansion is seen in a 41 percent increase in the money supply, well above 1971's 18 percent increase.

Recovery began in the second half of 1972, headed by exports. Commodity exports rose more than $0.5 billion from 1971 levels to $1.7 billion, imports grew less rapidly, and so the balance-of-payments deficit fell sharply to $371 million. Despite the second-half recovery, output rose only 7.3 percent, or less than in 1971.

Recovery continued and accelerated during 1973, led by expansion of world trade. Manufacturing output rose 31 percent as exports reached $3.2 billion. Imports grew too but at a lesser rate, so that the current-account deficit dropped to an unusually low $309 million while large capital inflows ($340 million) raised foreign-exchange holdings to over $1.0 billion by the end of the year. Although the money supply increased at the same high rate as in 1972, prices did not rise much until late in the year, when worldwide raw materials shortages and the oil embargo began to affect the Korean economy. The impact of these events was insufficient to offset growth, however, and output rose an unprecedented 16.5 percent in 1973.

The effects of worldwide recession and the oil embargo hit Korea in 1974. A series of Special Presidential Emergency Measures was initiated to offset the impact of foreign upheavals by stabilizing prices, strengthening export finance, and generating employment. Despite these measures, rising oil and raw materials prices contributed to domestic inflation as the GNP deflator increased 27 percent, well above the 9.6 percent of 1973. The value of exports rose 38 percent, but imports increased 68 percent, a small surplus on invisible trade was replaced by a deficit, and the current-account balance-of-payments deficit soared to a record $2.023 billion. Employment levels continued to rise through mid-1974, but average monthly man-days in mining and manufacturing began to drop and with them the growth of industrial output. Overall, domestic product increased 8.7 percent in 1974, or about half as much as in 1973.

This brief chronology reveals an alternating pattern of acceleration and deceleration around a high average growth rate during the first half of the 1970s. Acceleration phases have been associated with booming exports, monetary expansion, and, ultimately, domestic inflation. These features have been followed by restrictive government measures to end overheating or by international crises that slowed export growth, raised balance-of-payments deficits, and reduced output expansion. This sort of instability, concealed by subperiod averaging, was a significant characteristic of Korea's growth during the latter part of the second subperiod and on into the mid-1970s.

Though overrapid monetary expansion or premature credit restriction may have contributed to instability, the main causes appear to be changing international market conditions that affected raw material supplies or the demand for exports. Heavy involvement in trade and Korea's poor natural-resource base have clearly amplified the influence of international disturbances on the domestic economy.[15] One consequence of instability has been government intervention to ameliorate the effects of international disturbances. Another has been renewed emphasis on import substitution in the 1970s (see chap. 8) and continued public statements calling for the achievement of self-sufficiency in food production (see chap. 5).

PROSPECTS FOR GROWTH

The rate and pattern of Korea's economic growth during the next several decades are likely to depend upon the international economic situation and retention of comparative advantage in labor-intensive manufactures, or, possibly, development of new types of comparative advantage. Also, growth may be affected or even halted by internal and external political problems. Armed confrontation with the North has been an ever-present threat since the Korean War, while the potential for an internal uprising appears to have grown in recent years after President Park imposed martial law in the fall of 1972, rewrote the constitution, and adopted an increasingly authoritarian style of government. In addition, the future pattern of development is likely to be influenced by the sorts of imbalance that have resulted from the rapid growth of the second subperiod. Because efficiency must be sacrificed to achieve greater balance or equality insofar as greater balance requires comparatively inefficient resource allocation, any meaningful attempt to increase balance is likely to reduce future growth rates. There is now evidence of a shift in development strategy toward greater balance, but it is too recent to tell whether there is a real public commitment to the new strategy.

One characteristic of the Korean economy has been extensive involvement in foreign trade. This was apparent as early as the 1930s, when trade ratios (exports plus imports/commodity product plus imports) reached 50 percent, well above the average for small countries that typically had the highest ratios. Trade ratios fell to less than 20

15. Korea has no domestic oil supply, for instance. Demand for petroleum products rose rapidly during the late 1960s and early 1970s as oil replaced coal for heating, a highway network was built, new oil-fired electric generating plants were constructed, and a petrochemical complex was established. The oil embargo and subsequent jump in oil prices raised the cost of petroleum imports from $296 million in 1973 to $917 million during the first eleven months of 1974. The increase, due solely to higher prices because domestic use had been curtailed, was equivalent to almost a third of the commodity trade deficit in 1974.

percent in 1953–55 and 1960–62 before export-led expansion during the second subperiod increased the importance of trade and raised the ratios to 52 percent by 1970–72. Almost one-quarter of manufacturing output was produced for export at this time.

Cost–benefit relations appear to have favored importing and output for export rather than import substitution and production for domestic markets, and Third Plan (1972–76) projections call for continued expansion of both. Export earnings have been used to purchase the machinery and equipment needed to expand industrial capacity and to pay for the imported raw materials incorporated in the exports. These exports have been increasingly concentrated in labor-intensive manufactures so that relatively abundant labor was exchanged, in effect, for relatively scarce capital and raw materials. However, the process has limits that should slow future growth. Among these are a probable rise in relative labor costs and an increasingly unbalanced industrial structure. In addition, growth may be curbed by external forces or by increased efforts to reduce dependence on other countries.

Export advantage has been based primarily on relatively low labor costs. Costs have been low because labor has been abundant and unorganized and because the cost of wage goods has been kept down either by aid in the form of U.S. surplus wheat (PL 480 imports) or by government intervention in domestic markets to hold down prices of consumer necessities. Rapid employment growth and a declining rate of population increase should make labor increasingly scarce; besides, the era of American commodity aid ended in the mid-1970s as shortage replaced surplus. The cost of the subsidies required to hold down consumer prices is also likely to rise with increasing demand. Comparative advantage depends on *relative* costs so that Korea can retain advantage if wages rise more elsewhere, but this seems unlikely given Korea's low initial wages and the forces at work to raise them.

New emphasis on expanding heavy and chemical industry in the Third Plan is a reversion to the import-substitution projects that were proposed in the First Plan and then dropped when it was revised (1964). Such emphasis may be due to growth of domestic markets during the intervening decade, failure of heavy and chemical industries to keep up with new demand from expanding export industries, or some notion of "proper balance" that has been violated by a growth pattern centered on light manufacturing. Whatever the reason, expansion of the heavy and chemical industries, if implemented, is likely to divert resources from export activity and therefore slow export growth.

External forces that may alter future trade include the sort of world-wide recession and market disturbances that occurred in 1973–74 and long-term shifts in the growth rates of Korea's main trading partners. Three-quarters of exports and imports were shipped to or received from Japan and the United States at the end of the second subperiod. Growth of output, exports, and imports was generally greater in these two countries during the 1960s and early 1970s than in the 1950s and was substantially above rates for earlier periods. This more rapid growth can probably be credited with increasing supplies of goods available for export, provision of aid or credit to finance their purchase, and expanded demand for imports. The point gains support from what happened when growth has been interrupted in Japan and the United States. In 1974, for example, real GNP decreased in both the United States and Japan. The increase in U.S. import volume was infinitesimal, Japan's imports declined, and Korea's real export growth rate dropped substantially.

Global recession, the oil embargo, and raw materials shortages not only restricted Korea's export expansion but also led to deterioration in the terms of trade and created difficulties in borrowing to cover unusually large balance-of-payments deficits. Such deficits, which have financed a substantial share of total domestic capital formation, represent Korea's dependence upon American aid during the first subperiod and upon private loans (particularly from Japanese lenders) during the second. Both the benefit of aid for Korea's agricultural development and the more general relation between foreign resource inflows and economic growth have been questioned, but the real issue here is economic dependence rather than the role of foreign capital.[16] Dependence on aid or borrowing is regarded unfavorably, and fears of increased dependence have been responsible for attempts to achieve

16. See pp. 77–78. Japan's share of foreign capital invested in joint ventures rose from 21 percent in 1950–69 to over 90 percent in 1974 (*Korea Times*, 5 Dec. 1974). Adverse effects of importing U.S. agricultural surplus have been discussed by Chu Suk-kyun, for example ("Impact of U.S. Surplus Agricultural Products on Korean Agriculture"). A more general case against aid has been made on the grounds that "from South Korea to Southern Rhodesia, numerous additional examples of the tendency of capital imports to supplant domestic savings could be found" (K. B. Griffin and J. L. Enos, "Foreign Assistance: Objectives and Consequences," p. 322). Later work shows, however, that foreign capital inflows (both aid and private capital) are positively related to both savings and overall growth rates in Korea and elsewhere. See Gustav F. Papanek, "Aid, Foreign Private Investment, Savings, and Growth in Less Developed Countries," pp. 129–30; Constantin Voivodas, "Exports, Foreign Capital Inflow, and South Korean Growth," p. 484.

self-sufficiency in food production and to restrict or replace imports. Continued deterioration in the terms of trade or stiffer borrowing terms are likely to alter cost–benefit relations so as to lower benefits (raise costs) and thus increase the incentive to lessen dependence by reducing Korea's involvement in trade.

The Korean War and the ensuing confrontation with a hostile power north of the 38th parallel led to the military coup of 1961 and subsequent rule by an authoritarian government able to restrict consumption and for the most part ignore distributive issues in pushing for rapid growth. However, confrontation has had more direct economic consequences, for Korea has been a garrison state since 1953 with a military establishment of 600,000–700,000 men and 20–25 percent of government budgets, or 4–5 percent of GNP, allocated to defense expenditure. Economic costs have included reduction in potential civilian employment and GNP available for nonmilitary uses because resources allocated to military ends are largely lost for development purposes. Costs should not be measured according to numbers of soldiers or size of defense budgets, however, because published figures are incomplete, actual costs depend upon alternative uses (i.e., fungibility), and costs have been offset by foreign assistance.

Since the Marshall Plan period (1949–52), few other countries have received as much United States military support and economic assistance or generated such large-scale, defense-related foreign exchange earnings as Korea. Assistance can be explained in terms of strategic location between China and Japan, the heritage of the AMG era, the Korean War legacy, or Vietnam War requirements, but the apparent danger of attack from the North has undoubtedly shared responsibility for securing the economic as well as the military assistance provided by the United States. For this reason, costs to Korea of maintaining an oversize military establishment should be reduced by assistance received to support it and by any possible economic benefits of military activities.[17]

Confrontation with the North has not only had political consequences and a direct impact on resource allocation by diverting more

17. That economic as well as military assistance has depended upon confrontation or actual war can be seen by comparing the amounts and timing of U.S. economic assistance to Korea and Vietnam with the amount and time pattern of assistance to the Philippines, India, or other countries. The distinction between the two forms of assistance, or between assistance and military service earnings, is blurred in any event because these are nominal categories where any one type of receipt tends to free resources that can be used for other purposes.

resources to military activities than would otherwise have been the case, but it has also been used to justify the sacrifices associated with accelerated growth. Growth has an additional dimension when it is thought to contribute to national security and it can be argued that superior economic performance is needed for protection against incursions from the North. This does not mean that particular economic policies have been instituted for military or strategic reasons; export expansion, for instance, appears to be unrelated to the republic's defense posture. However, the restraints on current consumption and the sorts of increasing inequality associated with rapid growth have undoubtedly been more palatable when growth serves national or patriotic as well as economic ends.

Although consumption rose rapidly during the second subperiod, it still averaged only $220 per capita by 1970–72 while an increasing share of total resources was being allocated to investment and exports. A large portion of the expanding investment totals was used to build manufacturing and other industrial-sector capacity, which produced widening gaps in sectoral output per worker, growing disparity between rural and urban consumption, and increasing regional income inequality.

Rapid growth and the various forms of economic balance are not logically incompatible, but there are reasons for incompatibility in Korea. Small domestic markets, relatively abundant labor, and relatively scarce land and capital have made exports of labor-intensive manufactures the most efficient means of achieving rapid growth. Emphasis on rapid growth has therefore focused on industrialization and particularly on output for export. Export production has been concentrated in the Seoul–Inch'ŏn and Pusan areas because, among other attractions, they are efficient locations that offer minimum transport and transshipment costs. The result has been increasing imbalance, especially during the second subperiod, marked by growing differentials among sectors in output per worker and widening regional income disparities associated with the sectoral differentials.

Increasing income inequality may have resulted from growing sectoral and regional differentials during the second subperiod though, as noted earlier, the available data are inadequate for measuring changes in Korea's income distribution. Nevertheless, government labor and agricultural policies have discriminated against peasants and industrial workers, two major occupational groups at the bottom of the income-size distribution. The government has been active in agricultural markets, supplying fertilizer and other inputs and purchasing or importing grains. Pricing policies have been used to hold down the cost of food and other wage goods in the industrial sector. Similarly, the government has pursued labor policies that have restricted union activity and has also failed to enforce labor standards laws so that employers have been able to minimize costs by paying low wages, requiring workers to work long hours, and avoiding the expenses necessary to provide proper working conditions.[18]

The types of imbalance associated with rapid growth and the policies used to skim off a greater share of growing output for investment in further growth have sacrificed the immediate interests of major economic interest groups in Korea. This has only been possible because an authoritarian, military-dominated government has not had to make significant economic concessions for political support. There is a parallel here with Meiji Japan, where regressive fiscal policies were used in "taking up the slack," or reallocating "excess labour . . . and resources of productivity on the land" from agriculture to the new industrial sector.[19] The parallel lies in the direction of allocation and in action by an authoritarian government, however, and not in the means employed or results obtained. Reallocation in Korea has been achieved mainly through market intervention instead of through fiscal action since the government has been able to use many policy instruments that were not available in Meiji Japan. Also, the pace of industrialization has been much faster and the resulting imbalances have been much greater in modern Korea.

It is tempting to assume that only a communist or an authoritarian government can command the resources necessary for a less developed country to achieve rapid growth and that Korea's accelerated growth during the second subperiod was due to assumption of power by an authoritarian regime. Notwithstanding, comparison of growth rates among developing countries with and without authoritarian forms of government shows no correlation between growth and form of government. The particular strategies employed rather than simply the ability to impose unpopular or even consistent strategies must have been

18. See pp. 138–39; Robert Whymant's "Sweat-shops of Polyster Road" (*The Guardian*, 29 May 1973); and Bernie Wideman, "The Plight of the South Korean Peasant," in Baldwin, *Without Parallel*.
19. Gustav Ranis, "The Financing of Japanese Economic Development," p. 440.

responsible for the government's contribution to accelerated growth.[20] Furthermore, it may be more difficult for an authoritarian government to adopt new strategies when circumstances require or otherwise to possess the flexibility needed to deal with changing circumstances because such governments tend to be shielded from critical judgment.

When the undesirable by-products of rapid growth became painfully apparent during the late 1960s as migration to the cities accelerated and the combination of rapid urbanization and industrialization over-taxed available facilities, the government responded with a sharp increase in investment to break infrastructure bottlenecks. Increasing sectoral and regional imbalance also led to a shift in policy emphasis from rapid growth during the first two plans to less rapid growth combined with economic balance in the Third Plan. "Rather than merely emphasizing 'economic growth,' the Third Five-Year Economic Development Plan can be characterized by its attempt to promote a 'balanced economy' by 'expanding regional development,' 'developing and improving life in rural areas,' and 'improving the quality of life of workers.'"[21]

The discussion of Korea's growth prospects has emphasized the central roles of trade, confrontation with the North and possible internal upheaval, and the kinds of imbalance that increased with accelerated growth during the second subperiod. Export-led growth has been based on Korea's comparative advantage in producing labor-intensive manufactures and on the expansion of income and imports in Japan and the United States, Korea's principal trading partners. Demographic and employment trends and increasing costs of wage goods seem likely to reduce comparative advantage in traditional export lines but, more important, the sort of global recession and market crises that halted expansion in Japan and the United States during the mid-1970s threatened Korea's continued growth and raised new questions about a development strategy tied to export expansion and foreign capital inflows. These internal and external factors, espe-

20. See G. William Dick, "Authoritarian versus Nonauthoritarian Approaches to Economic Development," pp. 822–24. Of the 59 countries ranked according to real GDP per capita growth rates in 1959–68 and classified by form of government, Korea was among the authoritarian countries in the first quartile. Dick's work suffers from a specification problem since the form of government can follow from as well as determine the rate of economic growth. An authoritarian regime may assume power, for example, because prior economic performance was unsatisfactory.

21. Government of the Republic of Korea, *The Third Five-Year Economic Development Plan*, p. vi.

cially the increasing costs of dependence on foreign financing, suggest that trade will probably play a smaller role in Korea's future growth than it has in the past.

Confrontation with the North has imposed the economic burden of maintaining a large army. This burden is likely to decline, in relative terms, because troop levels have stabilized while the economy continues to grow. Any reversal of the decline is likely to depend on political or strategic developments that are difficult to foresee. Such developments might include a shift by the DPRK (Democratic People's Republic of Korea, or North Korea) toward a more adventurous military posture, possibly inspired by communist success in South Vietnam; withdrawal of American military assistance should failure of such assistance in Vietnam lead to withdrawal elsewhere or should the increasingly authoritarian government in Korea arouse political opposition in the United States; or, possibly, internal unrest sparked by political repression.

Rapid growth during the second subperiod generated growing sectoral and regional imbalance, and possibly increasing income inequality as well. Such imbalance, an undesirable by-product of rapid growth, evidently inspired a shift in policy so that the Third Plan, unlike its predecessors, emphasized a combination of greater economic balance and somewhat slower growth. The need to right imbalance also underlies the "new village movement" (*saemaul undong*), adopted early in 1972 to stress farm community development and improve rural life.

It is too early to evaluate Third Plan achievement as this is written but the attempt to "promote a 'balanced economy,' " if actually implemented, represents a radical change in development strategy with profound implications for Korea's future economic growth. The shift from rapid growth concentrated in the industrial sector, especially in manufacture for export, to a strategy that calls for achieving a "balanced economy" by "expanding regional development, developing and improving life in rural areas, and improving the quality of life of workers" requires redirection of resources to agriculture and other lagging sectors, to backward regions, and to peasants and industrial workers.

That such radical change will actually occur is open to doubt for a number of reasons. Goals such as "improving the quality" of life are difficult to measure and therefore may appear to be satisfied when, in fact, they are not. Also, the new goals involve institutional change, which is much more difficult to achieve than capacity expansion.

Finally, such radical change calls for new economic policies and a degree of flexibility in administration not hitherto required. If actual rather than nominal achievement is stressed, if the necessary institutional change is possible, and if the government proves sufficiently flexible to implement a new development strategy, increased balance and less rapid growth should mark Korea's economic future.

4

The Labor-Absorption Problem

A major issue in Korea and in other less developed countries is whether output expansion has been sufficient to absorb the increasing supply of labor. Evidence of widespread unemployment and underemployment in developing countries since the 1950s has generated an extensive literature on surplus labor, disguised unemployment, and the turning point (from labor surplus to labor shortage). Interest increased sharply in recent years because employment expansion proved disappointing in the 1960s, while projections for Colombia and other developing countries showed a future marked by rising unemployment levels and the likelihood that a growing proportion of the labor force would be unemployed.[1]

In Korea, surveys of the urban (actually nonfarm) labor force have shown high rates of unemployment among those aged 15–24, while "in Seoul in 1965, out of a total labor force of 1,012,000, the unemployed amounted to 230,000 or 23 percent."[2] Perhaps more important has been rural underemployment or surplus labor. Studies by Hong and Cho of farm labor utilization found an excess of workers on the order of one-third during 1958–64 (Hong) and revealed that approximately 30 percent of labor time available in 1959 was unutilized (Cho).[3] Unemployment and underemployment were undoubtedly major

1. See, for example, David Turnham, *The Employment Problem in Less Developed Countries*, pp. 114–20; International Labour Office, *Towards Full Employment*, pp. 45–46; Derek T. Healey, "Development Policy: New Thinking About an Interpretation," pp. 766–69.
2. Ro Chung-hyun, *Population and the Asian Environment* (1971), p. 9, cited in Healey, "Development Policy," p. 771.
3. Hong Young-pyo, "Agricultural Overpopulation in Korea"; Cho Yong-sam, *"Disguised Unemployment" in Underdeveloped Areas with Special Reference to South Korean Agriculture*.

problems during the first subperiod, but accelerated growth during the second should have absorbed a great deal of labor. The available estimates indicate, in fact, that employment increased by 3 million between 1963 and 1972, but this figure is significant only when related to the increase in the supply of potential workers.

The supply should vary with population growth, participation rates, and the factors that influence participation, whereas demand is likely to depend on output expansion, relative factor costs, and productivity increase. Absorption can be viewed as a function of the changing balance between supply and demand. Interest here lies primarily in the extent to which accelerated growth during the second subperiod contributed to absorption and in Korea's experience with problems of labor absorption compared with experience elsewhere.

Labor absorption tends to be obscured when economic-activity status, employment, and underemployment are difficult to specify, as is true of countries such as Korea with relatively undeveloped labor markets where a large portion of labor is provided within family units instead of by individuals working for wages. Many people have only casual attachment to the labor force so that inactivity rather than unemployment is the alternative to employment. Activity status is thus likely to change with changes in demand because more labor (workers or man-hours) would be available if demand warranted it. Unemployment, in turn, tends to be unimportant compared with inactivity or the partial activity seen in short workweeks. This means that measures of labor absorption ought to relate actual inputs to potential inputs where the potential is more broadly conceived than in standard labor-force definitions.

LABOR-FORCE PARTICIPATION, SUPPLY, AND POTENTIAL SUPPLY

Consistent estimates of Korea's economically active population based on a labor-force approach are available only for the period since August 1962. Anyone 14 years of age or older who works for pay or profit (or in the family business) during the survey week, who has a job but is temporarily absent, or who has no job but is looking for work is included in the economically active population. "Looking for work" is broadly defined so that people who do not actually try to find work (because of bad weather, temporary illness, or belief that no job is available) are included. Under this definition, 31–32 percent of Korea's population has been economically active, a rate that remained quite stable from 1963 to 1972. This is low when compared to rates in more industrially advanced countries, mainly because participation among men under 30 is substantially lower, as is participation among women aged 20–29 and among people of both sexes aged 55 and above. Low participation rates among young men are a statistical artifact; unlike other countries, soldiers are excluded from Korea's labor force. Relatively low participation among women in their twenties is probably due to child raising and limited opportunities for obtaining non-agricultural work (the gap is most marked among urban households), whereas low rates among older persons may result from shorter life expectancy and their household obligations in extended families.

Annual estimates are simple averages of quarterly surveys held during the middle weeks of March, June, September, and December. The averages conceal wide seasonal variation. Employment and total activity have been 3 million higher at June peaks than at December troughs, with most of the variation concentrated among women in farm households. In 1972, for example, 3.4 million women were engaged in agricultural activities during June but only 1.2 million in December.

The quarterly surveys may show wide variation, but it is not known whether they capture the full extent of seasonal swings in employment or whether an average of the four quarterly estimates typifies annual activity. The June survey may catch some of the extra labor needed to transplant rice, for example, but the September survey comes too early to reflect the additional labor needed during the rice harvest and the planting of winter wheat and barley.[4] Though subject to unknown bias, the quarterly estimates can still be used to explain variations in workweek and seasonal disappearance from the labor force.

One consequence of wide seasonal swings in agricultural activity is to reduce the average workweek in agriculture. The workweek grew since 1963, but it was only 44 hours in 1972, when the average workweek in nonagricultural occupations was 58 hours. Also, since seasonal movement in economic activity and employment is similar, the residual —unemployment—has been relatively constant. Estimated unemployment, furthermore, has been low in recent years (the rate averaged only

4. These quarterly surveys have been used to illustrate seasonality in employment levels because "one case where surveys are sufficiently frequent is that of Korea" (Turnham, *The Employment Problem*, p. 62). Although "sufficiently frequent" to show seasonality, the estimates are not frequent enough to ensure that the seasonality shown is accurate.

4.5 percent during 1970–72). This means that when seasonal work ceases, workers leave the labor force. They are not unemployed (e.g., looking for work), because there is no work for them.

"Unemployment" traditionally denotes a situation where supply exceeds demand at some given price, so the distinction between unemployment and inactivity is irrelevant insofar as the seasonally inactive are available for work. If they are available, seasonal disappearance of potential workers from the labor force is a form of disguised unemployment that has been much more important than open unemployment in Korea (3 million versus 0.5 million in 1972, for instance). Published unemployment estimates, in consequence, are likely to prove poor measures of the unemployment situation.[5]

Some sense of potential supply can be obtained from the quarterly survey estimates, in which the economically inactive population is grouped into those who are engaged in housekeeping, attending school, too old to work, or who have other reasons for inactivity. Over half the inactive population has consisted of women engaged in housekeeping and a million or more have been too old to work, while the number whose reason for inactivity is "something else" has diminished, probably because of better survey techniques. Students are the one major group that has been growing relatively and absolutely within the inactive population, from 1.1 million in 1963 to 2.1 million by 1972. Expansion of schooling accounted for half the increase in economic inactivity since 1963, and, since the cohort of 14-year-olds increased only 0.35 million from 1963 to 1972, increased schooling also restricted growth in the number of potential new labor force entrants.

In June 1972, the seasonal employment peak, 12.1 million persons were employed from an economically active population of 12.5 million. Employment and activity dropped to 9 and 9.5 million, respectively, in December. If all persons employed in June had been employed throughout the year, Korea's labor force would have risen by 1.5 million. Only 40 percent of farm household members otherwise engaged

5. Especially when small changes in the unemployment estimates are misinterpreted. An article entitled "Jobless Rate Down by 0.3 Percent," for example, noted that "this represents a decrease of 25,000 in the number of the nation's jobless persons from 471,000 in 1969 to 446,000 in 1970." The article concludes that "this percentage figure indicates that the nation's unemployment situation has much improved since 1969" (*Korea Times*, 23 March 1971). Not only is the unemployment figure well within the standard error of estimate for labor-force estimates in the 400,000–500,000 range (i.e., it is insignificant in itself), but it is also small relative to the increase in the number of economically inactive persons between 1969 and 1970 (155,000).

in housekeeping were inactive for this reason in June. If the June proportion is the minimum essential for housekeeping tasks and the remaining 60 percent of erstwhile housekeepers were occupied with other duties classified as "employment," the same proportion of nonfarm housekeepers should be available for employment in other months. If so, the labor force would have grown by another 1.9 million in 1972. Add the unemployed at the June employment peak (429,000), and maximum potential employment (or available supply) would have been 14.4 million, or 36 percent above the actual figure. Similar calculations for 1963 yield a maximum potential estimate of 10.9 million, or 43 percent more than actual employment in that year.

Speculative arithmetic of this sort is less useful for establishing magnitudes of potential employment or supply, which can be faulted for incompleteness and assumptions about possible activity of the inactive, than it is for illustrating the weakness of labor-force concepts in countries such as Korea. Most of the potentially active are engaged in housekeeping during the off-peak months; they would not qualify for unemployment assistance even if it were available. Because they function in a primarily subsistence segment of the economy, the usual reasons for unemployment—insufficient aggregate demand and technological unemployability—do not apply.[6] This is why the difference between actual and maximum potential labor supply is not labeled "unemployment" here, and why greater commercialization of household services and other institutional changes would probably be needed before potential could be translated into actual employment.

Estimates of the potential, it should be observed, depend upon arbitrary assumptions about who should or should not work. A number of inactive groups (students, those listed as too old to work, the disabled) that account for almost half the economically inactive population were excluded from potential supply here on the grounds that it would be socially undesirable for them to work, but different social values or national circumstances could easily alter these assumptions and the estimates that follow from them. Also, the estimates are probably too high because housekeeping activity is both postponable and seasonal, so that low June levels may be below minimum average inputs. (In November, for example, the *kimjang* [or making of *kimchi*, a pickled and fermented Chinese cabbage that is a staple of the

6. Difficulties of defining unemployment in less developed countries are treated in more detail (and with considerable sarcasm) by John Weeks in "A Brief Note on the Unemployment Crisis in Poor Countries."

Korean winter diet] is a conspicuously time-consuming household task.) In addition, the measures are incomplete because no allowance is made for changes in working hours. The average workweek rose 7 or 8 percent from 1963 to 1972, mainly because a growing proportion of the employed was working in nonagricultural jobs where the workweek is much longer than in agriculture. Adjustment for changes in working hours would reduce the growth of potential supply.

Korea's population grew 20 percent from 1963 to 1972, the number of economically active persons rose 33 percent, and employment adjusted for lengthening of the average workweek increased 48 percent. Potential supply expanded 31 percent during this interval. Difficulties of defining the supply make inferences hazardous, but it still appears that demand grew more rapidly than supply during the second subperiod. Rapid output growth from 1963 to 1972 not only served to increase employment but also seems to have absorbed an increasing proportion of the labor supply potentially available for work.

LABOR-ABSORPTION MEASURES

Output was related to employment in table 2.4 to measure output per worker and growth of output per worker. Where y represents income or output and n employment, y/n is the standard measure of output per worker, or labor productivity, and its reciprocal, n/y, is a measure of labor intensity. Labor absorption, in turn, varies with output growth and labor intensity. Because there were major differences among sectors in output per worker and a rapid overall increase in output per worker during the second subperiod, there should also be large differences in labor intensity among sectors and a marked decline in average labor intensity. Absorption, then, reflects the offsetting influences of rapid output growth and declining labor intensity.

Employment and income (output) estimates for the agricultural, industrial, and service sectors in 1963 and 1972 and measures of average and incremental labor intensity derived from these estimates are shown in table 4.1. In addition, the "labor-absorption rate of income growth" has been calculated and is also given in the table. More than four-fifths of the increase in employment from 1963 to 1972 (Δn) and in income or output (Δy) occurred in the industrial and service sectors (see cols. 3 and 7). Agriculture's contribution to employment and output growth was therefore relatively small (this is confirmed by the annual growth rates shown for each sector in cols. 4 and 8).

Average labor intensity at the beginning of the period, or n/y in

Table 4.1. Measures of Labor Absorption by Sector:
1963–72

A. *Employment* (n): *thousands*

	1963 (1)	1972 (2)	Change from 1963 to 1972 (Δn) (3)	Annual growth rate (G_n) (4)
1. Total	7,662	10,559	2,897	3.63
2. Agricultural	4,837	5,346	509	1.12
3. Industrial	997	2,212	1,215	9.26
4. Service	1,828	3,001	1,173	4.67

B. *Income* (y): *billion won*

	1963 (5)	1972 (6)	Change from 1963 to 1972 (Δy) (7)	Annual growth rate (G_y) (8)
5. Total	1,225.2	2,710.1	1,484.9	8.94
6. Agricultural	531.5	760.1	228.6	4.06
7. Industrial	239.0	988.7	749.7	17.09
8. Service	454.7	961.3	506.6	8.68

C. *Average labor intensity* (n/y), *incremental intensity* (Δn/Δy), *and the labor-absorption
rate of income growth* (G_n/G_y).

	n/y in 1963 (9)	Δn/Δy (10)	G_n/G_y (11)
9. Total	6.25	1.95	0.41
10. Agricultural	9.10	2.23	0.28
11. Industrial	4.17	1.62	0.54
12. Service	4.02	2.32	0.54

Sources: Income (gross domestic product at 1970 factor costs), same as in table 2.1;
Employment, EPB, *Annual Report on the Economically Active Population, 1972.*
Note: Sectors are defined as in table 2.3, and the sectoral employment distribution for
1970 is used to distribute employment in 1972.

1963, ranged from 9.10 man-years per million won of output in
agriculture to 4.17 for the industrial sector and 4.02 in services. These
labor/output ratios show that labor absorbed per unit of value added
(net output) in agriculture was more than double that in the industrial
and service sectors. Ratios of incremental employment, Δn, to the
increase in income (Δy), or $\Delta n/\Delta y$, are also given in table 4.1 (col. 10).
These incremental labor/output ratios are much lower for all sectors
than the average ratios in 1963, illustrating the sharp drop in absorption
that occurred during the second subperiod.

   The growth of employment was not simply a function of output expansion, since increasing output per worker among members of the existing labor force should reduce the need to hire more workers. Nevertheless, one can ask what employment would have been in 1972 if labor intensity (n/y) had remained the same in 1972 as in 1963 (i.e., if incremental employment per additional unit of output, $\Delta n/\Delta y$, equaled the 1963 average) and if output growth had not been influenced by increasing output per worker. If the incremental labor/output ratios had not fallen, employment would have risen by 7.2 million instead of by an actual 2.9 million.[7] The difference between actual and hypothetical employment increases in each sector results from differences between 1963 average levels and 1963–72 incremental ratios. The proportionate increase is largest for agriculture because of the relatively large drop in that sector's incremental labor intensity after 1963. Only 2.2. extra man-years were consumed per additional million won of agricultural output from 1963 to 1972 compared to an average of 9.1 in 1963.

Average annual (compound) growth rates for employment (G_n) and income (G_y) and the ratio of the two (G_n/G_y) are also given in table 4.1. These ratios, or labor-absorption rates of income growth, show the increase in employment relative to the rise in income, or the amount of labor absorption per unit increase in income. Unlike the average and incremental labor/income ratios, the labor-absorption rates are pure numbers that, because they are not influenced by the units used to measure income (output), can be compared with labor-absorption rates for other countries. These rates, shown in column 11, averaged 0.41 for all activities, 0.28 in agriculture, and 0.54 each in the industrial and service sectors. In other words, income had to grow at an average rate of 2.5 percent to support a 1 percent increase in employment. Income growth needed to generate a 1 percent increase in agricultural employment was almost 4 percent; the amount required to yield a 1 percent increase in industrial and service employment was a little less than 2 percent.

None of the employment estimates, average or incremental labor/output ratios, or labor-absorption rates of income growth have been adjusted for changes in the average workweek, because interest here is focused on labor absorption and employment rather than on labor

___

7. The hypothetical increase in total employment (Δn) was derived by multiplying 1963 labor intensity (n/y) by the increase in income (Δy) for each sector and then adding the hypothetical changes for the three sectors. Labor intensity for total employment in 1963 is equal to the sum of sectoral intensities weighted according to 1963 income shares, and cannot be used to derive the hypothetical total, because $\Sigma n/y \cdot \Sigma \Delta y \neq \Sigma(n/y \cdot \Delta y)$.

input as one of several factor inputs. Nevertheless, measures of output per worker would reflect actual hours worked rather than numbers of workers and so, for the same reason, should reciprocal measures such as the average and incremental labor/output ratios. Similarly, labor-absorption rates of income growth may be more accurate indicators of labor absorbed when adjusted for variations in average workweek because these variations can conceivably substitute for changes in employment. In Korea, as mentioned earlier, growth in the proportion of the labor force engaged in nonagricultural activities increased the average workweek after 1963. When the employment estimates are adjusted to a full-time equivalent (FTE), or 50-hour, workweek, the aggregate labor-absorption rate of income growth rises from 0.41 to 0.50. Adjusted estimates were not used here, because they cannot be compared to unadjusted measures for other countries, but the effects of adjustment are worth noting.

Labor-absorption rates of income growth in Korea, Singapore, Thailand, Taiwan, West Malaysia, and the Philippines (mostly during the 1950s and 1960s) have been examined by Oshima.[8] The simple average of the rates for the six countries was 0.41 for all sectors, 0.20 in agriculture, 0.52 for the industrial sector, and 0.51 in services. These rates are similar to those shown for Korea in table 4.1, which would indicate that Korea's experience with labor absorption from 1963 to 1972 was fairly typical of that in other developing countries in East and Southeast Asia during recent years.[9] If Korean experience was typical, this raises a number of issues that may have application elsewhere. In particular, why has aggregate absorption been limited and why, among sectors, has absorption been especially low in agriculture?

Determinants of Labor Absorption

Policies that affect the pattern of output growth or alter relative factor prices, and the potential for technical adaptation and its exploitation should have determined the extent to which accelerated output growth

8. Harry T. Oshima, "Labor Absorption in East and Southeast Asia: A Summary with Interpretation of Post-War Experience," p. 68.
9. Estimates for Korea shown in the Oshima article were taken from my "Labor Absorption in Korea Since 1963" (a paper presented before the conference on Manpower in East and Southeast Asia held in Singapore in May 1971). The estimates used by Oshima differ from those shown here partly because the periods covered are different (1963 to 1970 rather than 1972) but mostly because Korean labor-force estimates were revised at the end of 1973 to show much more rapid increase in employment. Revision has raised Korea's labor-absorption rates from below average to slightly above average for the six-country sample.

in Korea during the second subperiod was translated into increasing labor absorption.

Emphasis on import substitution during the first subperiod required the expansion of fertilizer, cement, petroleum processing, and other capital-intensive industries that provided relatively little direct benefit in the way of labor absorption. Devaluation, interest-rate reform, and other liberal policies adopted in the early 1960s served to redirect emphasis from import substitution to export expansion and thus encouraged more labor-intensive activities. Norton compared capital/output ratios in 1965 with ratios of export to import values in 1960 and 1968 and found that the manufactured products which displayed the most rapid export growth were among Korea's most labor-intensive manufactures.[10]

The switch in emphasis from import substitution to export promotion should have increased labor absorption, but industrialization and the industrialization bias in Korea's first two five-year plans probably did not. Average labor intensity was much higher for agriculture than for industry in 1963 (see table 4.1), though the sharp drop in incremental intensity for agriculture meant that agricultural output rose with relatively little additional labor input. Still, special features of Korean agriculture have served to absorb labor so that displacement of farm workers has been less than it might otherwise have been. Agriculture has been characterized by small average holding size and rice specialization. Comparatively high yields per hectare have been associated with exceptionally labor-intensive methods of cultivation.[11] In a sense,

10. The average labor coefficient (number of workers per billion won of gross product) for mining and manufacturing in 1966 was 1,457. Coefficients for import substitutes such as chemical fertilizer (593), iron and steel (324), and petroleum products (98) were much lower (see Bank of Korea, *Interindustry Relations Table for 1966*). Norton's capital coefficients are given in Irma Adelman, David C. Cole, Roger Norton, and Lee Kee Jung, "The Korean Sectoral Model," in Irma Adelman, ed., *Practical Approaches to Development Planning*, p. 120. Export/import ratios and the argument that Korea's trade has been increasingly oriented toward less capital-intensive products can be found in Roger D. Norton, "The South Korean Economy in the 1960's."

Indirect as well as direct inputs should be considered in evaluating the labor intensity of exports and import substitutes. When indirect inputs of transport and other traditionally capital-intensive overhead facilities are included, import substitutes might prove to be more rather than less labor intensive than exports. However, a recent study by Lim of total (direct plus indirect) labor requirements for manufactured exports and import replacements, based on the 1968 input–output tables, indicates that this is not the case. Manufactured exports have been more labor intensive than manufactured import replacements. See Youngil Lim, "Factor Contents of Foreign Trade in South Korea."

11. Korea ranks fairly high in cross-country comparisons of production per hectare but last in output per worker (see United Nations, FAO, *The State of Food and Agriculture, 1968*, p. 78).

agriculture has been a "sponge" for workers who could not be absorbed even by the massive growth of employment in other sectors during the second subperiod. The sponge thesis may also account for the low incremental labor/output ratio and labor-absorption rates of income growth found in agriculture after 1963. Production was already so labor intensive at the beginning of the second subperiod that output could be increased with relatively little additional labor input.

More stress on agricultural development might have increased labor absorption in Korea, but industrialization itself clearly reduced absorption since the incremental labor/output ratio has been particularly low in the industrial sector. The ratio is low because government policies designed to promote industrialization have reduced the relative cost of capital and encouraged the development of large-scale, more capital-intensive activities. Among these policies were a tariff structure that has favored machinery and equipment imports, import licensing tied to minimum export requirements, and provision of repayment guarantees to foreign suppliers. Foreign equipment has been comparatively inexpensive, Korean firms able to meet export targets (mainly large firms) could import, and those with access to imports benefited from government-guaranteed foreign currency loans. Benefits resulted from the perennial overvaluation of the won and the high domestic interest-rate policy after the fall of 1965, which have made imports and foreign loans (primarily suppliers' credits) cheap relative to domestic goods and loans. Also, the KDB and the government-controlled commercial banks provided funds for industrial enterprises (especially government-invested corporations) at rates well below those charged in the unorganized money market. Firms with access to these institutions, mainly large firms, have obtained domestic credit at what amounts to subsidized rates. Firm size is significant here because a number of possible proxies for capital intensity show that large establishments, and therefore large firms, tend to be more capital intensive, and thus absorb proportionately less labor, than small ones.[12]

The impact of government policies that have reduced capital costs is partly offset by other policies that have served to hold down labor costs. Korea has been a net food importer since liberation and the volume of food imports has risen significantly in recent years. The combination of increased food imports, fertilizer-crop purchase programs, and retail-level price controls has restricted food prices and therefore the cost of wage goods. Prices of other common con-

12. Kuznets, "Labor Absorption in Korea Since 1963," table 8.

sumption items provided by government monopolies or enterprises (cigarettes, for example) have also been kept down. There is little union tradition is Korea, and trade unions have been instruments of government labor control rather than organizations concerned with the economic welfare of their members. Membership is limited, there is no minimum wage law, and furthermore, an elaborate set of bargaining and standards acts inaugurated by the AMG in the 1940s has been largely ignored. This evidence of union weakness indicates, if only indirectly, that unions have had little effect on raising wage levels or limiting employment.[13]

Government policies have been credited here with influencing the pattern of structural change, relative factor prices, and therefore labor absorption. Such attribution may give policy action more credit than it deserves, partly because the switch from import substitution to export expansion or the rapid industrialization that marked the second subperiod required individual response to new signals as well as government action to alter the signals, and partly because policies imply purposive action that, in this instance, was directed toward goals other than increased labor absorption. There has been little in any one of the five-year plans to indicate that labor absorption was of concern or that employment expansion was a major policy goal. In fact, the main emphasis of the first two plans (1962–72) was to maximize output growth, and "in the Second Plan, employment was neglected in the various planning studies, partly because the available estimates of employment levels were so poor and partly because the planners felt that labor would not be a constraint to growth."[14]

If increased labor absorption had been a major policy goal, relatively more emphasis would have been placed on expanding agricultural output rather than on industrialization and, within the industrial sector,

13. Only "permanent" (regularly employed) workers qualify for union membership. Membership was 367,000 at the end of 1967, when the population of potential members (regularly employed, nonfarm household employees) was 1.37 million. (see *The Korea Annual, 1968*, p. 340, and EPB, *Annual Report on the Economically Active Population, 1967*, p. 72). Unions in Puerto Rico have probably been as weak as those in Korea, but minimum wages in certain manufacturing establishments tripled from 1949 to 1963. The price elasticity of employment was found to be − 1.0, that is, wages and employment varied equiproportionally and inversely (see Lloyd G. Reynolds, "Wages and Employment in a Labor-Surplus Economy," pp. 22–34). When reports by the Office of Labor Affairs on violations of the Labor Standards Act began to appear after the protest suicide of a market worker in November 1970, it became apparent that poor working conditions were the rule rather than the exception (see, e.g., *Korea Times*, 22 Jan. 1971).

14. Roger D. Norton, "Planning with Facts: The Case of Korea," pp. 62–63.

encouragement given to the most labor-intensive activities and to small rather than to large enterprises. Manufacturing, which accounts for most of Korea's industrial product, has been concentrated in relatively labor-intensive activities, average establishment size tends to be much smaller, and output per worker much lower (i.e., labor intensity much higher) than in more industrially advanced economies. Establishment size has been growing, however, and with it capital intensity and output per worker.[15] Labor absorption policies would have to reverse these trends, either by encouraging particularly labor-using activities or by making existing activities more labor intensive.

The first possibility requires that there be sufficient demand to warrant greater output of labor-intensive products. Substitution of modern for traditional goods during the course of industrialization suggests that demand may not always be sufficient. For example, half the workers in Korea's paper industry during the late 1950s were employed by small establishments that made Korean-style paper. A decade later, value added by these establishments had dropped from 15 to 3 percent and employment from 50 to 20 percent of the industry total. Korean-style paper, a traditional good produced on a small scale by labor-using means, was being displaced by the modern products of larger, more capital-intensive factories.

Existing activities may absorb more labor (the second possibility) if it is both technically feasible and economically worthwhile to increase labor intensity. Labor costs should be lower relative to capital costs in Korea than in most other countries, given what little we know of comparative factor endowments, though government policies have probably tended on balance to reduce labor's price advantage. When labor is relatively cheap, the economic incentive exists to substitute labor for capital. There is still a question, however, of whether it is technically possible to do this.

Surprisingly little is known of the potential for factor substitution or the adaptation of available technology to differences in relative factor costs. It has been commonly assumed that labor and capital can be freely and continuously substituted over a wide range and that

15. The least capital-intensive industries accounted for one-third of total manufacturing value added in 1966. The same industries, which also tend to be least capital intensive in other countries, contributed only one-quarter of total value added in U.S. manufacturing during 1967. In the mid-1960s, the average Korean manufacturing establishment had less than one-third the number of employees of its U.S. counterpart, while value added per worker was roughly 20 percent to one-third of Japanese levels, which in turn were one-third to 40 percent of American levels.

substitution will take place to minimize costs. The assumption has been eroded in recent years when firms in capital-scarce, labor-plentiful developing countries imported the latest and most capital-intensive technology and made little or no effort to adjust the new techniques to local factor endowments. Such contradictory behavior has been ascribed to market distortions that make capital too cheap, lack of entrepreneurial capacity, or, more likely, limited scope for factor substitution.[16]

The issue here is somewhat speculative; that is, what could be done, given optimal conditions, to adapt technology to domestic factor supplies? It is also partly a matter of historical fact: What has actually been done to adapt new techniques? The historical question should be easier to answer since there is no way to predict capacity for technical innovation, but the sort of information we now have and the difficulties inherent in measuring actual adaptation suggest that it may not be.

Ranis provides a number of historical cases of "capital-stretching" (i.e., labor intensifying) innovations from Japan and contemporary ones from Korea and Taiwan as evidence that "the current widespread skepticism concerning the supposed tyranny of the rigid technical coefficients may be seriously in error."[17] The Korean innovations relate to machinery and process (rather than plant) and include increasing the number of workers on plywood production lines or decreasing the number of looms per worker in cotton weaving relative to Japan. This was done in order to substitute cheap labor for high-quality raw materials. Also, given processes tend to be more labor using than in Japan or the United States because machinery is run more hours per day, because materials are moved by hand rather than by machine, and because higher machine speeds are used so that more product inspection and machinery maintainance is required.

The results of econometric studies by Clague and Williamson contradict Ranis's examples and tend to confirm the "tyranny of rigid technical coefficients." Clague used capital/labor ratios and factor prices to calculate the elasticity of substitution between labor and capital for a set of manufactured goods produced in both Peru and

16. Limited scope for factor substitution, in turn, may have a number of possible causes. For instance, it has been suggested that skilled labor rather than capital is the scarce factor in developing countries and that more capital-intensive techniques economize on the use of skilled labor (see Werner Baer and Michel E. A. Hervé, "Employment and Industrialization in Developing Countries," pp. 99–102).

17. Gustav Ranis, "Industrial Sector Labor Absorption," p. 408.

the United States. The elasticities, taken from actual plant and engineering estimates and calculated according to alternative assumptions about capital values and prices, were uniformly low. Another study by Williamson employs several different short-run labor demand models to test the speed with which manufacturing employment has adjusted to output growth in the Philippines. Employment response was quite slow and labor absorption therefore disappointingly low. Although Williamson's work is not directly addressed to measuring elasticities of factor substitution, low absorption was found to be due in part to "an extremely pronounced labor-saving bias in technical change" or, in the present context, rigid technical coefficients.[18]

Results of the econometric studies are sensitive to difficulties of measuring capital inputs, aggregation problems, and uncertain specification of the factors that explain demand for labor. Actual factor substitution or technical adaptation may therefore be greater than is shown in these studies. Ranis's cases are admittedly episodic; the kinds of capital-stretching innovation found in plywood or textile manufacture probably cannot be achieved in continuous process operations such as petroleum refining where opportunities to change machinery and process are likely to be more limited. These analytical difficulties and the nature of the subject indicate, at least for the present, that the sort of answers needed to assess the quantitative significance of factor substitution or technical adaptation cannot be expected. We clearly do not know enough to suggest that "substitutability between capital and other economic inputs is substantial."[19]

A potential conflict between maximizing output and maximizing employment exists where technical adaptation and capital-stretching innovation are possible. Conflict may occur if more labor-intensive methods involve slower expansion of income and output and therefore of the savings needed to increase capacity and generate future growth. On the other hand, it is conceivable that adoption of more capital-intensive techniques might yield maximum output and savings growth that would, in turn, permit more future employment.[20] The conflict also has important distributive implications because employment

18. Jeffrey G. Williamson, "Capital Accumulation, Labor Saving, and Labor Absorption Once More," p. 65; Christopher K. Clague, "Capital–Labor Substitution in Manufacturing in Underdeveloped Countries," p. 535.

19 Henry J. Bruton, "Economic Development and Labor Use: A Review," p. 25.

20. If continued indefinitely, however, the potential increase in employment would never be realized (see Frances Stewart and Paul Streeten, "Conflicts Between Output and Employment Objectives in Developing Countries," pp. 164–65).

maximization not only provides more work for the unemployed and the underemployed but, in providing work, also raises incomes at the lower end of the income scale.[21]

Labor absorption in Korea, as observed earlier, has been a function of two offsetting factors: rapid output growth and declining labor intensity. To summarize, output growth and labor intensity were influenced during the second subperiod by major structural changes and government policies that affected relative prices and firm size. The structural change with the greatest impact on absorption was undoubtedly the rising output and employment share of the industrial sector (low labor intensity), offset to some degree by a switch within the industrial sector from import substitution (low labor intensity) to export expansion (high labor intensity). Government policies designed to encourage industrialization and promote exports are not likely to have been neutral with respect to labor intensity either; they probably reduced the relative price of capital and thus stimulated more capital-intensive activities. Policies that favored large rather than small firms certainly had this effect. One development at least partly traceable to these policies was the marked decline in labor intensity after 1963 that is seen in table 4.1.

Were employment rather than output maximization the government's major economic goal, a different set of policies would have been employed to encourage particularly labor-intensive activities, promote small-scale enterprise, and raise the relative price of capital. How much labor absorption might have increased, given an employment-maximization or even an employment-neutral strategy, depends in part on the economic and technical potential for capital-stretching innovation and, more generally, on whether output and employment maximization are conflicting or complementary goals.

Employment climbed by 3 million from 1963 to 1972 so that labor was probably absorbed on balance during the interval because this

21. "To treat 'income' as a net total, without inquiring who gains and who loses, and then set this against 'employment,' is to miss the point" (ILO, *Towards Full Employment*, p. 49). In fact, the association among poverty, low output per worker, unemployment and underemployment, and the narrowness of the conventional unemployment concept when used in developing countries has inspired an income approach to measuring unemployment in which those with incomes below some acceptable minimum are classified as inadequately employed. See, for example, Turnham, *The Employment Problem*, pp. 18–21; Raj Krishna, "Unemployment in India." The income approach was not used here in measuring labor absorption or potential labor supply, because little is known of income by employment status in Korea.

increase was larger than the increase in potential supply. However, potential supply was still well above actual employment in 1972. If potential supply is an accurate indicator of the maximum employment that might be achieved were demand to warrant it, inadequate absorption remained a problem in Korea by the end of the second subperiod since one-quarter of potential workers were not employed. Any measure of potential is conjectural, so inferences based on the relation between employment and potential supply are essentially conjectural too. We do know, however, that Korea's labor-absorption rate of income growth was similar to that of other countries in East and Southeast Asia. We also know that actual rates of output increase (G_y) and employment expansion (G_n) were well above average. One benefit of the acceleration in output during the second subperiod, then, was to increase employment and reduce any potential conflict between employment expansion and output growth.

5

The Contribution of Agriculture

The agricultural sector accounted for half of domestic product and two-thirds of employment in 1953–55. Both product and employment rose in subsequent years, but agriculture's share in total product diminished as industrialization accelerated (see table 2.3). This secular decline in agriculture's output and employment shares is a major feature of economic development that has been observed elsewhere than in Korea. The declining output share has typically been explained by low income elasticity of demand for food, the declining employment share by the migration of surplus labor to new jobs in other sectors, or mechanization that permits output expansion with little or no increase in labor inputs. Also, the sectoral biases of modern technology have generally favored the industrial sector.[1] Diminishing importance and the sort of explanation offered for it have served to divert attention from actual increases in agricultural output, however, and the other contributions that agriculture has made to overall economic growth.

In addition to the output contribution, agriculture may provide labor and capital needed for the expansion of other sectors, additional income and foreign exchange derived from export of farm products, and a growing market for the output of other sectors. Several of these nonproduct contributions have undoubtedly been important in Korea's development, but interest here focuses on output growth and the extent to which the agricultural sector has been able to meet the increased demand for food and other agricultural products generated by population increase and rising per capita incomes. The impact of output growth can perhaps best be established by considering what

1. See Bruce F. Johnston and John W. Mellor, "The Role of Agriculture in Economic Development," p. 567.

might happen if growth were insufficient for the food supply to keep pace with the increase in demand. "[T]he result is likely to be a substantial rise in food prices leading to political discontent and pressure on wage rates with consequent adverse effects on industrial profits, investment, and economic growth."[2]

Although food prices began to increase more quickly than other prices in the late 1960s and a stabilization program slowed nonagricultural expansion in 1972, there was little sign that insufficient increase in agricultural production had adversely affected overall economic growth by the end of the second subperiod (1960–62 to 1970–72). In fact, the average annual increase in agricultural output rose from 2.3 percent in the first subperiod (1953–55 to 1960–62) to 4.2 percent during the second. Crop production (85–90 percent of total agricultural output) in 1972, a poor harvest year, was one-third more than the 1961–65 average. Korea's agricultural performance during the first subperiod was roughly the same as that of other countries in the Far East, where the annual increase in output of 12 major crops averaged 2.45 percent from 1953–55 to 1962–63. However, performance was considerably better than average in later years. Increases in both world and Far Eastern agricultural production from 1961–63 to 1970–72 averaged 2.6 percent while Korea's second-subperiod output grew at an annual rate of 4.2 percent.

Such performance is noteworthy given Korea's unpromising agricultural history and unfavorable physical setting. The inheritance from the colonial era, especially the agricultural institutions, was probably less favorable than Taiwan's, and the immediate postliberation years were marked by fertilizer shortages, crop failures, and even food riots (see pp. 18, 30).[3] Limited production, heavy immigration after 1945, and Korean War dislocation caused emergency or near-emergency conditions that were alleviated by large-scale grain imports obtained with U.S. aid. Because output rose from a low base and population

2. Ibid., p. 573. The causal chain here assumes inelastic demand for food, a large share of food in total consumer expenditures, imports to cover domestic supply shortage, and limited foreign-exchange holdings so that food imports can be increased only by reducing imports of machinery and the other products necessary to expand industrial output.

3. The tardiness of Korea's agricultural development, when compared with Taiwan's, has been attributed by Hayami to: (1) later annexation, (2) earlier development of irrigation in Taiwan for producing sugar cane, (3) suppression of Korean rice imports, which, unlike Taiwan rice, were directly competitive with Japanese varieties, and (4) Taiwan's revenue surplus of 1905–10, which allowed heavy investment in irrigation and other infrastructure (see Yujiro Hayami, "Green Revolution in Historical Perspective: The Experience of Japan, Taiwan and Korea," p. 28).

increase outstripped agricultural growth, it is hardly surprising that grain imports continued at high levels during most of the first subperiod.

Only one-fifth of total land area is arable because of the peninsula's mountainous topography. Limited cultivable area combined with rapid postliberation population increase has given Korea one of the world's highest man/land ratios. Rainfall is concentrated during the summer monsoon and much of the nonarable land has been stripped of forest cover for fuel. This situation makes irrigation difficult (only a small fraction of total water runoff can be used for irrigation) and flooding common. Fluctuations in rainfall have also been a recurrent cause of poor harvests. The climate is characterized by cold winters that shorten the growing season so that opportunities for multiple cropping are limited primarily to the southern part of the country.

Widespread tenancy, another colonial inheritance, was largely elim-inated by a series of land reforms that began in 1948, continued during the Korean War, and was completed in 1958. Average holding size after the reforms has been 0.9 cheongbo, or 2.2 acres, and the typical holding is divided into five or six plots. Such small holdings are a consequence of legal limits (no one can hold more than 3.0 cheongbo) and Korea's high man/land ratios. Small holding size has been res-ponsible for extremely labor-intensive farming in which land is the scarce factor and the object of maximization is the value of output per cheongbo rather than per worker. This is why crops have accounted for almost nine-tenths of agricultural production and livestock only one-tenth, and why crops have consisted mostly of cereals rather than other, more land-using crops. It is also why rice, the only high-value cereal, has dominated cereal production in Korea (see table A3).

Despite a historical and physical background that would appear to be particularly unfavorable, Korea's agricultural production acce-lerated during the second subperiod. Such acceleration raises questions of why output levels should have increased, why they did not increase more, and whether the increase was sufficient to meet the country's growing demand for agricultural products. These are the main issues examined in the remainder of this chapter.

INPUTS AND THE EXPANSION OF OUTPUT

Agricultural output depends on inputs of land, labor, and the different types of farm capital (machinery or draft animals, irrigation, fertilizer). Introduction of new seed strains and cultivation techniques (i.e., the products of research and extension activities), improved rural credit and marketing facilities, and cost–price relationships should also influence output. The established method of explaining output growth is to estimate a production function in which output trends are related to increasing inputs of land, labor, fixed capital (represented by area under irrigation, machinery or implements, stock of draft animals, and so on) and working capital (fertilizer).

A production function is not used here to explain accelerated growth during the second subperiod, because the available data show a time pattern of input expansion that is inconsistent with output acceleration. Also, it is either difficult or impossible to specify the nonphysical inputs so that they can be introduced into the production function. How, for example, does one derive an indicator for research inputs? Such inputs have been important enough in Korea and elsewhere that they cannot be ignored if output behavior is to be explained.[4] Since the relative contribution of each input cannot be determined without using the production-function approach, the explanation is necessarily nonquantitative.

A set of estimates for the main physical inputs in 1956, 1963, and 1972 and growth rates for the 1956–63 and 1963–72 periods are shown in table 5.1.[5] The number of farm households in 1956 and 1963 (see row 1) is given to supplement the employment estimates since consistent employment series are not available before 1963, but numbers of households is probably an upward-biased indicator of labor input because average household size has been decreasing. Nevertheless, the average annual increase in numbers from 1956 to 1963 was only 1.3 percent, census data on population of all *gun* (rural administrative units) indicate that the annual growth of rural population dropped from 2.1 percent in 1955–60 to 1.25 percent in 1960–66, and employ-

4. Increase in physical inputs accounted for only 42–50 percent of output growth in Korean agriclture during the 1955–68 period, according to Ban's estimates (Ban Sung Hwan, "Growth Rates of Korean Agriculture, 1918–1968," p. 36). Similarly, production functions for Taiwan (which differ according to input weights) during the years 1920–39 show that "upward of 25 percent of the output increases can be explained only by the unkown factor, technological change." See Samuel P. S. Ho, "Agricultural Transformation Under Colonialism: The Case of Taiwan," p. 325.

5. Agricultural estimates are not ordinarily shown with single-year end points, because natural catastrophes can influence harvests and, therefore, growth-rate calculations. This stricture applies to output rather than inputs, however, and since consistent estimates for most input series cannot be obtained for the years before 1956, it seemed best to use single-year end points in order to encompass the widest possible time span in calculating growth rates.

Table 5.1. Growth of Agricultural Inputs (1956 to 1963 and
1963 to 1970) and Outputs (1953–55 to 1960–62 and
1960–62 to 1970–72)

		1956 (1)	1963 (2)	1972 (3)	*Average annual growth rate (%)*	
					(1) to (2) (4)	*(2) to (3)* (5)
1.	Farm households	2,200.5	2,415.6	2,487.6	1.3	0.2
2.	Employment[a]	—	4,644	5,110	—	1.1
3.	FTE employment [a,b]	—	3,985	4,466	—	1.3
4.	Cultivated area	2,008.5	2,097.0	2,261.0	0.6	0.8
5.	Land utilized	3,020.0	3,178.8	3,291.6	0.7	0.4
6a.	Irrigation[c]	209.4	294.9	—	5.0	—
b.[d]		—	395.2	566.2	—	4.1
7.	Farm machinery[e]	265.2	862.6	1,031.6	18.4	1.9
8.	Fertilizer					
a.	Chemical elements[f]	170.8	307.1	647.7	8.7	8.6
b.	Total[g]	850.0	1,057.9	1,428.5	3.2	3.4
		1953– 55	1960– 62	1970– 72		
9.	Output[h]	421	493	744	2.3	4.2

Sources: MAF, *Yearbooks of Agriculture and Forestry Statistics*, multiple years; NACF, *Agricultural Yearbooks*; EPB, *Korea Statistical Yearbooks*; table 2.3 above.

Note: All units in thousands unless otherwise indicated. Land area: 1 cheongbo = 0.9917 hectares; fertilizer: metric tons.

[a] Agriculture and forestry (hunters and fishermen excluded).

[b] FTE (full-time equivalent) employment is adjusted to a 50-hour workweek.

[c] Benefited area completed by irrigation associations.

[d] Completely irrigated paddy fields.

[e] Plows (hand and power driven).

[f] The figure shown for 1956 is actually the 1957 estimate.

[g] The 1956 figure shows supply, not consumption.

[h] Gross domestic product at 1970 factor costs (billion won).

ment (with and without adjustment for hours worked) rose even less from 1963 to 1972. Migration statistics show heavy outmigration from rural areas in the late 1960s and early 1970s, large enough so that Ministry of Agriculture and Forestry (MAF) annual surveys reveal an absolute drop in farm population after 1967.

Information on numbers of households, farm population, or migration does not tell how labor inputs behaved and may understate possible increase in such inputs if substantial underemployment existed when output began to accelerate. On the other hand, adjusted (FTE) employment rose only 0.3 percent a year while survey data show an actual decline in average labor hours (family, employed, and exchange) per household after 1963. The evidence suggests that labor inputs grew little if at all during the second subperiod.

Data for cultivated area and land utilized (table 5.1, rows 4 and 5) show annual growth rates of less than 1 percent in 1956–63 and 1963–72. Both cultivated area and land utilized reached a maximum in the late 1960s before declining slightly in subsequent years so that there has been no discernible trend in utilization ratios (area used for particular crops/total cultivated area). Loss of land under cultivation to other uses was still minor by the end of the second subperiod and might, conceivably, have been offset by reclamation projects. Limited areas of tidal flat were in fact reclaimed, and another 200,000 hectares of upland (equal to 8 percent of land already cultivated) could have been developed, but the capital-intensive nature of such projects and their long gestation periods made them uneconomic in practice.[6] Land inputs can also be stretched by increased double cropping (raising utilization) as well as by reclamation but this has been limited, in turn, by climate and by low prices for the winter grains (wheat and barley) that have been the main second crops. Growth in second-subperiod agricultural output was achieved without any significant expansion of Korea's limited cultivable area or increase in utilization ratios.

Fully irrigated paddy and land benefited by irrigation associations increased 4–5 percent a year from 1956 to 1972 (table 5.1, rows 6a and 6b). Comparison of irrigated paddy, all paddy, and total cultivated area in Korea, Taiwan, and Japan in the mid-1960s shows that the ratio of irrigated to total cultivated area was much lower in Korea than in the other two countries. The proportion of irrigated paddy in total paddy was about the same in Korea as in Taiwan (60 percent)

6. See Agricultural Economics Research Institute (Ministry of Agriculture and Forestry)–Department of Agricultural Economics, Michigan State University (AERI—MSU), *Korean Agricultural Sectoral Analysis and Recommended Development Strategies, 1971–1985,* pp. 28–31. The Tongjin River project, a major reclamation work, began in 1963, took more than six years and 5.3 billion won to complete, and added 4,270 hectares of arable land and irrigation for another 7,200 hectares (*Korea Times,* 7 Aug. 1969). Additional output was an estimated 130,000 *suk* annually (about 19,000 metric tons), valued at 780 million won in 1965–66 farm prices; production costs averaged 65 percent of market prices, so annual net income attributable to the project would be 273 million won a year. Under the most favorable assumptions (zero depreciation, no time lapes between investment and return, and no further preparation costs), the implicit return on the project was only 5.2 percent a year.

but well below Japan's 96 percent level. Since yields on irrigated paddy average more than twice those of rainfed paddy, a substantial portion of paddy land had yet to be irrigated, and successive droughts in 1967–68 focused attention on the need for "all-weather farming" (the government's term for irrigation), one might expect more rapid extension of irrigation by the end of the second subperiod than is shown in table 5.1.

Again, as with reclamation, investment in new irrigation works has been limited by the heavy capital outlays involved and also by technical difficulties caused by Korea's highly seasonal rainfall patterns. Even under the most favorable assumptions, the annual rate of return on investment in irrigation was found to be less than 6 percent at a time when the discount on bills was 24 percent and the rate on NACF (National Agricultural Cooperative Federation) project loans, a variety of subsidized loan, was 10 percent.[7] It is hardly surprising, then, that irrigation was not expanded more rapidly.

Figures for plows (hand and power driven), the principal farm implements used in Korea, are given in row 7 of table 5.1 as an indicator of fixed capital inputs. Numbers of draft cattle (over a million in recent years) could also have been used since these animals have been the main source of nonhuman power in farming. The number of draft cattle rose at a 5.9 percent annual rate from 1956 to 1963 before declining in 1963–72. Difficulties of aggregation inevitably make it more difficult to measure capital inputs than the other inputs shown in table 5.1, but fixed capital appears to have increased little during the second subperiod, and at a slower rate than output.

Data on inputs of the basic fertilizer elements (nitrogen, phosphorus, and potassium) and total tonnage consumed are presented in rows 8a and 8b of table 5.1. Fertilizer is the largest single category of working capital, a significant component of grain production costs, and is generally regarded as the major determinant of yield levels.[8] All chemical fertilizer was imported before 1960, when the first of a number of urea plants was built. By the late 1960s, Korea was largely self-sufficient in producing nitrogenous fertilizers. This growth in capacity evidently encouraged domestic consumption, for unlike the other physical inputs,

7. Lee Kie-wook, "Efficiency of Resource Allocation in Traditional Agriculture: A Case Study of South Korea," chap. 5.
8. See UN, FAO, *The Response of Rice to Fertilizer*, p. 57. Data for Taiwan are employed to show a highly significant, positive correlation between rates of nitrogen applied and yield increases.

inputs of fertilizer elements increased more rapidly than did output during the 1963–72 period. Consumption also rose faster since the mid-1950s than in either Taiwan or Japan. Usage of phosphates and potash was still comparatively low, but inputs of nitrogen were approaching Taiwanese and Japanese levels by the early 1970s.

The increase in physical inputs shown in table 5.1 appears insufficient to explain any acceleration in the growth of agricultural output. The only exception is fertilizer, where inputs of the chemical elements increased more rapidly than production. It is possible that the input–output relationship is nonlinear or linear but greater than unity so that small increases in inputs generate large output increases; however, the law of diminishing returns suggests that this is not so, particularly in labor-intensive agriculture of the Korean type. A more likely explanation is that expansion of nonphysical inputs or more favorable cost–price relations were chiefly responsible for the accelerated growth of agricultural output during the second subperiod.

Besides physical inputs of land, labor, and capital, factors that might be expected to influence agricultural production include farm costs and prices, imports of competitive agricultural products, credit availability, and research and extension activities. Though these "nonphysical" inputs are difficult or impossible to specify in quantitative terms, it is still possible to evaluate their contribution to output growth.

In Korea, the government makes direct food-grain purchases, extends rice-lien loans to acquire rice and reduce seasonal price fluctuation, collects land taxes in kind, and runs a grain-fertilizer exchange program. All these programs are designed to collect grains in government hands; the grains, in turn, are used primarily to feed the armed forces. The government has also sponsored or subsidized reclamation projects, land consolidation activities, and domestic fertilizer production, and government funds have been a major source of National Agricultural Cooperative Federation (NACF) loans. In addition, government estimates of the supply and demand for grain are used to determine import requirements. Other economic measures ranging from tariff policies to labor-conditions laws should also influence agricultural output, if only indirectly.

Collection programs have probably been the main determinant of agricultural product prices. Government collection of rice and barley has never reached more than 10 percent of total output, but only 30–50 percent of rice and 15–30 percent of barley produced have entered market channels, so these collections represent much greater proportions of commercial production. The government has also distributed fertilizer through the NACF. The impact of the government's fertilizer sales and grain purchases is reflected in a parity index that relates prices received to prices paid by farmers. Other factors, such as abnormal harvests and the secular increase in demand for food, also affect the parity index so that it measures more than just the price effects of government policies. Nonetheless, government action has been crucial in establishing farm costs and product prices, so that the parity index is largely influenced by such action. The index (1965-100), which shows prices received/prices paid, rose from 78 in 1960 to 113 in 1963, dropped to 94 by 1968, and then advanced once more to 113 in 1972. The first increase was especially significant because it coincides with the beginning of the second subperiod.[9] It shows an improvement in cost–price relationships during the early 1960s that undoubtedly contributed to the acceleration in agricultural production which followed.

A large portion of agricultural transactions in Korea has been in kind rather than in cash, and of the remainder, most have been financed in unorganized (curb) markets rather than by regularly established financial institutions. This means that little is known about the volume and growth of total agricultural credit, but agricultural loans of commercial and specialized banks (including the NACF) increased more rapidly than the value of agricultural product (measured in current prices) from 1960 to 1972. Also, loan rates charged by private lenders dropped after the mid-1950s, which suggests that loans supplied in organized markets grew relative to demand. Insufficient credit undoubtedly continued to hamper agricultural development during the second subperiod, but probably to a lesser degree than in the first.

Research and extension activity in Korea can be traced back to Meiji Japan, where "veteran farmers traveled throughout the country after 1868, teaching improved methods of cultivation that were based . . . on their own experiences." In Korea, Japanese occupation was marked by "aggressive introduction of improved plant and animal stocks and cultural and protective methods from Japanese and Western

9. Note, however, that the effects of government programs on market prices are obscured by an estimating procedure that overstates actual prices. The NACF calculates annual market prices as the simple, unweighted average of monthly prices during the year, but since most crops are sold at harvest time when prices reach seasonal lows, published figures overstate the true average. Decline in seasonal variation should reduce bias in market-price measures, but part of the observed rise in prices during recent years may be due to reduction in bias as well as to actual increases.

sources."[10] Research and extension work was not revived until 1957 and was later placed under the MAF's Office of Rural Development (ORD) in 1962. More than a dozen research institutes were established, each province obtained its own research station, approximately 6,000 persons were engaged in extension work (half at the village level) by the late 1960s, and rural areas were covered by an extensive network of agricultural improvement and 4-H clubs, cooperatives, and soil improvement organizations. Growth of research and extension was also accompanied by expanded enrollments in the agricultural and forestry programs of colleges and universities, junior technical colleges, and high schools. These programs produced 124,000 graduates during the decade 1956–66 so that by 1966 there was approximately one graduate for each 20 farm households.

Growth was so rapid that by the mid-1960s, after only a decade of development, Korea's research, extension, and agricultural-education structure compared favorably with those in most other Asian countries. Both the recent development of this structure and the typically long gestation periods for investment in research and education suggest that benefits from this investment in the form of greater yields and overall output growth should have come more during the second rather than the first subperiod.

The output response to any increase in nonphysical inputs such as credit, research, extension and education or changes in government grain procurement programs is more difficult to determine than the returns to physical inputs. Such inputs cannot be easily specified and there is no necessary relation between input expansion and output growth.[11] Nevertheless, improved cost–price relationships, increased availability of credit, and expansion of the agricultural research–extension–education structure undoubtedly contributed to acceleration in the growth of agricultural output during the second subperiod. Their behavior, unlike that of most physical inputs, seems to have been

10. Hiromitsu Kaneda, "The Sources and Rates of Productivity Gains in Japanese Agriculture, as Compared with the U.S. Experience," p. 1445; United States, Operations Mission to Korea (USOM/K), "Rural Development Program Evaluation Report: Korea, 1967," p. 193. However, there was only "limited in-country basic research." See also Martin Wilbur, "Japan and the Korean Farmers."

11. It is therefore not legitimate to say, as has been said of Korea, that "most of the yield increase [for rice, barley, potatose] in each instance may be attributed to improved crop varieties and cultural practices produced or discovered through agricultural research which was applied [in 1956–66]" (USOM/K, "Rural Development Program Evaluation Report," p. 199).

consistent with the pattern of growth in agricultural output during the two subperiods.

Although agricultural production accelerated during the second subperiod, it would have grown more if it had not been limited by a set of barriers or constraints that restricted output expansion. Any increase in labor inputs, cultivable land, utilization ratios, the proportion of irrigated paddy, mechanization, or fertilizer inputs should have increased output, as would more favorable cost–price relations, ample credit, or increased investment in research–extension–education activities. Similarly, a decline in competitive imports such as the surplus wheat brought in under the PL 480 programs probably would have raised domestic grain prices and therefore increased both incentives and production. Even if the barriers to growth were eliminated, it does not necessarily follow that the potential increase in output would have been sufficient to meet domestic needs or, in other words, to have achieved self-sufficiency. In fact, as is suggested in the next section, self-sufficiency would probably not have been attained even if Korea's full agricultural potential had been reached.

Mechanization has perhaps been the most promising means of increasing output through expanding physical inputs since Korean agriculture was still virtually unmechanized by the end of the second subperiod. Power tillers (the major farm machine) are included in the farm-equipment total shown in table 5.1, but there were fewer than 25,000 of them by 1972. Japan, with not many more farm families than Korea (2.8 million versus 2.5 million) had 2.5 million garden tractors (i.e., power tillers) in 1966 while Taiwan, with only one-third the number of farm families, had more than two-and-a-half times as many in 1967.

Mechanization has been limited in Korea mainly because farm incomes were too low to purchase equipment without credit and credit has not been available, and because low wages and draft-animal costs and high machinery prices made mechanization uneconomic in a number of potential applications since machinery is essentially a substitute for labor or draft animals.[12] However, both wages of hired labor and costs of draft animals have risen more rapidly than equipment prices since 1965. If more credit is made available for purchasing

12. See Herman Southworth, ed., *Farm Mechanization in East Asia.*

equipment and the relative prices of labor and draft animals continue to rise, increased mechanization seems likely.

Reduction of fertilizer prices has been another potential means of increasing output through raising yields. Fertilizer distribution in Korea has been monopolized by the NACF, most of the fertilizer sales have been credit rather than cash sales, and fertilizer sold on credit has usually been sold under the government's grain-fertilizer exchange program, under which terms for repayment in kind have been pegged to government purchase prices. Consumption should vary with available supplies and the cost of fertilizer relative to yield benefits where the costs include effective interest charges on credit sales. Failure to recognize this last point can lead to erroneous conclusions.

The Agency for International Development (AID) evidently used average market prices for rice and cash prices of fertilizer when it found that the purchasing power of rice in terms of fertilizer elements was more favorable in Korea than in Taiwan or Japan. In November 1969, for example, the farm (market) price of rice was 5,700 won per bag, the government purchase price was 4,200 won, and loan repayments were set at 300 won above the government purchase price. This meant that farmers had to exchange rice for fertilizer at the rate of 4,500 won per bag, not 5,700 won, so that "the effective interest rate on short-term credit purchases of fertilizer was very high." The rice–fertilizer parity would therefore appear to have been less favorable than shown in the AID report. Furthermore, inputs have probably been suboptimal; supply–consumption data indicate that there was a continued and growing excess supply from the mid-1960s through the early 1970s.[13]

Relatively low government rice purchase prices not only raised effective interest charges on fertilizer credit sales but also reduced the volume of government rice collection because farmers could get better prices or more favorable terms when they sold their grain to private merchants. Farmers in the grain-fertilizer exchange program have faced an additional problem; because the price of rice at harvest is unknown when fertilizer is distributed in the spring, they have had to assume the risk of losses from poor harvests or unfavorable exchange terms when the purchase price is below the market price.

13. The AID report referred to in the text is USOM/K, "Rural Development Program Evaluation Report," pp. 132–33; the quote is from AERI–MSU, *Korean Agricultural Sector Analysis*, p. 33; fertilizer supply and consumption data are given in MAF, *Yearbook of Agricultural Statistics, 1972*, pp. 80–83.

In addition to mechanization and greater fertilization, increased credit availability should also have served to expand agricultural output. Limited credit and hight borrowing costs have been typical barriers to agricultural development, and Korea has been no exception. Moreover, "the detachment [of agriculture] from organized finance is especially notable in Korea."[14] This was written in 1965 after the particularly rapid inflation of the early 1960s had caused farmers and others to abandon money and other liquid assets but was still true by the end of the second subperiod. Fewer than half of farmers' receipts were received in cash, liquid assets comprised less than 5 percent of total assets, and over two-thirds of farm-household debt was held by individuals and others (mostly other farmers) rather than by financial institutions in the early 1970s. The NACF, along with the individual *gun* and city cooperatives, has been the farmers' main source of institutional credit. Farmers' deposits accounted for less than a quarter of total deposits, however, whereas deposits made up less than half the financial resources of the NACF system before 1972. A large proportion of farm activity was clearly nonmonetized, and in that which was monetized, institutions played a minor role.

There is nothing intrinsically wrong with the detachment of agriculture from organized finance unless detachment contributes to insufficiency of credit, high credit costs, or credit misallocation. The insufficiency of the institutional supply and the high cost of noninstitutional credit are revealed in a number of ways. For example, a 1964 survey showed aggregate demand for farm credit of 46 billion won (possibly 59 billion if debt repayment and other, unspecified requirements are included) when outstanding loans by cooperatives totaled only 27 billion won. Agriculture contributed one-quarter of GNP in the early 1970s yet received less than 10 percent of all institutional loans. In 1956, shortly after the Korean Agricultural Bank (predecessor of the NACF) was established, another survey found that over three-quarters of farm debt was obtained from individuals at rates of 10 percent or more per *month*.[15] Curb market rates subsequently dropped to 3–5 percent a month but remained substantially above the rates charged by the copperatives on most loans (15–25 percent per annum).

Low institutional loan charges may stem from subsidy rather than low costs, but loan charges are high in unorganized markets because

14. John G. Gurley, Hugh T. Patrick, and E. S. Shaw, *The Financial Structure of Korea*, p. 83.
15. NACF, *Rural Credit Survey in Korea*, pp. 71, 221; NACF, *Problems and Means of Improvement of Agricultural Credit in Korea*, p. 23.

of high costs and monopoly elements. Lenders usually advance a small number of small, short-term loans and borrowers typically can obtain credit only from those who know them.[16] High credit costs can therefore be blamed on the detachment of agriculture from organized finance. Moreover, allocation according to kinship or acquaintance instead of potential return and degree of risk is obviously inefficient. However, the case for organized finance (particularly if based on the NACF record) is not overwhelming.

The NACF has been funded through the government budget or borrowing from the BOK (government funds) and private deposits (banking funds). Repayment obligations limit the use of banking funds to short-term loans that carry much higher interest charges than loans made with government funds. There is no economic reason that rates should vary by source rather than use. Also, the NACF has not coordinated loan programs or supervised credit use. Loans are made against rice delivery at harvest under the rice-lien loan program, but farm operating loans have been granted without regard for whether the farmer has a rice-lien loan. Nor has guidance been provided for borrowers; consequently, there is no link between obtaining the means to increase production and acquiring the knowledge required for their proper use. In addition, failure to distinguish between loans for relief and loans for productive purposes may have weakened the NACF's financial strength. The NACF was charged with repaying usurious loans and collecting debts from farm debtors under the Usurious Debts Settlement Act of 1961. Eight years later, 1.56 million of the 2.87 billion won due from farmers was still uncollected. Loans have been extended to marginal farmers with little or no collateral, many of whom "regarded these loans as a government largesse for which repayment was unnecessary."[17]

If there is a case for expanding the role of credit institutions such as the NACF, it is that they have greater potential than private lenders for rational allocation, productive loan supervision, and efficient col-

16. See Anthony Bottomley, "The Cost of Administering Private Loans in Underdeveloped Rural Areas." The personal element is clearly evident in *kye* (a traditional Korean cooperative installment finance organization), generally formed by groups of relatives or acquaintances. The bulk of farmers' "circular" (i.e., liquid) assets have been in the form of loans and shares in kye (see Colin Campbell and Chang Shick Ahn, "*Kyes and Mujins*—Financial Intermediaries in South Korea").

17. "[I]t is no exaggeration to say that there is no system for giving suitable instructions and advice when [a] loan is granted" (NACF, *Problems and Means of Improvement*, p. 61). Figures on the NACF's uncollected loans were given in *Korea Times*, 1 March 1969. The quotation presented in the text is from USOM/K—University of Wisconsin, *Study of Agricultural Cooperatives in Korea*, p. 66.

lection. Expansion should also reduce oligopoly and monopoly exploitation in local loan markets and help to equalize loan rates among sectors. In Korea, where institutional loans have typically been made at subsidized rates, the share of institutional loans in total loans has evidently been higher in sectors other than agriculture so that average loan rates have been lower. Less than a third of farm debt was held by financial institutions in the early 1970s, as noted above, while loan status reports required of business and industrial firms in the summer of 1972 showed that these firms obtained three-quarters of their credit from such institutions.[18] Farmers who could not obtain NACF credit were, in effect, subsidizing nonagricultural borrowers who received loans from other lending institutions.

The barriers to output growth discussed so far have been due mainly to insufficient input. In contrast, the contribution of research, extension, and education to output growth appears to have been limited less by insufficient input than by inefficient utilization of input.

Experience elsewhere has demonstrated that the benefits from expenditures for research (and extension) can be substantial. For example, Griliches found that the annual net social return on expenditure for developing hybrid corn in the United States was 700 percent and estimated that returns on all agricultural research in the United States in 1950–60 ranged from 35 to 171 percent, depending upon the amount of input savings. Similarly high returns to rural education, research, and extension were also derived for the period 1880–1938 in Japan.[19] There is little or no evidence that the same inputs have yielded equally high benefits in Korea, however.

Returns on this type of investment have been limited by problems of direction, status, and application rather than by insufficiency of numbers. The principal difficulties seem to be lack of coordination, misdirection of research activity, low status of farming, and limited opportunities for applying new techniques. For example, direction of ORD activities by local political units has limited guidance work in favor of other government programs. University research and training

18. Evidence is fragmentary because there are no regularly published data on lending in unorganized financial markets, since such lending is illegal. The figures shown here for nonagricultural firms were released after the government cracked down on the unorganized market by threatening to fine borrowers who failed to report loans and by excusing the loans (rather than renegotiating them on more favorable terms) when lenders failed to report (see *Korea Times*, 11 Aug. 1972).

19. Zvi Griliches, "Research Costs and Social Returns: Hybrid Corn and Related Innovations," pp. 424, 430; Anthony M. Tang, "Discussion: U.S. Endeavours to Assist Low-Income Countries [to] Improve Economic Capabilities of Their People."

programs are under the direction of the Ministry of Education, not the MAF, so that "their potential contribution to an agricultural research program is virtually untapped."[20]

One notable aspect of Korean agriculture in recent years has been the delay in introducing the new "miracle" strains of high-yielding rice and wheat. High-yield rice varieties were introduced into the Philippines in 1966, yet the first demonstration plots for one of these varieties (IR 667) were not established in Korea until the 1970–71 rice crop year. Introduction may have been delayed by the need to adapt the strain to Korean conditions or by inadequacies of Korea's research establishment since it seemed to lack "a full understanding and appreciation of problem-oriented research."[21]

The low status of farming has been related to limited opportunity for applying agricultural education, and limited opportunity, in turn, accounts at least in part for the inferior status of agricultural schooling and the graduates of agricultural programs. Village surveys have shown that farmers are reluctant to educate their children because education is believed unnecessary for farming. Less than one-quarter of the farmers interviewed felt that farming was the best occupation for their children. But education, even agricultural education, is perceived as a means for achieving higher status. Agricultural high schools are considered inferior because they have been filled with students barred by poor records from academic programs, because graduates have had more than usual difficulty in gaining admission to college, and because there are few opportunities to use agricultural training. Consequently, a high proportion of graduates from these schools (and agricultural colleges as well) found work in unrelated fields and never used their agriculture-specific training. There have been few opportunities because government employment has been unattractive and parental prerogatives have prevented graduates from attempting to introduce new techniques.[22]

Another barrier to output expansion has been the depressing effect

20. AERI—MSU, *Korean Agricultural Sector Analysis*, p. 50.
21. Ibid., p. 189.
22. The village surveys are reported in John E. Mills, ed., *Ethno-Sociological Report of Four Korean Villages*, pp. 60,76, and Chang Shub Roh, *Four Villages in O'Sung Myun* (1966), quoted in USOM/K, "Rural Development Program Evaluation Report," p. 251. Problems of agricultural education are discussed in the USOM report (ibid., pp. 251–52). In another study (*A Korean Village Between Farm and Sea*), Vincent S. R. Brandt has observed that "about half of all irrigated rice land . . . is owned by men over 50 who are not only conservative, but insist strongly on their authoritarian prerogatives, both in determining land use and in controlling the actions of their sons" (p. 82).

of agricultural imports on domestic production. Much of the large-scale foreign assistance received after 1953 consisted of surplus American agricultural products shipped to Korea under PL 480. When aid levels declined in the early 1960s, commercial imports rose to replace aid. During the second subperiod, Korea imported wheat and wheat flour valued at approximately $850 million, $640 million worth of cotton, and $600 million of rice (mainly after 1966). Cereals imports made up 5–10 percent of domestic crop supplies from 1956 through 1968, and 20–30 percent afterward, when annual import levels reached 2 million tons or more.

Each year the MAF estimates demand, domestic output, and the shortage to be covered by imports during the following year. Actual imports since 1959, with few exceptions, have exceeded anticipated shortages. This discrepancy has inspired charges that excess imports have depressed domestic prices and, more generally, that agricultural imports have harmed Korean agriculture.[23] It is not evident whether excess imports were brought in to increase carryover (domestic stocks) or whether the MAF estimates suffered from continued downward bias but, more importantly, neither does it appear that imports have been wholly harmful to Korean farmers.

For example, domestic cotton production doubled from the early 1920s to the late 1930s, but imports were still required to meet the needs of an expanding textile industry. Because both area planted in cotton and cotton production declined in recent years, it seems reasonable to conclude that cotton producers suffered from surplus-cotton imports. The harmful effect of wheat and flour imports on wheat farmers is less obvious because both area planted in wheat and wheat prices rose during the 1960s; moreover, surplus food imported under PL 480, Title II, has been used as payment in kind to rural workers engaged in land reclamation and other agricultural projects. Such projects serve to increase capacity rather than to depress income and output.

Although imports may not necessarily harm Korean agriculture and although the argument against imports can be an argument for self-sufficiency when there is no previous record of ability to meet domestic needs, imports have probably served on balance to limit the growth of

23. For example, "the fact that heavy reliance on foreign aid and excessive importation of U.S. surplus farm products have adversely affected the agricultural production and ravaged the rural economy can hardly be refuted" (Chu Suk-kyun, "Impact of U.S. Surplus Agricultural Products on Korean Agriculture," p. 231).

agricultural production. This is because imports increase the supply of food, demand for which is typically inelastic. Prices should therefore fall more (or rise less) with imports than without, and lower prices can be expected to reduce farmers' incomes and thus their incentive to expand output. Also, access to imports relieves pressure on the government to develop domestic production. In addition, food imports provided through aid serve as a form of investable surplus that may be used to promote industrialization rather than to raise agricultural output.[24]

This last point is a reminder that government resource-allocation measures may also influence agricultural output growth. Investment allocation in Korea's five-year plans and the actual pattern of investment suggest that aid and the other forms of investable surplus have been used to develop industry instead of agriculture. There is also definite evidence that the government has attempted to restrict food prices, most likely in order to limit wage costs and maintain the competitiveness of industrial exports.[25] In short, the import of food and other agricultural products is only one of several policy instruments that have had the incidental effect of delaying agricultural development in Korea.

SUFFICIENCY OF GROWTH

Agricultural output accelerated during the second subperiod, but the increase was clearly not enough to meet domestic requirements as demand rose with population and per capita income. Population grew at an annual rate of 3.0 percent in the first subperiod and 2.3 percent during the second; annual rates for per capita income (domestic product) growth were 0.8 and 6.3 percent, respectively. Though the expenditure elasticity of demand for food is typically low (it was 0.55

24. Note, however, that the elasticity of commercialized supply can be perverse in Korea. Higher rice prices, for example, allow farmers to sell less rice (the preferred grain) and switch their own consumption to rice from barley (an inferior one). Nevertheless, the long-run effect of importing should be to lower prices through increased supply.

The idea that imports of surplus agricultural commodities form an investable surplus is adapted from the concept of "agricultural slack" used in the Ranis–Fei (and Arthur Lewis) models to finance reallocation of labor from the traditional to the modern sector of a dualistic economy. See Gustav Ranis and John C. H. Fei, "Agrarianism, Dualism, and Economic Development," in Irma Adelman and Eric Thorbecke, eds., *The Theory and Design of Economic Development.*

25. In June 1972 at the time of the barley harvest, for example, the government announced that barley purchases would be lower than previously stated and also began sales from government barley stocks (*Korea Times*, 20 June 1972).

for all foods in the mid-1960s), food consumption still rises with per capita income, even if less than proportionally. The average increase in per capita food consumption during the first subperiod was insignificant but not in the second; per capita consumption rose 3.5 percent a year. Growing population and rising individual consumption levels combined to increase real private expenditure on food at an annual rate of 3.1 percent in the first and 5.9 percent during the second subperiod. Output growth, in contrast, averaged only 2.3 percent and 4.2 percent a year, respectively, during the two periods.[26]

Divergence of output from consumption created a widening gap between supply and demand that was filled by imports. Since nonfood production, agricultural exports (except fish), and food imports other than cereals are negligible in Korea, a rough proxy for domestic supply can be derived by adding grain imports to domestic crop production. This proxy shows that imports accounted for 5–10 percent of domestic supply in most years from 1956 through 1968 before increasing to 20–30 percent in 1969–72. Crop production rose gradually from 5 or 6 million tons a year in the mid-1950s to 10–11 million tons in the early 1970s (see table A3) while cereal imports ranged between 600,000 and 800,000 tons until 1969, when they jumped to 1.3 million tons, and then increased further to almost 3 millions tons a year in 1971–72.

The growing food deficit is ironic because two decades earlier an FAO mission to Korea concluded that "South Korea could be self-sufficient in respect to food by the start of the 1956 Food Year." Self-sufficiency in food or food grain production has also been a major goal in each of Korea's five-year plans and one goal that accelerated growth has conspicuously failed to achieve.[27]

There is no economic justification for self-sufficiency, but it is politically attractive because "the basic requirements for national living no longer will be dependent on foreign aid" and because "the pressure of food imports on the nation's balance of payments has

26. Elasticity estimates are given in Pak Ki Hyuk and Han Kee Chun, *An Analysis of Food Consumption in the Republic of Korea*, tables 5.5–5.7, and U.S. Department of Agriculture, *Changing Food Consumption Patterns in the Republic of Korea*. Comparison of food consumption (demand) and agricultural output (domestic supply) might be misleading if substantial proportions of the output were exported or used as industrial raw materials, but this is not the case in Korea.

27. See UNKRA–FAO, *Rehabilitation and Development of Agriculture, Forestry, and Fisheries in South Korea*, p. 12; Republic of Korea, *Summary of the First Five-Year Economic Plan*, pp. 25, 41; Government of the Republic of Korea, *The Second Five-Year Economic Development Plan*, p. 33; Government of the Republic of Korea, *The Third Five-Year Economic Plan*, p. 2.

become heavier."[28] Korea's factor endowments and relatively unfavorable physical setting make self-sufficiency a potentially expensive and therefore an economically unfeasible goal. The government apparently recognized this (and seems also to have understimated the increase in demand for food as growth accelerated), for proportionally less was allocated to investment in agriculture than had been called for in either of the first two plan periods.

Pressure from the growing food deficit on the balance of payments became heavier after 1966 as virtually free U.S. PL 480 imports were replaced by commercial imports. However, food imports as a proportion of total merchandise exports dropped from two-thirds in 1960–62 to less than 10 percent of a much larger export total in 1970–72. The increase in exports, and thus the means to pay for food imports, makes the balance-of payments argument unconvincing. Another possible reason for limiting food imports would be deterioration in the terms of trade so that more exports are needed to pay for each ton of imported food, but there was no evidence of this by the early 1970s. In neither instance would net food imports have to be reduced to zero, as is required for self-sufficiency.

Self-sufficiency is likely to be unattainable as well as expensive. Korea's agricultural potential can be estimated by applying Japanese yield levels for major crops (rice, barley, and wheat) to planted areas in Korea since Japanese yields have been significantly higher than yields in the other countries of East and Southeast Asia. This estimate assumes that the extra resources needed are available and that differences in soils, climate, and other factors would not prevent Korea from attaining Japanese yield levels—all heroic assumptions. Given these assumptions, the hypothetical increase in 1970–72 output would have been sufficient to cover only half the actual deficit.

Increase in agricultural output has been too small to achieve self-sufficiency but this goal, as suggested above, is likely to be economically unfeasible and technically unattainable. Performance should therefore not be faulted for failure to reach such a goal. Perhaps a better standard of performance is the increase in product during the first subperiod. If output had grown no faster in the second than in the first subperiod, 1970–72 production would have averaged 8.7 million tons a year rather than the 10.6 million actually recorded. Slower growth would

28. Government of the ROK, *The Second Five-Year Plan*, p. 34; Government of the ROK, *The Third Five-Year Plan*, p. 33.

have probably reduced incomes and therefore demand, but if it had not, food imports would have had to rise 70 percent to meet demand in 1970–72. Alternatively, accelerated output growth served to reduce potential food imports by more than 40 percent. However viewed, this was a significant contribution to Korea's development during the second subperiod.

6

The Rapid Growth of Manufacturing

A fragmentary picture of manufacturing activity emerges from the earlier discussion of the causes of acceleration, changes in sectoral shares, and the behavior of investment and exports. During the first subperiod (1953–55 to 1960–62), the fairly rapid growth in consumer-goods and materials manufactures for the domestic market was beginning to reach its limits by the early 1960s. New emphasis on industrial development, heavy investment in manufacturing and infrastructure, and a redirection of manufacturing output from import replacement to export changed the picture during the second subperiod (1960–62 to 1970–72).

Accelerated growth during this subperiod was concentrated in the industrial sector, the sector was dominated by manufacturing, and manufacturing in turn was led by output for export. To designate this pattern as "export-led growth" would be correct but not particularly instructive. The sudden acceleration in output, the very high growth rates achieved, and the importance of manufacturing in establishing these rates are sufficiently unusual (if not unique) that the role of manufacturing is central to any explanation of Korean development. Of special interest in this context are questions of what explains the increase in output of manufactures, in what ways the characteristics of Korean manufacturing are typical, how these characteristics have changed, and what the consequences of rapid growth in manufacturing are for the rest of the economy.

ACCELERATION IN MANUFACTURING OUTPUT

Industrial production indices include mining and electric generation as well as manufacturing in Korea. These indices increased at an

Table 6.1.
Industrial Production: Average Annual Growth Rates

	1970 Weights[c]	1954 to 1960–62	1960–62 to 1970–72
All items	100.00	14.3	16.6
Mining	8.44	25.3	6.4
Electricity	5.63	10.5	19.2
Manufactures	85.93	12.7	17.5
Food	8.81	13.2	12.0
Beverages	5.17	16.6	11.2
Tobacco	4.54	4.8	12.3
Textiles	16.32	8.7	21.0
Apparel	3.39	—	21.8
Leather products	0.21	4.3	9.8
Wood, cork products	3.60	3.8	20.0
Furniture, fixtures	0.44	—	6.5
Paper and paper products	2.77	17.7	13.8
Printing, publishing	3.45	12.6	12.9
Chemicals[a]	11.51	24.7	23.0
Plastic products	1.10	—	92.2
Petrol, coal products	1.70	—	12.9
Petrol refining	3.89	—	28.1
Rubber products	2.40	9.7	8.6
Stone, clay, glass products	6.52	17.1	17.7
Basic metals	4.97	22.4	18.2
Metal products	2.84	18.0	11.4
Nonelectrical machinery	2.22	5.2	4.7
Electrical machinery	4.06	29.1	25.5
Transport equipment	5.71	9.2	27.5
Miscellaneous[b]	3.54	4.3	8.3

Sources: BOK, *Economic Statistics Yearbook*, various years; EPB, *Annual Reports on the Current Industrial Production Survey*.
[a] Weighted average (using 1970 weights) of industrial and other chemicals.
[b] Includes instruments, plastic products in first subperiod, but not in second.
[c] Excludes footwear, 0.36 (included with apparel in earlier years), and instruments (0.48), formerly included with miscellaneous manufactures.

average annual rate of 14.3 percent during the first subperiod and 16.6 percent in the second (see table 6.1). Manufacturing, which accounted for 86 percent of industrial value added in 1970, grew at annual rates of 12.7 and 17.5 percent, respectively, during the two subperiods. Some of the growth in output of manufactures during the first subperiod simply restored production lost during the Korean War, but statistics for the principal manufactures show that prewar output levels were already reestablished for many products by 1953 so that reasons other than recovery must be found to explain most of the growth observed during these years.

The primary type of manufacturing growth during the first subperiod involved import replacement. This is not surprising, since Korea inherited an incomplete economy at the time of liberation that was further fragmented by division into North and South so that imports were needed to replace production where domestic capacity no longer existed. Also, any domestic output to meet already established demand necessarily involved substitution for imports. The standard two-digit production-index categories are of little help in identifying import substitutes, and consistent output series are not available for earlier years to show how far the substitution process had gone by 1954. Nonetheless, a characteristic pattern of output that involves replacement of consumer nondurables and the intermediate products needed to produce them can be seen in Korea during the first subperiod.

Domestic production of flat glass, newsprint, woolen yarns, and rubber tires reached 80 percent or more of total supply (domestic output plus imports) by the end of the first subperiod. Output of such consumer goods as processed foods and beverages grew more than the all-manufacturing average. One consequence of replacement was that imports of processed foods, finished textiles, and apparel had become insignificant by the early 1960s.

Economic measures employed by the Rhee government had been designed primarily to maximize aid inflows rather than to generate domestic development. The new military regime, preoccupied with worsening inflation and balance-of-payments problems, was mainly concerned with import restriction, a complex multiple exchange-rate system, and other stopgap measures required to deal with balance-of-payments crises during the early 1960s. If the import substitution during the first subperiod was related to any one scheme for development (and it is not at all evident that any set of policies employed before the end of the period constituted a coherent development policy), it was to an inward-looking strategy in which growth is generated through easy substitution. Substitution is "easy" when the particular goods involved (food, apparel, and other consumer nondurables) can be produced on a small scale by labor-intensive means with relatively unskilled labor and without employing particularly advanced technology.[1]

This strategy, if it was in fact a strategy, worked fairly well until

1. See Bela Balassa, "Industrial Policies in Taiwan and Korea," p. 55.

it began to break down toward the end of the first subperiod as most of the opportunities for easy substitution became exhausted. By the early 1960s, substantial overcapacity had developed in sugar refining, flour milling, and other consumer-goods or consumer-materials industries. When the era of easy substitution ended, there were three conceivable means of stimulating growth. One was to expand agricultural exports, a second was to develop exports of manufactures, and the third was to replace imports of consumer durables, machinery, and their intermediate products with domestic production. The first two alternatives would require a switch to an outward-looking strategy that provided new incentives for exporting while the third continued the inward-looking approach but now applied to a new range of products. Expansion of agricultural exports was unpromising because the Japanese market was no longer open to Korean farm products and because international prices were depressed by large American agricultural surpluses, but mainly because Korea's small supply of arable land and relatively large population limited potential growth of any surplus needed for export. Continued import replacement did not appear very promising, because the next stage of substitution required the manufacture of goods either that were unsuited to Korea's factor endowments or that could be produced efficiently only on a scale too large for small domestic markets. This left manufacture for export as the most promising alternative and, as we shall see later, much of the acceleration in output, the especially high growth rates, and the changes in the structure of manufacturing during the second subperiod can be traced to rapid expansion of manufactured exports.

IMPORT SUBSTITUTION

The continued significance of import substitution in Korea during the second subperiod tends to be overlooked because of heavy emphasis on export expansion and the exceptionally rapid growth of manufactured exports. But the rapid increase in output of import substitutes such as woolen yarns, chemical fertilizer, oil refining, and assembled autos and the above-average growth of the major industry groups that produce them indicate that such neglect is unwarranted (see table 6.1). It is also unwarranted because all three five-year plans have called for large-scale investment in new capacity to produce import substitutes such as fertilizer, cement, steel, and petrochemicals.

Although the integrated steel mill and petrochemical projects set forth in the First Plan had to be postponed, they were started toward the end of the Second Plan period (1967–1971). One immediate consequence was the exceptionally rapid growth in output of plastic products shown in table 6.1. New emphasis on heavy and chemical industries in the Third Plan (1972–76) suggests that import substitution should continue to play a major role in the growth of manufactures after the end of the second subperiod.

Devaluation of the won, fiscal reform, and an increase in bank interest rates were among a series of measures adopted in the mid-1960s to end Korea's chronic inflation and stabilize the economy. Direct controls were typically replaced by indirect ones and steps were taken to liberalize imports. Despite such liberalization, an impressive array of devices remained that has been used by the government to restrict undesirable or unnecessary imports and to protect domestic producers, particularly producers of import substitutes. Such devices include a prohibited list, quotas, a special customs duty (intended to eliminate excess profits of importers), tariffs, and commodity taxes (imposed mainly on imported materials). The government also limits imports through a registration system in which all foreign-trade enterprises are required to register with the Ministry of Commerce and Industry (MCI) and must meet export minima in order to import. Local sales by foreign-owned firms are usually prohibited. In addition, imports have been controlled by limiting access to foreign credit that might be used to finance imports since foreign loans are secured by repayment guarantees issued by the KXB.

Published tariff rates have been high, especially rates for consumer goods, but the actual average rate was relatively low (less than 10 percent) because most imports, particularly imports of unprocessed materials and investment goods, have been exempt. The actual rates are nominal, however, and do not reflect the effects of tariffs on materials inputs or of taxes and subsidies on outputs. Two sets of estimates designed to account for these effects (and the influence of commodity taxes and special customs duties on inputs) have been derived to measure effective rates of protection in 1965. This was done by relating actual value added to *real* value added (i.e., valued added in the absence of taxes, tariffs, and subsidies). Effective rates on finished and semifinished manufactures were found to be relatively high, while rates on primary exports were either low or negative.

Comparison with effective rates elsewhere showed that the rates have been high for intermediate goods and low for investment goods.[2] In brief, the tariff–tax–subsidy structure is consistent with a pattern of import substitution that has emphasized replacement of manufactured materials.

The restrictive devices outlined above plus favorable credit treatment and other positive measures have encouraged import substitution, which in turn accounts for some of the change in the pattern of manufacturing output. Substitution was responsible for the above-average growth of consumer nondurables in the first subperiod and for the particularly rapid increase in output of several intermediate-goods (manufactured materials) industries during the second. Effects of import substitution are also reflected in the changing structure of Korea's imports.

Trade statistics show that half to two-thirds of total imports were manufactured imports from the mid-1950s until the close of the second subperiod, with no discernible trend in the proportion. Despite the usual difficulties of allocating commodities by economic grouping, it is evident that consumer goods made up a fairly constant 10 percent of manufactured imports during these years and that the proportion of materials dropped from three-quarters to less than half, but this decline was offset by a tripling in the share of investment goods. The distribution of manufactured imports at the end of the second subperiod indicates that the potential for future substitution, unless there are significant changes in the pattern of demand, lies mainly with chemicals other than fertilizers, basic metals, transport equipment, nonelectric machinery, and synthetic fibers and yarns.

Both the replacement record and the scope for future substitution reveal, with several notable exceptions (the auto assembly plants and oil refineries), that substitution has been directed toward the earlier stages of multistage production. Instead of importing finished textiles to make apparel, for instance, domestic production has been pushed back to include weaving, fabric finishing, and yarn spinning. This sort of backward linkage benefits from already established demand in domestic markets or demand that can be assured by imposing tariffs on competitive imports. The pattern of substitution and changes in the distribution of manufactured imports also show that little effort has been made to develop domestic production of investment goods.

---

2. Korean Development Association, *Effective Protective Rates of Korean Industries*; Faculty Members of Seoul National University, *Analysis of Korea's Import Substitution Industries.*

This is confirmed by the depressed state of the domestic nonelectric machinery industry (see table 6.1) and can be explained by the relatively small size of the domestic market, which limits demand for any one type of machine and therefore the opportunities for the sort of specialization that characterizes engineering (machine tool) firms.[3]

Small market size and unsuitability of Korea's factor endowments were mentioned earlier as reasons that, once opportunities for easy replacement had been exhausted, continued import substitution did not appear to be an attractive strategy at the beginning of the second subperiod. The market for manufactures, which has been defined as domestic output plus imports less exports, was only a billion dollars or so in the early 1960s, when domestic markets in other developing countries were much larger (India, $23 billion; Brazil, $14 billion).[4] Also, some of the main import-substitute activities such as the production of chemical fertilizers and oil refining are highly capital intensive, and capital is scarce and therefore relatively expensive.

An ample literature now exists on the problems caused by inappropriate factor proportions and limited markets and, more generally, on the inefficiency or high cost of import substitution as a development strategy. Among such costs have been loss of comparative advantage, improper resource allocation, encouragements of monopolistic practices, and the threat to exports when exporters are dependent upon high-cost import substitutes.[5] A number of these costs have already been incurred in Korea.

3. "It is obvious that one of the outstanding features of underdevelopment is the inability to produce the machines for modern industry" (Meir Merhav, *Technological Dependence, Monopoly, and Growth*, p. 55). The typical machine-tool firm is a small-scale operation that produces a narrow range of specialized machinery and maximizes productivity through repetition or variation of a familiar product. Limited market size reduces the opportunities for specialization rather than limiting economies of scale (see Nathan Rosenberg, "Capital Goods, Technology, and Economic Growth," pp. 219–20).

4. Estimates of the domestic market for manufactures (in 1960) are from Bela Belassa and Helen Hughes, "Statistical Indicators of Levels of Industrial Development," table 12. Gross domestic product originating in the manufacturing sector is adjusted by the ratio of value added to value of output (from the nearest census year) and then converted to dollars before adding imports and subtracting exports, both of which are denominated in dollars. The estimate for Korea in 1960 ($1.011 billion) was later reduced to $736 million (see Balassa, "Industrial Policies in Taiwan and Korea," table 1). Both this revision and the difficulties of making realistic conversions from national-currency estimates to dollar values suggest that measures of the domestic market given in the text are subject to large errors. The differences among Korea, Brazil, and India are so large, however, that orders of magnitude may be correct even if the specific estimates are not.

5. See, for example, John H. Power, "Import Substitution as an Industrialization Strategy"; Santiago Macario, "Protectionism and Industrialization in Latin America".

For example, government threats to impose price controls on nylon yarns, soap, and rubber shoes indicate that manufacturers of these import-substitute products have been exercising monopoly power. Production of PVC (polyvinyl chloride, a material used mainly for plastic pipes, other construction products, and kitchenware) began in the late 1960s, but plants were still operating at 60 percent or less of capacity in 1970 because demand was insufficient relative to the minimum efficient size of output. The best illustration of this problem, which is essentially a matter of poor resource allocation, was the need to expand planned capacity of the proposed integrated steel mill (after the proposal was turned down by a World Bank consortium) before the Japanese would agree to finance the project. Most plywood produced in Korea is exported and domestic production of urea, a plywood material, has been ample (sufficient, in fact, to permit exports of urea fertilizer to Chile and Vietnam). However, plywood makers sought permission from the MCI to import urea from Japan because the local price was higher than the Japanese price.[6]

Benefits of greater domestic capacity, increased employment, better availability of materials, and foreign-exchange saving must exist to offset the costs listed above; otherwise there would be no economic justification for import substitution. The domestic market for manufactures, stimulated by accelerated output growth during the second subperiod, grew from $1 billion a year in 1960–62 to approximately $4 billion by 1970–72. Also, the high rate of investment during the interim undoubtedly increased the relative supply of capital. Both developments should reduce costs without reducing benefits of import substitution and so promote the attraction of this strategy for increasing growth.

EXPORT EXPANSION

To reiterate briefly, the description of Korea's exports presented earlier showed that the export-promotion program initiated in 1962 encouraged exports, particularly exports of manufactures (see table 2.9). The principal exports during the second subperiod were plywood, finished textiles, electronic equipment, wigs, and other miscellaneous manufactures. A large and increasing share of these and other exports was shipped to the United States. Export has been promoted by tax

6. *Korea Times*, 8 and 11 May, 8 June, 7 Aug., 27 Sept., 4 and 15 Nov., 1969; 28 March 1970; 8 June 1971.

exemption, easy access to low-cost credit, subsidies, foreign-loan guarantees, and import licensing. Exports are among the most labor intensive of Korea's manufactures, and their import content has typically been high. The first of these characteristics has contributed substantially to labor absorption and the second, when combined with heavy subsidies, to high costs of foreign exchange. Policies used to encourage exports, the volume and characteristics of exports, and costs and benefits of exporting merit further consideration and are discussed below.

The increase in exports during the second subperiod, most notably manufactured exports, has been phenomenal. The dollar value of exports (Korea's trade statistics are denominated in dollars rather than won) rose from 27 million a year in 1953–55 to 43 million in 1960–62 and then soared to 1.176 billion by 1970–72. This represents an increase from 5 percent of GNP at the start of the first subperiod to almost 20 percent by the end of the second. Manufactures accounted for less than 20 percent of total exports in 1960–62 but more than 80 percent in 1970–72. Output for export, in turn, constituted 22 percent of total manufacturing output in 1970–72.

Direct subsidy and an import-linking system that permitted exporters to obtain otherwise prohibited imports for use as raw materials or for resale were the chief means of encouraging export before 1964. A major devaluation in 1964 made export more attractive relative to domestic sales, and though subsidies and the link system were retained, tax exemption and credit incentives became more important means for expanding exports. Profits earned on exports have been exempt from corporate or individual income taxes (whichever was paid by the exporter), the business activities tax has not been levied on gross receipts from exports, and furthermore the exporter could be excused from paying commodity taxes if his bank could provide export certificates to the tax office. Also, any liability for customs and special customs duties on imports used in producing exports has been canceled at the time of export.

Credit allocation has particularly favored export activity. Exporters could use letters of credit (guarantees of foreign importers' credit worthiness) as collateral for 6 percent won loans in the late 1960s, when the bill rate was 24 percent. (These loans, incidentally, covered the dollar value of the exports, which includes not only domestic won costs but also the costs of imported materials, profits, and other components of value added.) Raw-material importers received import payment guarantees from commercial banks (guarantees by the BOK, later the KXB) that foreign exchange needed for payment would be available; guarantee charges were 9 percent a year. Actual credit for raw material imports (domestic usance credit) has been supplied by the BOK (KXB) for an annual 6 percent "commission." The major source of funds for export, however, has been suppliers' credits. Foreign suppliers of plant, equipment, and raw materials, who have been protected by KXB repayment guarantees, provided more than $1.5 billion of credit during 1967–69 alone. Acceptances and guarantees issued by the KXB totaled 651 billion won at the end of 1972.

Export loans of deposit-money banks (mainly commercial banks) came to less than 10 percent of their total loans in 1970–72, but customers' liabilities for acceptances and guarantees rose from 4 billion won at the end of 1963 to 422 billion by the end of 1972, or from 15 to 57 percent of total loans and discounts outstanding (the proportion was even higher in 1970–71). Not all acceptances and guarantees constituted export credit, and export loans, acceptances, and guarantees of deposit-money banks were not the only source of export credit. The KDB, not a deposit-money bank, also makes long-term domestic loans and issues acceptances and guarantees for foreign-financed capital projects that contribute to exports. Although export loans cannot always be distinguished from other loans, one may conclude that "export industries have received the highest priority in the government's allocation of foreign borrowings and 'foreign-exchange loans.'"[7]

Beside tax exemptions and easy access to credit, exporters received direct subsidies before 1964 (in the form of exchange premia on export earnings up to 25 won per dollar) and discounts on railway and electric costs in subsequent years. Exporters have also benefited from leakage. Standard breakage allowances set on transformation of imported raw materials into finished exports have been sufficiently generous so that sales of exempt exports in domestic markets have been a significant source of profits. Costs of leakage and the import-linking system cannot be determined, but the value of measurable subsidies per dollar of exports in 1968, when the exchange rate averaged 277 won per dollar, was estimated by the Korea Traders' Association at 50.86 won. Profits on exports were only 2.12 percent in that year, despite subsidies, while the profit margin on domestic sales averaged

7. S. Kanesa-Thasan, "Stabilizing an Economy: The Korean Experience," in Irma Adelman, ed., *Practical Approaches to Development Planning*, p. 270.

9.49 percent, according to the Korea Productivity Center. This meant that the value of direct subsidy and profits forgone was such that it cost 348 won to produce a dollar's worth of exports in 1968. Since exports had an average import content of 50 percent, 1 dollar of imports cost 1.5 dollars in terms of domestic inputs valued at the then prevailing exchange rate.[8]

If output for export has been relatively unprofitable, as noted above, why do Korean entrepreneurs produce for export? One reason is that firms exported in order to import. The MCI issues import licenses that can be retained only if licensees meet minimum export requirements ($200,000 in 1970). The main reason, however, is that the government's "export-first" program has placed great stress on export production, so that good export performance is an established way to maintain government favor, which can be essential for business success. In short, the entrepreneur has not faced a simple choice between exporting or not exporting but a more complex calculation that balances low profits or losses on exports against the benefits of cheap credit, opportunities for shifting export financing to more lucrative uses, and gains from linkage and leakage.

Costs and benefits of exporting can be evaluated in the aggregate as well as for individual entrepreneurs. The combination of subsidies and low profits has made foreign exchange expensive in terms of domestic inputs. This calls for reduction of subsidies, reduction of imports, or a combination of the two. The MCI's export-first policies have been conspicuously successful in meeting and raising export goals, but the MCI has been accused of being so preoccupied with formal achievement that basic reasons for exporting, including the acquisition of foreign exchange as cheaply as possible, have been neglected.[9]

Insofar as net rather than gross exports is the variable to be maxi-

8. The subsidy and profit estimates are reported in *Korea Times* (15 Aug. and 21 Dec. 1969), as is the average import content of manufactured exports (31 March 1970). This last estimate is subject to downward bias because only the import content of direct materials inputs is included. USOM/K, "Growth Prospects in Manufacturing," rates manufacturing industries according to balance-of-payments effects (i.e., the dollar-earnings rate). The rate for knitting mill products (derived from the 1960 input–output table) was 0.05, for instance. But the major intermediate input (almost 80 percent of total inputs) was cotton yarn, and over half the value of inputs into cotton yarn, in turn, was composed of imported raw cotton. Accordingly, downward bias in estimating import content is likely to be greater the more highly fabricated the product.

9. For example, "the export promotion policy of the Ministry of Commerce and Industry which places stress on nominal achievement . . . should be thoroughly reviewed" (*Korea Times*, 31 March 1970).

mized, this criticism is justified because easy access to import-payment guarantees has encouraged exporters to substitute imported for domestic materials, because credit has been provided to cover gross rather than net costs, and because no apparent effort has been made to relate subsidy to net foreign-exchange earnings. Exports rose rapidly during the second subperiod, but so did imports, with the result that the average merchandise deficit increased from $318 million a year in 1960–62 to $1.1 billion in 1970–72. Not all this increase was due to import of materials for export production that might otherwise have been obtained on competitive terms in Korea, but some of it certainly was. The growth of foreign debt and of annual debt-service obligations led the government to restrict foreign commercial borrowing after 1970. Continued increase may also force the MCI to shift its target from gross to net exports.

Another cost, a result of failure to liberalize imports sufficiently as well as of export growth, has been expansionary pressure on the money supply. Foreign-exchange reserves began to build up in the late 1960s, partly as a result of fast growth in suppliers' credits and foreign capital inflow and partly because payment was made for goods and services without a corresponding increase in their supply. Export loans, which were outside loan ceilings, contributed directly to monetary expansion before 1966. Since then, the BOK sharply increased marginal reserve requirements, sold stabilization bonds to the banks, and otherwise tried to offset the expansionary pressure of foreign borrowing (including export loans) on the money supply by restricting domestic credit.[10]

Export expansion has generated a number of benefits, including the building of industrial capacity, labor absorption, and the means to purchase goods and services that could not be obtained domestically. Other less measurable but potentially important benefits were the learning effects, increased exposure to competition, and access to borrowed technology that have been associated with export production.[11]

Manufacturing production, led by output for export, quintupled during the second subperiod. Industrial capacity may not have quin-

---

10. "In the latest several years when tremendous increases in the overbought foreign exchange position brought about most of the money expansion, the expansionary pressures from the foreign sector meant that credit contraction in the private sector had to be immoderately forced" (BOK, *Review of the Korean Economy, 1968*, p. 26).

11. See Donald Keesing, "Outward-Looking Policies and Economic Development."

tupled but probably increased by a similar order of magnitude. As aid receipts began to fall during the early 1960s, they were replaced by large-scale private or commercial loans, particularly after 1966. Such loans, which were used in part to buy the materials and equipment needed to build new industries and infrastructure, could have been financed only with the additional foreign exchange provided by the growth of Korea's exports. The growth of exports has also contributed to labor absorption.

Rapid export growth, especially when concentrated in labor-intensive products, must have generated additional employment, but how much? Watanabe has attempted to estimate the overall employment effects of manufacture for export in 1969. These include not only direct employment in export industries but also the new jobs created in supporting industries (linkage effects) and the employment required to supply the additional demand for consumer goods and services created by the first two types of added employment (multiplier effects). His estimates show that exports of manufactures and semimanufactures provided direct and indirect employment in all sectors of half a million workers. Also, exports accounted for 29 percent of manufacturing employment, or twice their share in manufacturing output. If "labor intensity of exports relative to that of production as a whole remained unchanged ... then about 50 percent of the increment in Korean manufacturing employment [from 1963 to 1969] ... was a direct result of export expansion."[12] The underlying assumption here is questionable, as the author is careful to note, but Watanabe's estimates were designed to avoid overstatement, whereas the size of possible error appears to be small relative to the large magnitudes involved. The export boom during the second subperiod evidently contributed greatly to labor absorption.

Korea's exports have been relatively labor intensive, as observed earlier, especially when compared to import substitutes. Moreover, as export volume has grown, output has become increasingly concentrated in more labor-intensive products. Norton compared capital coefficients for a number of manufacturing sectors in 1965 with export/import values in 1960 and 1968 taken from the BOK's input–output tables. Without exception, he found that ratios declined for sectors with capital coefficients of 0.3 or more while sectors with coefficients

---

12. Susumu Watanabe, "Exports and Employment: The Case of the Republic of Korea," p. 515.

of less than 0.3 (finished textiles, lumber and plywood, miscellaneous manufactures, and other of the more labor-intensive categories) had rising ratios. The same process was seen within industry groups. In textiles, for instance, the trade ratio for fibers and yarns (capital intensive) declined while the ratio for finished textiles (labor intensive) rose sharply.[13] Such increasing specialization according to labor intensity has been consistent with Korea's comparative advantage and with increased efficiency of resource allocation.

This sort of increasing specialization has also been associated with the rising shares of Korea and other developing countries of the UN Economic Commission for Asia and the Far East (ECAFE) region in the market for labor-intensive manufactures traditionally dominated by Japan. Wages and labor costs advanced with output and employment in Japan during the mid-1960s. Value added per worker was lower in the other ECAFE countries, but wages were even lower so that the decline in relative labor costs increased their comparative advantage in the more labor-intensive manufactures. An Asian Development Bank (ADB) survey of trade shares, wages, value added per worker, and labor costs (wages and salaries/value added) for textile, clothing, and plywood production in Japan, Korea, Taiwan, and a number of other ECAFE countries (primarily from 1962 to 1967) shows an inverse relationship between shifts in relative labor costs and export shares. In plywood manufacture, for example, Korean wages were one-third of Japanese wages in 1967 and value added per worker 43 percent of the Japanese level, so that Korean labor costs were only three-quarters of Japanese costs. As wages (relative labor costs) increased in Japan's plywood industry, Japan's share of ECAFE plywood exports to the rest of the world dropped 21 percent from 1962 to 1966 while Korea's share rose 12 percent.[14]

INPUTS AND SCALE OF OPERATIONS

Little has been said so far of the special attributes of the major manufacturing industries. Among those of special interest are capital intensity, labor intensity, and establishment size. Measures of each for mining, total manufacturing, and 22 manufacturing categories in 1972 are shown in table 6.2. The measures given here are only three

13. Roger D. Norton, "The South Korean Economy in the 1960s," pp. 5–6.
14. Asian Development Bank, *Changing Asian Trade Patterns and Opportunities in Industrial Exports.*

Table 6.2. Capital Intensity, Laboi Intensity,
and Establishment Size: 1972

	Capital coefficient[c]	Labor coefficient[d]	Establishment size[e]
Mining	.0707	.452	28.3
Manufactures[a]	.0830	.235	37.9
Food	.0743	.203	25.1
Beverages[b]	.0466	.196	28.1
Tobacco[b]	.0284	.079	1,824.8
Textiles	.0831	.284	51.4
Apparel	.0309	.334	11.1
Leather products	.0586	.531	18.8
Wood, cork products	.0732	.190	29.1
Furniture, fixtures	.0421	.435	3.3
Paper and paper products	.1812	.297	43.9
Printing, publishing	.0270	.448	18.1
Chemicals	.1055	.207	110.4
Plastic products	.0616	.184	69.8
Petrol, coal products	.0423	.210	28.2
Petrol refining	.0902	.063	2,160.5
Rubber products	.0911	.376	91.6
Stone, clay, glass products	.2580	.222	45.2
Basic metals	.2248	.235	97.1
Metal products	.0925	.424	12.3
Nonelectrical machinery	.0656	.412	13.8
Electrical machinery	.0456	.337	82.1
Transport equipment	.0416	.320	43.1
Miscellaneous	.0643	.422	28.5

Source: EPB, Report on Mining and Manufacturing Survey, 1972.
[a] Includes footwear and instruments, which are not included in the separate components shown.
[b] Value added in each case was adjusted to exclude indirect taxes, estimated from 1965 indirect tax/value added ratios (see BOK, Monthly Statistical Review, March 1967).
[c] Costs of fuel and purchased electricity as a proportion of value added.
[d] Employees remuneration as a proportion of value added.
[e] Average value added per establishment (in millions of won).

of many that might be used or that have already been derived, including capital coefficients based on a 1968 national wealth survey and labor coefficients estimated from 1966 input–output tables. All such measures are subject to a host of conceptual and estimating difficulties; the ones shown in table 6.1 were chosen because they refer to a consistent set of categories in the same year and because they seem to be as good or better in important respects than the alternatives.

The capital coefficients shown in table 6.2 were estimated by combining costs of fuel and purchased electricity in 1972 as a percentage of value added. The coefficients range from 3 percent for the manufacture of apparel and tobacco products to 26 percent in the production of stone, clay, and glass products. Some of these categories combine very dissimilar components and so the coefficients cannot be considered to represent the capital intensity of each activity included. For example, the coefficient for chemical fertilizer and pesticides was 20 percent whereas the all-chemical average was 11 percent. Also, since fuel and electricity can be used for heating and lighting as well as for running electric motors, this measure does not distinguish between direct and indirect uses of power in manufacturing. In addition, the measure fails to include self-generated electricity, though this may be reflected in costs of purchased fuels. Only 10 percent of all electricity consumed in manufacturing was self-generated in the early 1970s, but the ratio of self-generation to total electric consumption varied considerably from industry to industry. For instance, more than one-quarter of the electricity used to produce chemical fertilizers was self-generated. On the other hand, the coefficients used here are not subject to the errors and biases associated with coefficients based on direct measures of capital, where book values have to be adjusted for depreciation and obsolescence and then further adjusted to reflect differences in rates of capacity utilization.[15]

Labor coefficients given in table 6.2 show employees' remuneration as a proportion of value added. This runs upward from a low of 6 percent for petroleum refining to 53 percent in the manufacture of leather products. Labor coefficients based on input–output data are also available (for 1966) that show man-years per billion won of gross output. The coefficients here seem preferable, however, partly because they relate labor inputs to activity within the industry rather than to gross value of product, which also includes processing elsewhere of purchased materials, and partly because employees' remuneration (i.e., the wage bill) weights man-years by relative wages. Man-years of high-paid employees should represent more labor input than man-years of workers who earn less. On the other hand, employees' remuneration fails to include the labor contribution of working proprietors

15. See Young Chin Kim and Jene K. Kwon, *Capital Utilization in Korean Manufacturing, 1962–1971*, pp. 15, 107. Kim and Kwon calculated utilization rates based on a 24-hour working day for 30 manufacturing categories and found that such rates averaged 27–32 percent in 1971, with the highest rates more than eight times the lowest (ibid., table 4). Failure to adjust for such differences is probably the major source of error in capital coefficients derived directly from book values of capital stock.

and unpaid family workers. This means that the labor coefficients are biased downward, particularly for small-scale establishments where the owner's work or work by his family is likely to be important. However, most such establishments have been excluded from Korea's manufacturing censuses and annual surveys because coverage is limited to establishments with five or more workers.

Establishment size is measured according to average value added per establishment. In 1972 this varied from almost 2.2 billion won in petroleum refining and 1.8 billion for tobacco products (a state monopoly) to only 3 million won in the manufacture of furniture and fixtures. These extreme values, equivalent to 5.5 million and 8,400 U.S. dollars, respectively, show the difference between a modern factory industry and an industry still operating with traditional, handicraft methods. Modern factory production typically requires large minimum plant size for efficient operation, so when factory production replaces handicraft methods (as in the case of Korean-style paper: see p. 123), establishment size should increase. It should also increase as a result of government policies that have favored large firms, especially policies regulating the allocation of credit.[16]

There is good evidence that the scale of manufacturing activity has been growing and that output has become increasingly concentrated in large establishments. Those with fewer than 20 (but more than 4) workers accounted for 29 percent of total employment and 19 percent of value added in manufacturing during 1963; the figures for establishments with 200 or more workers were 34 and 47 percent, respectively. By 1972, only 16 percent of manufacturing employment and 7 percent of value added were provided by such small establishments while the employment share of large establishments had risen to 55 percent and the value-added share to 72 percent. Despite the increase in average size and concentration, Korean establishments were still small by international standards; the average U.S. manufacturing plant in the mid-1960s, for instance, had three times as many workers as its Korean counterpart.

Establishment size is of interest partly because it is closely associated

16. In 1963, for example, small-scale enterprise accounted for 60 percent of manufacturing output but received less than 27 percent of domestic loans ("small-scale" was defined to include firms with less than 30 million won in assets or, in manufacturing, with fewer than 200 workers). See Medium Industry Bank (MIB), *An Introduction to Small Industries in Korea*, pp. 14, 77. The same has been true for foreign loans. For instance, only 1 billion won in MIB acceptances (the local currency equivalent of guarantees to foreign lenders) was outstanding at the end of 1970. At the time the figure for the KDB, the main source of institutional funds for large firms, was 424 billion won.

with firm size. The combination of relatively small domestic markets and increase in average firm size has led to monopolistic practices that have, in turn, provoked the government to respond with threats to impose price ceilings or open markets to competitive imports.[17] More relevant for present purposes, however, is the relation between establishment size and the capital intensity or labor intensity of operations. Technological necessity, possible economies of scale, and government policy have all combined to increase plant size. Modern technology, in particular, is often highly capital using so that plant size tends to be positively associated with capital intensity. Also, since the same technological or engineering considerations apply in Korea as in other countries, industries that are especially capital intensive elsewhere are likely to be capital intensive in Korea too.[18] However, aggregate manufacturing can be even less capital intensive in Korea than in countries better endowed with capital either because relatively more output originates in the less capital-intensive industries or because individual activities may be less capital intensive than in other countries.

Capital intensity is measured here by the costs of fuel and purchased electricity as a proportion of value added but can also be evaluated in terms of book value of capital per unit of gross output or indirectly according to value added per worker, value added per unit of fixed assets, or the wage bill as a proportion of production costs or value added (the last two are inverse measures). Whatever the measure, capital intensity is found to increase with establishment size.[19]

Manufacturing will be less capital intensive in Korea than in other countries if relatively more output originates in less capital-intensive industries. For example, in 1968 the five industries with the lowest capital coefficients in Korea accounted for 34 percent of total manu-

17. For example, the EPB planned to curb price increases of 37 manufactures (including soap, nylon yarn, PVC, electrical appliances, cement, and pig iron), where more than 45 percent of the local market was controlled by a single firm (see *Korea Times*, 11 May 1969).

18. When Han compared Korean capital coefficients (for 1968) with coefficients for the same manufacturing industries in Japan (in 1955), he found a positive rank correlation between the two sets of estimates of + 0.61 (see Han Kee Chun, *Estimates of Korean Capital and Inventory Coefficients in 1968*, p. 204).

19. In table 6.1, for example, the coefficient of rank correlation between capital intensity and establishment size is + 0.37 (see also P. W. Kuznets, "Labor Absorption in Korea Since 1963," table 8). Increase in size and in capital intensity are not perfectly correlated, so that as size increases, the capital coefficients "jump a great deal," but it does not follow that "the tendency is for the capital coefficients to be inversely related to size" (Harry T. Oshima, "Labor Force 'Explosion' and the Labor-Intensive Sector in Asian Growth," p. 166).

facturing value added. The contribution of these industries in the United States (during 1967) was only 24 percent. Such bias in favor of less capital-intensive industries has been explained in terms of technological capacity and the income elasticity of demand. Manufacturing in poor countries such as Korea tends to be concentrated in "early" industries such as the food, beverage, tobacco, textile, and leather-products industries whose output meets essential needs, where income elasticity of demand for the products is low, and where manufacture is characterized by simple processes.[20] Capital coefficients shown in table 6.2 for four of these five industries are below the all-manufacturing average.

Manufacturing should also be less capital intensive in Korea than elsewhere if individual production processes are less capital intensive or more labor using. Examples of capital-stretching innovation gathered by Ranis suggest that specific activities are, in fact, less capital intensive in Korea than in other countries (see p. 124). However, it is difficult to show that this is generally true because intercountry comparisons either involve aggregation problems (capital coefficients differ because the composition of activities differs, not because particular activities are more or less capital intensive) or require exchange-rate conversions that fail to reflect differences in the relative costs of capital.[21]

Table 6.2 shows that industries with the lowest capital coefficients are usually among those that have the highest labor coefficients, although the relation is by no means perfect (the coefficient of rank correlation is −0.18). Since capital and labor are substitutes in the usual production-function formulation, there is a question here of why this inverse correlation is so low.

One possible reason is that an industry group may be particularly efficient or inefficient in the utilization of either capital or labor. Also, capital includes buildings and other structures as well as machinery. Labor may be substituted for machinery but not for buildings. In addition, the relation between capital and labor coefficients can be nonlinear, and such nonlinearity will reduce correlation coefficients because the rank-correlation method makes no allowance for distance

20. See Hollis B. Chenery and Lance Taylor, "Development Patterns: Among Countries and Over Times," pp. 409–12.
21. Differences between Korean and U.S. capital coefficients for the same industries are evidence of this last point (see p. 69). The conversion problem is analyzed in Milton Gilbert and Irving B. Kravis, *An International Comparison of National Products and the Purchasing Power of Currencies.*

between ranks. For example, the capital coefficient for paper and products in table 6.2 is 6.7 times as large as that for printing and publishing. However, the labor coefficient for printing and publishing is less than twice as large as that for paper and products. The likeliest reason why this correlation is so low is that the coefficients used here are imperfect proxies for actual capital and labor inputs. It is difficult to believe that petroleum refining is less capital intensive than production of paper products, for instance, or that the manufacture of tobacco products, after petroleum refining, is least labor intensive among the 22 industry categories shown in table 6.2.

PROBLEMS AND CONSEQUENCES OF RAPID GROWTH

The consequences of swift increase in manufacturing output during the second subperiod could be discerned in the discussion of import substitution and export expansion. For example, replacement of materials imports by domestic production meant that an increasing share of a growing import total could be allocated to imports of investment goods. Production for export, which has been increasingly centered on more labor-intensive products, was responsible for a significant portion of employment growth in recent years.

Rapid growth of manufacturing also heightened the demand for construction, electricity, transport, and the other inputs essential for manufacturing production. The supply of these inputs could not always be expanded fast enough, so bottlenecks resulted. In addition, rapid growth increased the share of manufacturing in total economic activity from less than average (for a country of Korea's population and per capita income) possibly to average or more than average. Moreover, uneven growth of the different industry groups altered the structure of manufacturing itself, but the abnormally large share of textiles in the total appears to have been preserved. Finally, rapid growth changed the overall structure of employment and contributed to the increasing concentration of economic activity in Korea's two major metropolitan areas.

Construction is a highly labor-intensive activity in Korea that has benefited from low labor costs and an ample supply of most building materials except lumber. For instance, Norton and Lee found not only that Korean capital coefficients were significantly lower than comparable U.S. coefficients but also that this difference was due to lower construction costs (p. 69). Construction costs were lower, in turn, because labor rather than materials costs were lower. The pace of construction activity rose sharply from the first to the second sub-periods with acceleration in the rate of capital formation (see tables 2.3 and 2.5). In fact, real product originating in the construction sector tripled during the construction boom that lasted from 1965 to 1970. Other construction (harbors, waterworks, and highway projects) multiplied especially quickly. Much of this and the other types of nonresidential investment was a response to rising demand from the industrial sector. The industrial sector accounted for over half of fixed capital formation during the second subperiod, with an increasing share allocated to the transport–storage–communications category (see table 2.8). Since construction costs rose no more rapidly than other prices during the late 1960s, construction-industry capacity was evidently sufficient to meet new demand for factories, highways, and the other infrastructure requirements of an expanding industrial sector.

Construction proved to be no bottleneck in the growth of manu-facturing output during the second subperiod, but the same cannot be said of electric output. Electric generation grew at about the same pace as manufacturing output after the early 1960s (see table 6.1) and power loss was reduced so that consumption increased even more rapidly; moreover, the industrial sector's share of total consumption rose from half in the mid-1950s to three-quarters by the early 1970s. Electric consumption rose rapidly, but output increased from a low base, increase came in stepwise fashion, and there were periods of shortage. In the summer of 1967, for example, drought reduced hydro generation and electricity had to be rationed.

One reason for shortage is that the elasticity of demand for electricity with respect to income or output is extremely high. Output growth that only matches the growth of manufacturing output is therefore insufficient to provide enough extra power to meet demand. Another reason is that both generation and transmission are particularly capital intensive and lumpy so that large-scale outlays are needed to build new capacity.[22] Investment has consequently been uneven

22. High elasticity of electric demand is found in the United States, where electric generation grew eleven fold from 1920 to 1955 while GNP tripled, and in India, where during the same period (1953–54 to 1962–63) national output rose 35 percent, industrial production 85 percent, and electric consumption tripled. See United Nations, ECAFE, *The Role and Application of Electric Power in the Industrialization of Asia and the Far East*, pp. 14–15. The capital coefficient for electricity in 1968 was higher than all except six of the coefficients for 117 sectors (see Han, *Estimates of Korean Capital and Inventory Coefficients in 1968*, table 3.7).

(outlays in 1968–71, after the 1967 shortage, were almost four times the 1964–67 level) and sporadic shortages have resulted.

Transport has been another barrier in Korea that limited manufacturing growth as well as the development of other sectors. Railways, the main form of transport, were built by the Japanese around the turn of the century to connect with Manchuria. Modern highways did not exist before 1945. Despite postliberation railway expansion, which centered on construction of East–West and industrial lines, a World Bank survey mission found as late as 1966 that "transportation in Korea is characterized by a general undercapacity of all modes of transportation." Examples could be seen in 1969, when the new minister of transport took a bus through Seoul's "traffic hell" and emerged with "soiled trousers, bitter smile," and during 1969–70, when the government, inspired by an acute shortage of railway rolling stock, urged cement manufacturers to build their own freight cars and announced that business firms would be allowed to import locomotives.[23]

Demand for transportation, like demand for electricity, is highly elastic with respect to output, and transport services are very capital intensive. These characteristics, failure to anticipate the rapid second-period increase in demand, and, possibly, a mistaken transport-development strategy were responsible for shortages. The bulk of First and Second Plan transport investment was allocated to railways; Korea had one of the world's lowest ratios of motor vehicles to population in 1965. A series of major projects was undertaken to expand transport in the late 1960s and, in particular, to construct a national highway network. The stock of motor vehicles doubled from 1965 to 1968 (and rose another 85 percent from 1968 to 1972) while fixed investment in the transport sector rose fivefold from 1966 to 1969.[24]

Building ahead of demand may be uneconomic, but the costs of

23. Ministry of Transport (MOT), "Korea Transportation Survey," 1:12; *Korea Times*, 14 Nov. 1969; 17 and 20 Jan. 1970.

24. A unit increase in final demand for the product of other sectors has typically required an increase in transport of 1.4 to 1.7 units (BOK, *Economic Statistics Yearbook, 1969*). A survey of incremental capital/output ratios for transport during the late 1950s and early 1960s shows ratios ranging from 8.3:1 for Korea to 19.1:1 for the United Kingdom (see MOT, "Korea Transportation Survey," p. 34). The actual portion of investment allocated to transport during the Second Plan period was almost double the planned level, a clear sign of failure to anticipate increased demand. The main thrust of the MOT's "Korea Transportation Survey" (the World Bank mission report) was that Second Plan targets were unbalanced because too much was provided for railways, too little for highway development.

transport shortage have required a major investment push. Because 40 percent of transportation services were utilized as inputs by manufacturing industries (according to the 1970 input–output tables), unexpectedly rapid growth of manufacturing output was probably responsible for much of the unanticipated increase in transport demand.

The relative importance of manufacturing (and mining) among sectors and the structure of activities within manufacturing were shown earlier in tables 2.3 and 6.1. Comparative studies by the United Nations, later extended by Chenery and Taylor, allow comparison of manufacturing in Korea with manufacturing in other countries. Chenery and Taylor examined data for industrial production (manufacturing and construction output) in 1950–62 and found that "among the large countries ... Nigeria and Korea are appreciably lower than their predicted industrial values." Although the authors "investigated the effect of a country's initial position on its postwar growth pattern with essentially negative results, in a few countries such as ... South Korea ... the subsequent growth pattern was obviously affected by initial disequilibrium in its productive structure. The tendency was for industry and primary production to converge toward the average cross-section pattern."[25] Above-average growth of the industrial sector during the second subperiod raised the share of manufacturing output in Korea so that by 1972 it may have been above, not below, its predicted value.

A United Nations study of industrial growth employs large samples of countries in 1953 and 1958 to establish regressions that can be used to relate the structure of manufactures for any country to a structure which would be "normal" for countries of its population, per capita income, and degree of industrialization.[26] When the actual and normal distributions of manufacturing value added for Korea in 1965 are compared, the main deviation from normality is found in textile

25. Chenery and Taylor, "Development Patterns," pp. 399, 402–03.
26. United Nations, *A Study of Industrial Growth.* The term "normal" is unfortunate here because it is used in a descriptive sense to mean "average" rather than with the normative connotation of "what ought to be." Byun has criticized the structure of Korean manufactures as "unintegrated," for example, because growth has centered on textiles and other light manufactures so that production remains dependent on imports of materials and equipment. He holds that balance is desirable and requires greater emphasis on heavy industry, but "the policy for heavy industrialization and the export-oriented policy contradict each other." See Byun Hyung-yoon, "Industrial Structure in Korea: With Reference to Secondary Industry," p. 67. This sort of normative evaluation may be correct but does not necessarily follow from comparison of actual with "normal" structures.

production, which accounted for 29 per cent of value added, or twice the normal level. The share of textiles was still above normal in 1970, primarily because the elasticity of textile output with respect to income is below the all-manufacturing average so that the normal share of textiles declines as per capita income rises. Abnormality here can be explained by Chenery and Taylor's "initial disequilibrium" since the disproportionate share of textiles dates back to the colonial era, and by comparative advantage in textile exports that has served to maintain the disequilibrium.

Above-average growth of the industrial sector, dominated by manufacturing, has radically altered the structure of employment and output in Korea in a relatively short time span. Industry's share of gross domestic product increased from 11 percent in 1953–55 to 35 percent in 1970–72; industrial employment rose from 13 to 22 percent of total employment between 1960–62 and 1970–72 (see tables 2.3 and 2.4). Much of the increase has been concentrated in Seoul, Korea's one really large city, and in Pusan and the area around Seoul (Kyonggi Province). In 1963, 30 percent of manufacturing employment was in Seoul, 57 percent in the combined Seoul–Pusan–Kyonggi region. The figures for 1972 were 33 and 63 percent, respectively. Since these are shares of rapidly expanding totals, the result has been increasing concentration of economic activity in an urban, industrial milieu.

Individual benefits of location in established industrial areas are responsible for concentration of manufacturing in urban locations but concentration, in turn, has overburdened public services, created pollution, and generated other social costs. There is nothing unusual about such costs and benefits except that it took only a decade of accelerated growth to create them; economic transformation of the sort that took place in Korea during the second subperiod typically extends over much longer time periods.[27] The unusual rapidity of growth, along with geographic concentration, placed demands on electric generation, the transport system, and other overhead services that were difficult to anticipate. Such growth was also a factor in heavy rural–urban migration and the social stress that usually accompanies migration. In short, success created problems that are implicit in the Third Plan (1972–76) goals. These problems are discussed further in chapter 8.

27. See p. 50.

7

Money, Prices, and Monetary Policy

The value figures that have been discussed here are usually denominated in constant prices in order to evaluate changes in real magnitudes. This diverts attention from the possible influence of inflation in an economy where annual price increases averaged more than 16 percent during the 1953–1972 period and where the average conceals wide variation. Inflation of this magnitude had to affect growth, structural change, and income distribution. Before the mid-1960s, much of the increase in Korea's money supply was generated by government borrowing from the central bank (BOK), and to the extent that inflation was caused by excessive monetary expansion, government borrowing was the major source of inflation. Inflation in this instance was a form of hidden taxation that increased the public sector's command over resources.

Inflation is usually attributed either to excessive increase in the money supply at given levels of demand for money (the monetarist view) or to rigidities in economic structure that prevent the supply of goods and services from responding to increases in demand (the structuralist view). Structural inflation, in turn, may result from price inelasticity of supply (cost push) or shifts in demand that fail to reduce prices in sectors where demand declines (demand shift).[1]

A cross-section study by Argy of structural factors responsible for inflation tends to discredit structuralist explanations but, as the author notes, it is "extremely difficult to devise appropriate indicators of structuralist ideas."[2] Lim found that prices in Korea are related, with a

1. A comprehensive but dated review of the literature on inflation is Martin Bronfenbrenner and Franklyn D. Holzman, "A Survey of Inflation Theory," in American Economic Association—Royal Economic Society, *Surveys of Economic Theory*, vol. 1 *Money, Interest, and Welfare*.
2. Victor Argy, "Structural Inflation in Developing Countries," p. 73.

Chart 7.1 Year-to-year Change in Prices and Money Supply

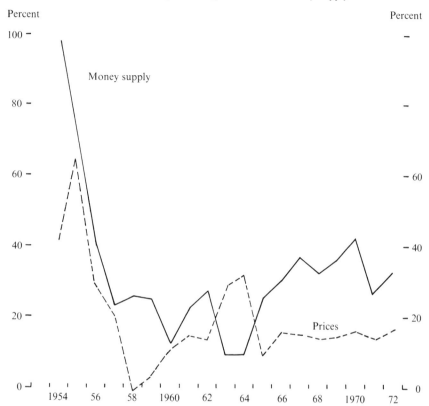

Source: Table 7.1.

lag, to changes in the money stock (currency plus demand deposits).[3]
However, a sizable portion of the variation in prices is not explained
by changes in Lim's money stock. Chart 7.1 shows annual changes in
the money supply (Lim's money stock) and in prices (the GNP deflator,
1970 = 100) for the 1953–72 period. Both this chart and Lim's
results suggest that other factors as well as changes in the money supply
have been responsible for inflation in Korea.

Money supply, the demand for money, and several measures of

3. Lim Youngil, "*Price Formation Process and Stabilization Policy in Korea*," pp.
21–24.

financial development are examined below. Determinants of the money supply are of particular interest, especially when grouped according to whether they can be controlled by the monetary authority. Monetary policies are also evaluated, as is the influence of Korea's financial structure on these policies. Although the causes of inflation cannot be fully specified and the effects of monetary policies on growth, structure, and distribution cannot be isolated from the effects of fiscal, commercial, or other policies, analysis of the money supply and the instruments of monetary policy is still worthwhile. It is worthwhile because it reveals the key role that the government, operating through the banking system, has played in mobilizing and allocating resources.

The pattern of resource or credit allocation cannot be detailed here, but industrial activities, large-scale enterprises, and firms producing for export have generally been favored in the distribution of credit (see pp. 157–58). Among nonindustrial, small-scale, and non-exporting enterprises, credit shortage has been particularly apparent in agriculture (pp. 140–41). Reliable data are not available to evaluate the changes in income distribution that undoubtedly occurred during the second subperiod, but rapid growth may have contributed to increasing inequality as sectoral disparities grew (see tables 2.3, 2.4, and chap. 3, pp. 96–99). If so, policies involving credit allocation by Korea's financial institutions were responsible, at least in part, for the lagging agricultural development and a possible increase in income inequality as well as for rapid industrial growth and spectacular export expansion.

MONEY SUPPLY AND THE DEMAND FOR MONEY

Figures for currency in circulation and demand deposits, adjusted to remove checks and bills in the process of collection, are combined under the heading of *Money supply* and shown in table 7.1. This is a conventional definition of money, but it can be expanded to include time and savings deposits (the *Total money stock*, col. 5 of table 7.1). Trust accounts, roughly equivalent to 10 percent of the total money stock in recent years, might have also been included but were not. Table 7.1 shows that the money supply rose rapidly. It tripled from 1953 to 1955, quadrupled from 1955 to 1962, rose little from 1962 to 1964, but then tripled from 1964 to 1968 and more than tripled from 1968 to 1972. Demand deposits (which include a form of savings deposit [*jo-chuk-yeh-gum*] that was essentially a checking account before being abolished at the end of 1967) grew more rapidly than currency until

Table 7.1. Money Supply, Prices, and Monetary Ratios
(In billion won)

End of year	Currency in circulation (1)	Demand deposits (adjusted) (2)	Money supply (3) = (1) + (2)	Time and savings deposits (4)	Total money stock (5) = (3) + (4)
1953	2.23	0.80	3.03	—	—
1954	4.00	1.81	5.81	0.39	6.20
1955	5.88	3.48	9.35	0.70	10.05
1956	7.33	4.76	12.09	1.42	13.51
1957	8.61	5.91	14.52	1.51	16.03
1958	11.11	8.15	19.26	1.62	20.88
1959	12.36	10.93	23.29	3.20	26.49
1960	13.93	10.58	24.51	3.10	27.61
1961	16.66	17.75	34.41	5.90	40.31
1962	18.00	22.81	40.82	12.70	53.52
1963	18.25	23.11	41.36	13.22	54.58
1964	24.90	23.68	48.58	14.79	63.37
1965	31.62	33.08	64.70	31.67	96.37
1966	42.88	41.30	84.18	71.77	155.95
1967	57.61	62.42	120.03	130.84	250.87
1968	81.86	67.98	149.84	259.99	409.83
1969	111.23	106.72	217.95	453.47	671.42
1970	133.34	173.13	306.47	580.48	886.95
1971	162.76	198.09	360.85	710.38	1,071.23
1972	218.92	290.45	509.37	911.51	1,420.88

End of year	Stabilization bonds and A/C[a] (6)	Reserves: all banking institutions[b] (7)	Currency issued (8)	High-powered money (9) = (6) + (7) + (8)	GNP (10)
1953		0.32	2.31	2.63	48.18
1954		0.59	4.17	4.76	66.88
1955		1.52	6.24	7.77	116.06
1956		2.59	7.85	10.44	152.44
1957		2.74	8.96	11.70	197.78
1958		2.46	11.63	14.09	207.19
1959		2.94	13.22	16.16	221.00
1960		3.01	14.63	17.64	246.34
1961		7.09	18.06	25.15	297.08
1962		8.83	20.72	29.55	348.89
1963		5.93	21.86	27.79	488.54
1964		4.70	27.94	32.64	700.20
1965		13.11	35.19	48.30	805.32
1966	4.57	43.62	46.46	94.65	1,032.45
1967	14.62	42.78	68.06	125.46	1,269.95

Table 7.1. (continued)

End of year	Stabilization bonds and A/C^a (6)	Reserves: all banking institutions[b] (7)	Currency issued (8)	High-powered money (9) = (6) + (7) + (8)	GNP (10)
1968	15.05	60.40	95.72	171.17	1,598.04
1969	22.72	91.54	129.90	244.16	2,081.52
1970	1.37	144.40	158.92	304.69	2,589.26
1971	24.57	102.84	186.80	314.21	3,151.55
1972	45.71	178.83	245.02	469.56	3,860.00

End of year	GNP deflator (11)	Money supply (adj.)[c] (12)	Currency ratio (%) (13) = (1) ÷ (3)	Money ratio (%) (14) = (12) ÷ (10)	Year-to-year change (%) in (12) (15)	in (11) (16)
1953	5.3	2.23	74	4.6		
1954	7.5	4.42	69	6.6	98	42
1955	12.4	7.58	63	6.5	71	65
1956	16.2	10.72	61	7.0	41	31
1957	19.5	13.31	59	6.7	24	20
1958	19.4	16.89	58	8.2	27	-1
1959	19.9	21.28	57	9.6	26	3
1960	21.8	23.90	57	9.7	12	10
1961	25.1	29.46	48	9.9	23	15
1962	28.6	37.62	44	10.8	28	14
1963	36.8	41.09	44	8.4	9	29
1964	48.6	44.97	51	6.5	9	32
1965	52.6	56.64	49	7.0	26	8
1966	60.1	74.44	51	7.2	31	14
1967	68.5	102.11	48	8.0	37	14
1968	76.6	134.94	55	8.4	32	12
1969	86.7	183.90	51	8.8	36	13
1970	100.0	262.21	44	10.1	43	15
1971	111.5	333.66	45	10.6	27	12
1972	127.7	440.12	42	11.4	32	15

Sources: BOK, *Economic Statistics Yearbook*, various years.

Note: Monetary statistics for the period since 1960 were revised in Feb. 1974 to conform with IMF standards. Because differences between revised and unrevised figures are insignificant (for present purposes), the figures used here were not revised.

[a] Stabilization bonds are sold by the BOK to banking institutions. The Monetary Stabilization Account (A/C) was opened in March 1967 to absorb excess bank reserves. Both are a form of reserve.

[b] These are "deposits of banking institutions" listed under BOK liabilities, and not the daily averages shown elsewhere. Reserves include import guarantee money.

[c] Average during year (calculated from successive end-of-year figures).

1962–63, increased at about the same pace through 1969, and then rose faster once more from 1969 to 1972. Time and savings deposits expanded very little until the interest-rate reform in the fall of 1965. Since then, their growth has been phenomenal (see table 7.1, col. 4).[4]

Both annual increases in the adjusted money supply and the GNP deflator are shown in chart 7.1; the deflator itself is shown in table 7.1, column 11. Prices tripled from 1953 to 1957, remained fairly stable from 1957 to 1960, tripled from 1960 to 1966, and more than doubled from 1966 to 1972. Both prices and money supply rose substantially during the 20-year period, so that some correspondence between movements in the two is inevitable but, as chart 7.1 reveals, the rate of inflation was considerably less than the rate of increase in the money supply after 1964. Such lack of correspondence suggests either that increases in money supply and increases in prices are not directly related or that the relationship has changed over time.

Price levels should vary with the demand for money relative to the supply at any given level of real output, and demand, in turn, should rise with real output and development of the financial structure. As GNP increases, more money is typically needed both to finance growing production of goods and services and to meet the requirements of an increasingly elaborate financial structure that mediates between savers and investors. Consequently, changes in the relationship between inflation and money supply shown in chart 7.1 may be associated with output expansion and the development of financial institutions. Two measures of this financial development, the currency ratio (currency in circulation/money supply, or c) and the money ratio (money supply/ GNP, or M/Y), are shown in table 7.1, columns 13 and 14.

The currency ratio has declined substantially since the mid-1950s. Korea's recent c-values of approximately 45–50 percent are similar to those observed among other developing countries but considerably above c values found in more economically advanced nations.[5] The relatively high c-values stem from limited use of checking accounts.

4. Most financial statistics used here, including those for currency, demand deposits, and money supply, are year-end figures. Loan ceilings have created an end-of-year credit squeeze so that the money supply (old definition, which excludes *jo-chuk-yeh-gum*) at the end of 1964, for example, was 43.1 billion won, but 46.7 billion at the end of November 1964 and 45.2 billion at the end of January 1965. This credit squeeze will bias year-end figures if they are used to represent behavior during the year but should not have much influence on the trends shown in table 7.1.

5. See Park Yung Chul, "The Role of Money in Stabilization Policy in Developing Countries," table 1.

There are a number of reasons for this, including reluctance of banks to accept checks drawn on other banks or even other branches of the same bank, owing to fear of forgery and experience with dishonored checks, and the banks' requirement of good credit standing and substantial collateral before a checking account can be opened.

High c-values have been coupled with relatively low money ratios. Korea's M/Y values of approximately 10–11 percent in recent years (see table 7.1, col. 14) were only one-fifth the level of those in the United States, for example. Relatively low money ratios have been found in other developing countries too. Factors believed responsible for low M/Y values include low per capita income or wealth, and hence low transactions demand for money, high expected rates of inflation, and thus high anticipated opportunity costs of holding cash balances or checking deposits, and a relatively large rural population, much of whose output is consumed at home rather than marketed. Insofar as these factors determine the demand for money, it would be surprising to find anything but low money ratios in Korea.[6]

The supply of money is relatively easy to calculate; the main problem is to decide what should be included. There is no regularly published information on the demand for money, however, and estimates can be derived only indirectly. Once derived, estimated demand is compared with actual supply to obtain estimates of excess supply or excess demand. These estimates, in turn, can be checked against changes in the price level to see whether the two sets of data are consistent or not. For instance, excess supply should be coincident with periods of above-average price increase.

Estimates of the demand for money are typically obtained from estimating equations in which the demand for money is calculated as a function of the level of per capita income, expected price change, the

6. J. J. Polak, "Monetary Analysis of Income Formation and Payments Problems," p. 47. The money ratios shown here are the inverse of the income velocity of money (Y/M). One cross-section study has revealed "a significant inverse relationship between levels of velocity and levels of income," which implies that a significant direct relationship exists between Y and M/Y (Hannan Ezekiel and Joseph O. Adekunle, "The Secular Behavior of Income Velocity: An International Cross-Section Study," p. 237). The relation is ambiguous, however, because another study shows that "the level of economic development is not an independent influence on income velocity" (Jacques Melitz and Hector Correa, "International Differences in Income Velocity," p. 12). Melitz and Correa found that their development variable (real per capita income) was significant only when their proxy for the degree of monetization was omitted. Income evidently influences income velocity (and the money ratio) through changes in the degree of monetization.

degree of monetization, and interest rates. A number of different definitions of money and the explanatory variables have been employed but, as one pair of authors has observed, "further investigation is needed to improve demand-for-money equations."[7]

That money-demand estimates need to be improved is understandable. There is a problem of disentangling the statistical effects of rising income levels and growing monetization of the economy on the transactions demand for money. Also, little is known of how price expectations are actually formed. Previous price change is used in all the estimates as a proxy for price expectations. This is crude because it implies that people are wholly regressive in forming expectations, and, clearly, it cannot explain sudden shifts or turning points in expectations that are logically unrelated to previous price changes or rates of price change.

Although demand estimates may be unsatisfactory, evidence of excess supply or demand can be inferred and their influence on prices explained when the nominal money supply is compared with the real supply. For example, the nominal money supply increased 19 percent from the end of 1962 to the end of 1964, but the real supply (denominated in 1965 prices) fell approximately 20 billion won, or 28 percent. The financial system, in effect, supplied more nominal liquidity than people were willing to hold. Spending units increased their spending on goods, services, and existing assets with the result that prices increased and the real value of liquid assets fell.[8]

The fall in the real value of liquid assets is reflected in the money ratio, which also declined in 1963 and 1964. Acceleration in the pace of inflation during the early 1960s evidently raised the opportunity cost of holding liquid assets so much that it offset any increase in the transactions demand for money that would have accompanied rising incomes. The consequence was a decline in the money ratio or, viewed differently, an increase in its reciprocal (Y/M), the income velocity of money. People were able to reduce their real holdings of liquid assets by speeding up turnover or the pace of transactions.

7. Kim Mahn Je and Nam Duck Woo, "A Statistical Model for Monetary Management," p. 17. Other estimates of the demand for money in Korea have been derived by John G. Gurley, Hugh T. Patrick, and E. S. Shaw, *The Financial Structure of Korea*, and by Ahn Seung Chul, "A Monetary Analysis of the Korean Economy, 1954–1966, on the Basis of Demand and Supply Functions of Money." A more general work on the subject is Joseph O. Adekunle's "The Demand for Money: Evidence from Developed and Less Developed Economies."

8. See, for example, Gurley, Patrick, and Shaw, *The Financial Structure of Korea*, pp. 9–11.

Determinants of the Money Supply

The key to the money supply is either bank reserves or "high-powered" money, a category that combines both reserves (including vault cash) and currency in circulation. Money is high-powered when "one dollar of such money held as bank reserves may give rise to the creation of several dollars of deposits."[9] Currency in circulation is a major component of the Korean money supply, so high-powered money rather than reserves would seem the more appropriate base for analyzing the money supply.[10] Both reserves of all banking institutions (end-of-year deposits with the BOK) and high-powered money are shown in table 7.1.

Currency issued, reserves (mainly commercial bank deposits), stabilization bonds, and Monetary Stabilization Account deposits form the bulk of BOK liabilities, which taken together are the accounting equivalent of central-bank lending and capital (assets). These liabilities form a reserve base for the money supply. The money supply is a multiple of the reserve base, equivalent to the product of the reserve base and the money multiplier. The money multiplier, in turn, is a function of the currency ratio (c) and the reserve ratio (the ratio of bank reserves to total deposits). Where M = the money supply, L = the reserve base, k = the money multiplier, c = the currency ratio, the r = the reserve ratio,

$$M = k \cdot L, \text{ and } k = \frac{1}{c + r(1 - c)}, \text{ so } M = \frac{1}{c + r(1 - c)} \cdot L.[11]$$

Actual values for c and r, and therefore k, depend on which definition of M obtains. If the money supply is broadly defined, c should be derived by relating currency to time, saving, and demand deposits, not demand deposits alone, while bank reserves should be divided by total deposits (not just demand deposits) in calculating r.

The purpose of dividing the money supply into a reserve base and a money multiplier is to distinguish between primary determinants of the money supply or net lending by the central bank (the reserve base), and secondary determinants, which include the currency and reserve ratios. The reserve base is primary in that central banks are assumed to control the size and composition of their liabilities. The currency ratio is determined by the public's preferences for cash as opposed to bank

9. Milton Friedman and Anna Schwartz, *A Monetary History of the United States*, p. 50. The authors note that the term *high-powered money* did not originate with them.
10. See Homer Jones, "Korean Financial Problems," pp. 18, 21.
11. For a mathematical derivation of k, see Richard Goode and Richard S. Thorn, "Variable Reserve Requirements against Commercial Bank Reserves," p. 43.

Table 7.2. The Reserve Base
(In billion won)

End of year	1954	1955	1956	1957	1958	1959	1960	1961	1962
Net lending to govt.[a]	3.83	7.05	6.30	5.68	8.09	10.89	7.71	14.25	24.85
Net lending to banks[b]	.95	1.40	3.50	4.79	2.78	1.90	5.43	.35	.30
Net purchase of foreign exchange	.15	.22	1.39	2.60	3.92	3.70	4.43	13.43	11.16
Won deposits of foreign organizations	.14	1.26	1.43	2.13	1.93	1.44	1.09	2.85	4.23
Other (net)[c]	-.03	.36	.64	.76	1.23	1.10	1.16	-.03	-2.01
Total[d]	4.76	7.77	10.40	11.70	14.09	16.15	17.64	25.15	30.06

	1963	1964	1965	1966	1967	1968	1969	1970	1971	1972
Net lending to govt.[a]	28.76	24.92	33.41	33.19	33.70	35.13	45.80	42.11	43.70	136.01
Net lending to banks[b]	4.05	7.62	4.51	.21	-4.46	2.71	6.80	83.12	83.84	123.32
Net purchase of foreign exchange	—	6.16	12.39	44.86	81.25	111.64	153.29	158.77	122.47	112.75
Won deposits of foreign organizations	6.75	8.10	5.95	3.35	3.18	5.78	6.18	4.46	3.10	4.49
Other (net)[c]	1.82	2.04	3.94	4.18	2.03	12.41	16.09	20.02	41.27	49.54
Total[d]	27.88	32.64	48.30	79.08	109.34	156.12	215.80	299.56	288.18	417.13

Sources: BOK. Economics Statistics Yearbook, various years.
[a] Government overdrafts, bonds, and loans to government agencies less government deposits.
[b] Loan to banking institutions minus export–import guarantees, monetary stabilization A/C, and stabilization bonds. The guarantee function was transferred from the BOK to the Korea Exchange Bank (KXB) in 1967.
[c] Includes industrial finance debentures before 1962 and the BOK's capital subscription to the KXB in 1966.
[d] Equivalent to currency issued, reserves of deposit-money banks, and reserves of the KDB and Central Federation of Fisheries Cooperatives (CFFC).

deposits. The reserve ratio depends partly on central bank reserve requirements, but it is also a function of individual banks' loan policies and demand for liquidity (excess reserves). The currency and reserve ratios (and money multiplier) are therefore considered to be secondary determinants of the money supply.

The reserve base, or high-powered money, is equivalent to bank deposits with the BOK plus currency issued by the BOK.[12] Components of the reserve base are given in table 7.2. Net lending to government was responsible for almost four-fifths of the increase in the reserve base from the end of 1954 to the end of 1964. Although the pattern of fiscal deficit was irregular, most of the increase came during 1961–63, when bond sales were increased and government deposits with the BOK were drawn down to finance the government's growing deficit.

The reserve base was fairly stable from 1961 through 1964 but grew more than tenfold from the end of 1964 to the end of 1972. The foremost source of growth after 1964 was rapidly rising net purchases of foreign exchange, or what in Korea is termed increase in the BOK's "overbought" position. This increased because the won value of foreign exchange bought by the BOK exceeded the won value of foreign exchange sold by the BOK. The overbought position also grew with devaluation. Devaluation raises won receipts from the sale of aid goods and thus reduces net lending to the government (aid receipts are a BOK liability credited to the government's counterpart-fund holdings), but it also increases the BOK's won payments for foreign exchange. The sale of aid goods (primarily agricultural surplus brought in under the United States PL 480 program) has been the main source of won deposits of foreign organizations. Unlike the other categories here, these won deposits serve to absorb rather than to expand the reserve base.

---

12. Currency issued = currency in circulation + vault cash of banks. Since vault cash plus bank deposits with the BOK constitutes bank reserves, the reserve base equals bank reserves plus money outside banks (currency in circulation). The distinction between currency issued (a BOK balance-sheet liability) and currency in circulation is quantitatively important (i.e., vault cash is substantial: see table 7.1). The reserve base was abandoned in early 1970 as an indicator of monetary control and replaced by "domestic credit" (money supply plus time and savings deposits, or the money stock: see the BOK's *Review of the Korean Economy, 1970*, p. 12). Sectoral categories were also modified to exclude the foreign sector. The reserve base is still used here, however, in order to provide consistent estimates for the whole period covered.

Perhaps the principal finding which emerges from table 7.2 is that the BOK extended surprisingly little credit to the banking system before 1970. This conclusion is partly illusory because shortages of commercial-bank reserves could be covered by borrowing from the BOK. Borrowing does not appear in the reserve base, and as shown below (see table 7.3, col. 5), such borrowing reached substantial proportions during the late 1960s. Nevertheless, net lending to banks (including borrowing from the BOK) was little higher during the early 1960s than in the mid-1950s; it increased significantly only in 1964 and afterward. BOK lending to banks was unusually low in 1961–62 because of the uncertain business outlook following the military coup (1961) and the blocking of bank deposits at the time of the currency reform (1962). Both events reduced the demand for loans. More recently, a substantial part of the BOK's lending to the banking system has gone to special (government) financial institutions. In 1968, for example, borrowing by the NACF for its business operation fund (i.e., fertilizer loans) rose 7.8 billion won. As a consequence, lending to private borrowers has expanded less than might be inferred from the figures shown for net lending to banks.

Expansion of the reserve base (and money supply) occurs because increases in net lending by the BOK to some sectors are not offset by decreases in lending to others. In this sense, demand for credit in one sector is competitive with demand from other sectors. This can be seen in table 7.2, where growth in government-sector borrowing was regularly offset until year-end 1965 by contraction of BOK lending to the banking sector, and vice versa. Competition has also been recognized in annual financial-stabilization programs, which have divided the targeted increase in money supply into separate targets for the public, foreign, private (e.g., banking), and fertilizer sectors. (The last represents BOK credit to the NACF.) Allocation among sectors is determined by government policy, and within the private sector, bank assets (loans) are controlled by a schedule of priorities for different industries and types of loans.

The money supply, reserve base, and multiplier concepts used here are all consistent with a broad definition of money, so that the money supply is actually the money stock of table 7.1. The reserve base is related to the money supply by a multiplier that has risen secularly from around 1.3 during the mid-1950s to an average value of over 3.3 in the early 1970s. This upward trend in multiplier values means that a unit rise in the reserve base has had an increasing impact on the money supply and also indicates that currency ratios must have dropped, reserve ratios fallen, or both.[13] The currency ratios listed in table 7.1 declined steadily from 1953 to 1962–63, rose in 1964, displayed no discernible trend during 1964–69, and then declined again through 1972. Reserve ratios, which are shown in table 7.4, dropped irregularly from 1955–56 to 1964–65, jumped in 1966–67, then dropped once more in 1972. Because the trend behavior of each series is irregular and the long-term decline in each case is roughly proportional, neither the currency ratio nor the reserve ratio can be assigned primary responsibility for the upward trend in the multiplier.

Once values for the reserve base and the money multiplier are established, it is possible to determine how much each has contributed to growth of the money supply. More generally, the relative significance of discretionary factors (the reserve base) as opposed to nondiscretionary factors (the multiplier) can be evaluated. Given the secular rise in multiplier values since the mid-1950s, one might expect that nondiscretionary factors have played a major role or at least a larger role in the growth of the money supply, but this is not the case.

Annual changes in the money supply (stock) are partitioned in table 7.3 to determine how much change was due to change in the reserve base and how much to change in the multiplier. There is also a small part of the change, a joint product of reserve base and multiplier

---

13. Let M equal money supply, L the reserve base, C currency in circulation, D bank deposits, R bank reserves, k the multiplier, c the currency ratio, and r the reserve ratio. Also, $c = C/M$, $r = R/D$, and $D = (1 - c)M$. Then, where $k = M/L$, substitution for L gives $k = M/(C + R)$ and substituting for C and R yields

$$k = \frac{M}{c \cdot M + r(1 - c)M} \text{ or } k = \frac{M}{c + r(1 - c)}.$$

If the multiplier (k) is to rise, then c, r, or both must fall.

Since here M equals money stock rather than money supply, an appropriate definition of c relates currency in circulation to total money stock, not just the money supply. Addition of a rapidly growing component such as time and savings deposits to the denominator of the currency ratio would produce a more pronounced and continuous downward trend in c. Similarly, the reserve ratios (r's) from table 7.4 are not really suitable for explaining multiplier behavior. They are based on daily averages instead of year-end values, for one, and also exclude the stabilization bonds and the Monetary Stabilization Account that are included in high-powered money and hence the reserve base. If stabilization bonds and the Monetary Stabilization Account were included with reserves, r values would be higher in 1966 and afterward. Adjustments were not made here, because it seemed best to retain the conventional definitions of c and r.

Table 7.3. Money Multiplier and Components of Increase in Money Stock: 1955–72

Year end	Money multiplier (k)[a] (1)	Change in reserve base (ΔL)[b] (2)	Change in money multiplier (Δk)[c] (3)	Change in money stock (ΔM) (4)	Increase in money stock due to:[d]		
					Change in reserve base (5)	Change in multiplier (6)	Both (7)
1954	1.30						
1955	1.29	3.01	−.01	3.85	3.92	.05	.03
1956	1.30	2.67	.01	3.46	3.45	.01	—
1957	1.37	1.26	.07	2.52	1.69	.74	.09
1958	1.48	2.39	.11	4.85	3.27	1.31	.27
1959	1.64	2.06	.16	5.61	3.05	2.23	.33
1960	1.57	1.49	−.07	1.12	2.44	−1.21	−.11
1961	1.60	7.51	.03	12.70	11.75	.67	.28
1962	1.78	4.91	.18	13.21	7.87	4.47	.87
1963	1.96	−2.18	.18	1.06	−3.88	5.32	.38
1964	1.94	4.76	−.02	8.79	9.32	−.47	−.08
1965	1.99	15.66	.05	33.00	30.39	1.76	.85
1966	1.97	30.78	−.02	59.58	61.40	−1.11	−.71
1967	2.29	30.26	.32	94.92	59.68	25.47	9.75
1968	2.62	46.78	.33	158.96	107.31	36.19	15.48
1969	3.11	59.68	.49	261.59	156.66	75.88	29.01
1970	2.96	83.76	−.15	215.53	260.57	−32.37	−12.57
1971	3.72	−11.38	.76	184.28	−33.69	226.47	−8.60
1972	3.41	128.95	−.31	349.63	479.35	−89.62	−40.10
				1,414.68	1,164.55	255.79	−4.83

[a] $k = M/L$, where M = total money stock from table 7.1, L = reserve base from table 7.2.
[b] From table 7.2.
[c] From col. 1.
[d] Increase in the money stock due to change in the reserve base, change in the multiplier, and change in both may not equal the change in money stock shown (ΔM) because of rounding errors. These terms correspond, respectively, to $k\Delta L$, ΔkL, and $\Delta k\Delta L$ in the expression $\Delta M = k\Delta L + \Delta kL + \Delta k\Delta L$ (see n. 14).

changes, that can be allocated between the two in an arbitrary fashion.[14] The totals shown at the bottom of columns 5–7 indicate that more than four-fifths of the growth in money supply has been associated with changes in the reserve base. Changes in the money multiplier are therefore relatively unimportant.[15] Table 7.3 also reveals evidence of an inverse relationship between changes in the reserve base and changes in the money multiplier. Relatively large increases in the reserve base (in 1961 and 1972, for example) are accompanied by small or negative increases in the money multiplier, and vice versa (1967 and 1971). This suggests that discretionary monetary policy, to the extent that it is reflected in reserve-base changes, is partly offset by the nondiscretionary elements that affect the money supply.[16]

OPERATION OF MONETARY POLICY INSTRUMENTS

Though monetary policies may be counterbalanced by nondiscretionary factors that influence the money supply, table 7.3 shows that most of the increase in Korea's money stock has been associated with changes in the reserve base. The reserve base, as noted, is subject to control through currency issue and reserve requirements. Discretionary factors would therefore seem important in explaining inflation in Korea. Since monetary policy is traditionally the province of the central bank (the Bank of Korea), examination of policies and the policy instruments used to implement them centers on the BOK's powers

14. If M equals $k \cdot L$ (as before), where M is money stock, k the multiplier, and L the reserve base, then

$$M + \Delta M = (k + \Delta k)(L + \Delta L), \text{ or } M + \Delta M = kL + k\Delta L + \Delta kL + \Delta k\Delta L.$$

Subtracting M from the left side and $k \cdot L$ (M) from the right side of the last expression yields $\Delta M = k\Delta L + \Delta kL + \Delta k\Delta L$. Here $k\Delta L$ is the increase in money stock due to expansion of the reserve base, and ΔkL represents the increase in money stock due to change in the money multiplier. The cross-product term ($\Delta k\Delta L$) is small and can either be ignored or distributed between the other two terms (see Joachim Ahrensdorf and S. Kanesathasan, "Variations in the Money Multiplier and their Implications for Central Banking," table 2).

15. Ahrensdorf and Kanesathasan found the average reserve-base effect (for 12 countries in 1952–58) to be about twice as large as the average money-multiplier effect (ibid., p. 133). This accords with Korean experience until 1972, when the large positive change in the reserve base overwhelmed the negative multiplier change and altered the column totals to increase the reserve-base effect.

16. When the increase in the reserve base is large, for example, banks may not be pushed to lend as they otherwise might (r would therefore rise) while individuals might attempt to limit their holdings of liquid assets (c would also rise). The last situation is a possible result of the price increase (and expectations of further price increase) associated with the expansion of the money supply.

and Korea's financial structure. What is crucial is how much power the BOK has to set policy, and whether the country's financial structure provides much scope for policy action.

Korea's current financial system dates back to the Bank of Korea Act, which was passed by the National Assembly a few months before the outbreak of the Korean War. The act was based on the work of several advisers from the Federal Reserve Bank of New York who recommended a system similar to that of the United States: an independent central bank governed by a Monetary Board (Board of Governors of the Federal Reserve System).[17] They understood the difficulties that had limited the success of the BOK's predecessor (the Bank of Chosŏn) and so provided for a system which would be sufficiently flexible to meet Korea's needs. But they did not foresee that the minister of finance would dominate the Monetary Board, or that the act would be amended in 1962 to limit explicitly the powers and functions of the board and place the BOK under government control.[18]

Korea had five nationwide commercial banks in 1972 whose ownership was vested in the government, six branch offices of foreign banks, and ten local banks, plus a group of government institutions designed to handle specialized financial transactions. The government-bond market was narrow, the stock market had been stagnant, and the insurance business was still in its infancy. However, there was a large unorganized (curb) market. When the government moved to reduce curb-market loan rates in the summer of 1972, 356 billion won in private loans were reported to the authorities.[19] The amount was

17. Arthur I. Bloomfield and John P. Jensen, *Banking Reform in South Korea.*
18. Kim Byong Kuk, *Central Banking Experiment in a Developing Economy*, pp. 23–24, 75–98. Kim feels that the statutory independence provided under the Act of 1950 was unrealistic (p. 96). Kim's book describes financial developments in Korea through the early 1960s. More recent developments (through the first half of 1969) are discussed in Bank of Korea, *The Banking System in Korea.*
19. The six branches of foreign banks and the local banks were of minor importance. Specialized government financial institutions included the Korea Development Bank (which lends mainly to large firms and government-invested corporations), the Medium Industry Bank (small business), the National Association of Cooperative Federations (farm loans), and the Korea Exchange Bank. This last organization assumed the BOK's foreign-currency loan business and repayment-guarantee function in 1967. Also, there were the Citizens' National Bank (installment deposits, small loans, and *mujin* business [see Kim, *Central Banking Experiment*, p. 67]), the Korea Housing Bank, the Korea Trust Bank, the CFFC (Central Federation of Fisheries Cooperatives), which provided credit for fishing much as the NACF does for agriculture, and several other minor institutions.
Only 55 billion won in government bonds were outstanding at the end of 1972, two-thirds of which were held by the BOK. Trading volume on the Korea Stock Exchange

equivalent to total lending by all special banks at the time and to roughly one-third of outstanding loans of deposit-money banks.

Gurley, Patrick, and Shaw had previously noted that only one-fifth of primary securities (stocks and bonds issued by investors) were financed by financial institutions at the end of 1963. Although the government financial sector held large amounts of primary and indirect securities (the latter include currency, demand deposits, and other claims on financial institutions issued to savers), over four-fifths of these constituted self-finance. Given the low money ratio and the high rate of deposit turnover that prevailed at the time, they concluded that "organized finance . . . has built itself an elaborate house to live in, but it has had only minimal contact with the private domestic sectors."[20]

Korea's financial structure was radically altered by the interest-rate reform of September 1965. The quantum jump in time and savings deposits of commercial banks (see table 7.1) greatly expanded the contact of organized finance with the private domestic sectors. The effects of the reform can also be seen by comparing the money stock with GNP or by deflating the money stock to show increases in the real money stock. Both are indicators of the growth of organized finance. McKinnon has shown, for example, that the money stock/GNP ratio rose from a low of 9 percent in 1964 to 33 percent by 1969, while the real money stock increased sevenfold during this period.[21] The share of organized finance in total finance probably expanded once more after August 1972. There was no spectacular leap in time and savings deposits of the sort that followed the interest-rate reform in 1965, but government action to reduce curb-market loan rates undoubtedly shifted some saving from the curb market to the banks.

Two conclusions follow from these characteristics of Korea's

(including transactions in national bonds) was less than 84 billion won, down from 98 billion in 1962. Most of the shares listed were those of government-invested corporations, and the government owned a large portion of the listed shares outstanding. Much of the trading was in the shares of the exchange itself (BOK, *Review of the Korean Economy, 1968*, pp. 55–58). Reserves of the National Life Insurance special account and assets of life and nonlife insurance companies had grown rapidly but still totaled less than 96 billion won by the end of 1972.

20. *The Financial Structure of Korea*, pp. 44, 47, 50. The government granted curb-market debtors a three-year moratorium in early August 1972, reduced interest rates, and required both debtors and creditors to report their borrowing and lending. See BOK, *Annual Report, 1972* [1973], pp. 26–28.

21. Ronald I. McKinnon, *Money and Capital in Economic Development*, pp. 108–09.

Table 7.4. Reserve Conditions of Banking Institutions
(Average of daily figures in billion won)

	Total deposits[a] (1)	Reserves (total)[b] (2)	Required reserves (3)	Excess reserves (4) = (2) − (3)	Borrowings from BOK[c] (5)	Reserve ratio (6) = (2) ÷ (1)	Net free Reserves (7) = (4) − (5)
1955	3.34	0.77	0.63	0.14	1.31	23.2	−1.17
1956	5.98	1.59	1.42	0.17	2.50	26.6	−2.33
1957	7.28	1.58	1.43	0.15	3.50	21.7	−3.35
1958	9.77	1.92	1.78	0.14	3.74	19.6	−3.60
1959	14.37	2.80	2.54	0.26	1.27	19.5	−1.01
1960	14.85	2.64	2.40	0.24	2.46	17.8	−2.22
1961	18.08	3.38	2.57	0.81	3.51	18.7	−2.70
1962	31.67	7.35	4.68	2.67	2.31	23.2	+0.36
1963	36.26	6.36	5.51	0.85	4.92	17.5	−4.07
1964	37.05	5.19	4.61	0.58	8.09	14.0	−7.51
1965	48.90	6.46	6.00	0.46	14.26	13.2	−13.80
1966	91.38	21.28	20.69	0.59	24.33	23.3	−23.74
1967	158.48	37.87	35.81	2.06	32.35	23.9	−30.29
1968	265.68	60.45	59.61	0.84	43.55	22.8	−42.71
1969	478.59	100.41	101.04	−0.63	70.78	21.0	−71.41
1970	643.47	135.59	134.76	0.83	—	21.1	—
1971	823.48	140.96	140.41	0.55	—	17.1	—
1972	1,029.64	139.22	137.12	2.10	—	13.5	—

Sources: BOK, *Economic Statistics Yearbook*, various years.
[a] Includes uncleared checks and bills (except period from latter half of Feb. 1960 to first half of Jan. 1966).
[b] Includes cash.
[c] Includes NACF's business operation fund.

financial structure. First, the typical assumptions of traditional monetary analysis do not always apply. Control of the Bank of Korea by the Ministry of Finance and government ownership of banks, to take two examples, means that the central bank cannot determine its own liabilities and that bank behavior is not necessarily governed by profitability or the other usual market considerations. Second, private lending on the curb market has played an important role in total finance, particularly before the interest-rate reform of 1965, thereby limiting the share of organized finance and thus the share subject to control by the BOK.

Reserve requirements, maximum interest-rate limits, rediscounting of commercial bank loans, and loan (and rediscount) ceilings are major instruments of monetary policy in Korea. Banking institutions (which include the commercial banks and all special banks except the KDB—the KDB is not considered a bank) have been compelled to maintain reserves with the BOK equivalent to at least 10 percent of time and savings deposits and 20 percent or more of demand deposits. (Vault cash has been credited toward a portion of these reserves.) Requirements steadily increased after 1965 so that by 1968 levels were almost double those that prevailed in the early 1960s. In late 1966 and early 1967, a form of marginal reserve was also employed so that much higher reserves had be held against new deposits. These requirements are reflected in the reserve conditions of banking institutions shown in table 7.4.

Table 7.4 reveals that banking institutions have been loaned up most of the time. Not only have excess reserves been negligible, but also borrowing by banks from the BOK (rediscounting) has been substantial and increasing. In consequence, net free reserves (excess reserves less borrowing from the BOK) were large and negative in most years. This is inconsistent with monetary restraint. Similarly, the fact that reserve ratios were no higher in 1969–71 than in 1955–56 is also inconsistent with monetary restraint. Why has the BOK been such a liberal lender at the rediscount window? Why have reserve ratios not been raised?

Both questions can be answered with reference to the interests of the banks and the government. The BOK paid no interest on reserve deposits from mid-1957 until 1966. Because commercial banks were able to lend all available funds, any attempt to raise reserve requirements would lower profits and be resisted by the banks. Such resistance was probably responsible for the creation of the Monetary Stabilization

Account and the sale of stabilization bonds to banks after 1966 since both are a form of interest-yielding reserve.[22] Reserve requirements were raised after 1965 but reserve ratios remained stable through 1970. This anomaly was caused by the great surge in time and savings deposits that followed the interest-rate reform in 1965. The increase in time deposits (low requirements) relative to demand deposits (high requirements) held down the ratios.

Liberal BOK rediscounting that lowers effective reserve ratios, if not nominal ratios, has resulted from pressure to provide funds for borrowing deemed worthy by the government. Only one-quarter to one-third of the deposits and reserves shown in table 7.4 are those of special banks, yet these banks accounted for well over half of total bank borrowing from the BOK. Extension of credit to special banks is regulated by the BOK, but the BOK can hardly withhold funds when approached by a special bank or a commercial bank to rediscount a high priority loan. A substantial proportion of the reserve base represented by net lending to banks is therefore not actually under BOK control.

Loan and rediscount ceilings were used by the BOK to supplement reserve requirements before the interest-rate reform. These ceilings were intended to limit so-called secondary credit expansion, or the successive rounds of deposit creation that occur after an initial loan is extended. They were not wholly successful, because the actual loans outstanding exceeded ceiling levels and because banks were able to shift loanable funds to securities, real estate, and other types of asset not subject to ceilings.[23]

Difficulties encountered by the BOK in limiting credit expansion due to excessive rediscounting and avoidance of loan ceiling are symptoms rather than causes of overexpansion of the money supply. The basic problem has been excess demand for loans; this, in turn, has been aggravated by the Monetary Board's interest-rate ceilings. When interest rates on deposits or loans are compared with increases in prices, one finds that the real return on savings placed with banking institu-

22. Gurley, Patrick, and Shaw should also be credited. They proposed a stabilization account in 1965 similar to the one later adapted (see *The Financial Structure of Korea*, pp. 31–36).

23. Nam, Lee, and Kim note a jump of 700 million won in "suspense receivable" (a commercial-bank asset) during 1964. Conversation with bank officials revealed that this represented credit in the form of advance deposits of guarantee money required by the BOK of importers who opened letters of credit with the BOK to foreign firms. If the banks had to make repayment (when importers defaulted), the suspense account rather than the loan account was debited because "the commercial banks could not exceed the ceiling up to which they had already loaned" (*Determinants of Money Supply and the Scope of Monetary Policy*, pp. 114–15).

tions was negative during much of the period from 1953 to 1965. Savers, in effect, were asked to subsidize borrowers. As a result, savers placed their savings elsewhere than in banks, which reduced the supply of loanable bank funds, limited the scope of organized finance (noted by Gurley, Patrick, and Shaw), and encouraged government deficit financing and the various forms of BOK lending that expand the reserve base.

The interest-rate reform at the end of September 1965 was a significant attempt to overcome the adverse effects of artificially low rates. The basic loan rate (on bills) was doubled, while rates on a number of time and savings-deposit categories more than doubled. The result was a dramatic increase in deposits. Time and savings deposits jumped from 32 billion won at the end of 1965 to 72 billion by the end of 1966; subsequently, they rose more than 12-fold to the end of 1972. The stated goals of the reform were to increase the quantity of private saving placed with the organized sector, raise loan and deposit rates to more realistic levels, and improve the efficiency with which savings were allocated among investments.[24] The reform was definitely successful in meeting the first goal. However, success in achieving the other two has not been so evident.

Published interest rates in Korea are legal maxima set by the Monetary Board; actual rates have been established by the Korea Bankers' Association and tend to be below these maxima. With reform, the increase in actual deposit rates was large enough to encourage savers to place their funds in banks rather than in the unorganized money market since, for the first time in many years, real returns (nominal yields adjusted for inflation) were positive. Although loan rates were increased in 1965 too, a weighted average of actual rates would have been well below the new basic rate (the bill rate) because suppliers' credits, export loans, and other preferential (low cost) lending constituted a large proportion of total lending. Deposit rates may have been raised to "more realistic levels," but loan rates were not.

One consequence of low-cost credit and government repayment guarantees to foreign lenders was an upsurge in export loans and suppliers' credits and a sharp rise in net foreign exchange purchases after the interest-rate reform. This increase is reflected in the reserve base. Much of the reserve-base expansion after 1965 took place in the foreign sector and later in the banking sector as export loans and other forms of export credit rose rapidly (see p. 158). A second consequence

24. BOK, *Monthly Statistical Review*, Oct. 1965, p. 62.

was an inverted rate structure in which average deposit rates were higher than loan rates. The inverted structure adversely affected bank profits and led to a series of downward rate revisions initiated by the Monetary Board in the spring of 1968.[25]

Perhaps the main consequence of low-cost, essentially subsidized credit has been excess demand for loans. Since markets are not cleared at prevailing interest rates, rationing has been required. In fact, organized finance in Korea provides a textbook case of rationing. Government priorities that favor exports (foreign loans must be repaid) and five-year-plan targets regulate the rationing. Thus, the banking system serves as the agent for allocating credit according to government priorities.

Efficient allocation requires that resources be allocated to maximize returns on investment, that returns are calculated to reflect actual resource scarcity (also, where possible, external economies and diseconomies), and that markets be cleared. Prices are expected to adjust to eliminate excess supply or demand. These conditions definitely have not applied when there was excess demand at prevailing prices (interest rates). Also, there is no reason to expect that loans have been allocated so as to maximize returns. Instead of asking How high a return can be expected on this loan?, banks have asked Who is the prospective borrower? and Do you have government approval?[26] The interest-rate reform might have increased allocative efficiency by transferring resources to the organized market, where lenders may be more experienced than lenders in the unorganized market.[27] Government priorities may also better reflect externalities or better offset monopoly elements than market-determined allocation. Nevertheless, govern-

25. Revision was justified on the grounds that lower loan rates would increase Korea's competitiveness in world markets (by reducing interest costs) and diminish the attractiveness of foreign borrowing, while lower deposit rates would eliminate the inverted rate structure and encourage the development of capital markets (since securities sales had been limited by high deposit yields). See BOK, *Financial Development Since Interest Rate Reform*, pp. 5–6.

26. Another practice that has limited allocative efficiency has been the banks' insistence that borrowers possess real estate or other physical capital as collateral for loans. This has encouraged investment in essentially unproductive assets. See Gurley, Patrick, and Shaw, *The Financial Structure of Korea*, pp. 63–64.

27. "Presumably there has been some improvement in this area [allocative efficiency] since more of the investment is now channeled through banks and other financial institutions where a higher degree of financial experience [than in the unorganized market] prevails" (Robert F. Emery, "The Korean Interest Rate Reform of September 1965," p. 6). However, three years later, Jones observed that "the interest rate structure in Korea is at present highly distorted in violation of economic principles" (Jones, "Korean Financial Problems," p. 1).

ment priorities have not been designed to maximize returns and markets have not been cleared. For these reasons, it is unlikely that organized finance would score very well in terms of market efficiency.

Excess demand can be eliminated either by increasing supply or by raising prices (in this case, lending rates). The jump in deposit rates with the interest-rate reform increased the supply of saving in banking institutions. Part of this increase probably represented switching of funds previously held in the unorganized market but most of it, especially during subsequent years, was undoubtedly made up of new saving. Real private saving rose from an annual average of 37 billion won in 1960–62 to 297 billion by 1970–72, or 23 percent a year (see table 2.11). Private saving is usually viewed as a function of per capita income rather than of interest rates, yet a positive, statistically significant relation between real interest rates and saving has been found for Korea whereas the relation between income and saving has yet to be properly established.[28] Interest rates conceivably influence saving by a circular mechanism in which lower rates of inflation serve to increase real yields on saving deposits and increased yields stimulate saving while greater saving reduces aggregate demand and thus inflation.

The goals of the interest-rate reform may not have been wholly achieved, because the monetary authority's power to regulate credit was supplanted by a rationing system to control excess demand for loans. However, when monetary policy has been free to operate, particularly in increasing the supply of private saving, it appears to have been quite successful. Fiscal reform and a more liberal commercial policy, as well as higher incomes, are other probable determinants of the saving–inflation—inflation–saving mechanism so that monetary policy would not have been solely responsible for the increase in saving and the greater price stability that marked the second subperiod. Nevertheless, it undoubtedly deserves substantial credit for these achievements.

28. The accepted view of the saving–interest rate relationship can be found, for example, in John Maynard Keynes, *The General Theory of Employment, Interest and Money*, p. 94. (Keynes is actually discussing individual spending here, but what he says applies equally to its inverse, saving.) Kim Kwang Suk found in Korea that "the increase in real deposit rates was not only a major factor for increase of money saving, but also a significant factor positively affecting aggregate domestic saving" ("An Appraisal of the High Interest Rate Strategy of Korea," p. 24). Cross-section tests of income–saving relationships in a number of countries during the 1950s by Johnson and Chieu failed to yield a statistically significant relationship between household or private saving and income (see D. W. Johnson and J. S. Y. Chieu, "The Savings-Income Relation in Underdeveloped and Developed Countries").

8

The Three Five-Year Plans

The Korean plans, like plans elsewhere, set forth public goals for economic growth. They reveal the priorities attached to different goals, how problems are perceived, and, to a lesser extent, the means chosen to cope with them. Annual GNP levels and growth rates are included, as are private and public consumption targets. The saving (domestic and foreign) and investment (government and private) needed to meet these goals are also specified. Export, import, and balance-of-payments targets are provided. Population projections are given and the increase in per capita income and consumption is derived. Changes in economic structure can be seen in the estimates of income originating in each sector and in the sectoral distribution of employment and investment. Each plan has also included a list of major projects, grouped by sector. Later plans provide more information and reflect the increasing sophistication gained from experience with earlier plans, but the main features of all the plans are essentially the same.

These plans are valuable for the analyst because they show which problems are of public concern and, by omission, which are not. *Public concern* in this context means that there is sufficient consensus for the problem to be raised in an official document and, further, means that planners believe that specific goals can be set which, if reached, should solve the problem. Planners may pose problems and set goals with no intention of meeting them, but this follows from the official nature of planning documents and the need to deal with issues planners believe to be of popular interest. With the exception of this type of anomaly, where there is a discrepancy between actual and ostensible goals, the plans can be taken at face value as expressions of the country's major economic problems and goals.

The plans are of interest at another level. The host of economic aggregates, their interrelations, and the lists of specific projects required to meet goals reveal both the sophistication and understanding of the planners and the realism and consistency of the plans. For example, projections can be compared with past experience to see if they are realistic or not. Required expenditures can be compared with available resources to check consistency.

In addition, the policies necessary to implement the plans can sometimes be assessed. In particular, do they appear appropriate, and is there any provision for periodic checking and adjustment? Unfortunately, though Korea's plans show savings, revenue, and other targets, they do not specify the policies needed to achieve them.[1]

Such omission suggsts that although the plans have analytic value, this value is limited and ought not to be extended. It is clearly inappropriate to judge plans according to policies later adopted to implement them. Similarly, the plans' significance depends upon subsequent developments, especially unanticipated events that can make a plan irrelevant. Given these limitations, however, Korea's plans are very useful documents for assessing the goals of growth, the success achieved in meeting them, and the effects of growth as evidenced in the selection of new goals in later plans.

Planning in Korea dates back to the Nathan (UNKRA) program of 1954, but the Nathan Plan and subsequent plans lacked the support necessary for their implementation until the military coup of 1961 gave power to a government committed to both economic development and economic planning. A summary of the First Five-Year Plan (FFYP) was released in Januarry 1962. An adjusted version (the Revised FFYP) was adopted in the spring of 1964. Both cover the period 1962–66. Although the FFYP "did not present a well-worked-out set of economic policies, it did imply a number of policy directions that were subsequently followed," and "some of the investment programs of the First Five-Year Plan were influential." However, poor performance and "fruitless efforts . . . to scale down the plan" meant that

---

1. What may appear to be a policy can be a goal in the guise of policy. For example, the "high growth of financial savings" to be achieved in the Second Five-Year Plan was to be attained by "increasing monetization and commercialization of rural areas, encouraging 'banking habits' of the general public, more efficient intermediation" and so forth (Government of the Republic of Korea, *The Second Five-Year Economic Development Plan*, p. 59).

the "First Plan as such was hardly referred to until work was started on the Second Plan."[2] Neither the FFYP nor the Revised FFYP should therefore be credited with much influence over actual events in 1962–66.

The Second Five-Year Plan (SFYP, begun in 1965 for the period 1967–71) was much more sophisticated than earlier plan documents. Despite earlier planning experience, the SFYP proved influential because it was the first installment of a long-range plan extending to 1981 and because a succession of annual overall resource budgets (ORBs) was used to adjust the plan when targets and results diverged and to make particular policy decisions consistent with overall, long-term targets.

The first two plans cover roughly the same years as the second subperiod (1960–62 to 1970–72) used here to evaluate the acceleration evident in Korea's growth path. Coincidence of planning and more rapid growth is not wholly fortuitous, but to conclude that planning was responsible for acceleration may overstate the role of planning. Planning is significant not only for its economic consequences but, in this case, as a sign that government priorities had shifted in favor of economic development goals. Similarly, the Third-Five-Year Plan (TFYP, for 1972–76) can be viewed either as a guide to the future or as an expression of the new priorities required by earlier successes and failures. The retrospective implications are particularly interesting because the TFYP differs from the SFYP both in construction and in emphasis. Whereas SFYP formulation was centralized, employed a formal, multisectoral planning model, and goals were consistent with maximizing growth, the government abandoned comprehensive planning in framing the TFYP, formulation was decentralized, and relatively more emphasis was placed on efficiency and equity of resource allocation.[3]

THE FIRST FIVE-YEAR PLAN

The "gist of the first five-year economic plan" was the attempt to "build an industrial base principally through increased energy produc-

2. David C. Cole and Young Woo Nam, "The Pattern and Significance of Economic Planning in Korea," in Irma Adelman, ed., *Practical Approaches to Development Planning*, p. 34.
3. Larry E. Westphal and Irma Adelman, "Reflections on the Political Economy of Planning: The Case of Korea," in Sung-Hwan Jo and Seong-Yawng Park, eds., *Basic Documents and Selected Papers of Korea's Third Five-Year Economic Development Plan*, pp. 14–15.

tion."[4] Attainment of self-sufficiency in food grain production was another major goal. Import-substitute industries were also to be developed. Gross national product was to grow at an accelerating rate, with an average annual (compound) increase of 7.1 percent (see table 8.1). Little increase in consumption was scheduled, but investment was expected to rise 51 percent during the period. Capital coefficients differ among sectors and a sector's investment share does not necessarily equal its output share, but sectoral distributions of investment and output (table 8.1) reveal a pattern appropriate for "building an industrial base."

Because investment was concentrated in the industrial sector and would be affected by the lumpiness associated with the construction of large-scale projects, investment ratios were to rise from 1962 to 1964 before falling back in 1965–66. This reflects a big-push approach to planning in which top-priority projects are scheduled first so that they will have the best chance for completion if the plan should not work out as anticipated.

The government's role in the plan was ambiguous. There was to be "a form of 'guided capitalism' in which the principle of free enterprise ... will be observed, but in which the government will either directly participate in or indirectly render guidance to the basic industries and other important fields."[5] The government would account for less than 20 percent of consumption in the FFYP but provide one-third of total investment (see table 8.1), or more than half if measured by source of funds since the government acts as an intermediary between foreign savers and domestic investors. This intermediary role has been a major instrument of government control and perhaps is what was meant by "guided capitalism."

Fiscal and saving targets were ambitious. A large deficit on current account in 1962 was to be replaced by a large surplus in 1966 as government revenues rose by two-thirds. The growing current-account surplus would be available to finance capital expenditures since current expenditure was to increase by less than 10 percent. Sources of saving are not shown in the plan, but consumption was to absorb over 90 percent of GNP during the plan period and investment ratios averaged 23 percent, thus making substantial foreign saving necessary. However, increased domestic saving was to reduce dependence on foreign saving.

4. ROK, *Summary of the First Five-Year Economic Plan*, p. 24.
5. Ibid., p. 28.

Table 8.1. Five-Year Plan Ratios

	Annual GNP growth rate (1)	Investment ratio[a] (2)	Saving ratio[b] (3)	Revenue ratio[c] (4)	Investment shares Pvt. (5)	Govt. (6)
1. FFYP (1962–66)	7.1	22.7	9.6	18.7	65.2	44.8
2. Revised FFYP	4.8	16.9	5.2	15.4	—	—
3. Actual 1962–66	9.4	17.3	7.4	11.4	75.8	24.2
4. SFYP (1967–71)	7.0	19.1	11.7	18.2	59.1	40.9
5. Actual 1967–71	11.9	30.9	15.6	13.3	73.7	26.3
6. TFYP (1972–76)	8.6	24.9	19.6	22.1	57.5	42.5

	Consumption shares Pvt. (7)	Govt. (8)	Primary[d] GNP (9)	Invest. (10)	Secondary[e] GNP (11)	Invest. (12)	Tertiary[f] GNP (13)	Invest. (14)
1. FFYP	81.5	18.5	36.0	17.2	—	34.0	48.7	48.8
2. Revised FFYP	83.2	16.8	32.5	16.1	23.2	42.9	44.3	41.0
3. Actual 1962–66	86.4	13.6	39.4	14.7	22.7	37.6	38.0	47.7
4. SFYP	84.5	15.5	35.2	16.3	25.2	30.7	39.6	53.0
5. Actual 1967–71	86.7	13.3	27.7	7.1	26.6	24.2	45.7	68.7
6. TFYP	75.0	25.0	24.1	13.6	26.1	27.5	49.8	58.9

Sources: ROK, Summary of the FFYP; ROK, FFYP, Adjusted Version; Government of the ROK, The SFYP; ROK, The TFYP; BOK, Economic Statistics Yearbook, various years.
[a] GDCF/GNP.
[b] Domestic saving/GNP.
[c] Consolidated government revenues/GNP.
[d] Agriculture, forestry, and fisheries.
[e] Mining and manufacturing, construction, electric generation (the last two categories were shifted to the tertiary sector during the SFYP, actual 1967–71, and TFYP).
[f] Transport, trade, and services.

This can be seen in a projected decline in balance-of-payments (current account) deficits from $310 million in 1962 to $247 million by 1966. Of the total projected deficit of $1.4 billion, two-thirds would be covered by "public donations" (mainly U.S. supporting assistance and PL 480 imports).

Population, labor force, and employment projections given in the FFYP receive surprisingly little emphasis. The rate of population increase was to fall fractionally each year, and it was anticipated that "population control measures will be required."[6] Expected growth of the labor force of 11 percent and a 26 percent increase in employment would reduce unemployment from 2.4 million in 1962 to 1.8 million by 1966. The plan document does not explain how any of these figures were derived and there is no evidence that they were employed in constructing the plan projections.

Projections for GNP, available resources, consumption, saving, and investment appear consistent. The projected growth of private consumption, for example, was slightly above the expected increase in food grain output in accordance with typically low income elasticities of demand for food. Several FFYP features are not so reasonable, however. A decline in projected private consumption from 1960 to 1962 seems unrealistic for a country with very low income levels such as Korea in the early 1960s. The marginal capital/output ratio of 4.1:1 implied by the projected increase in GNP, even allowing for the long gestation periods associated with large-scale projects, looks too high given evidence at the time of substantial excess capacity. The time shape of planned saving also appears questionable. A drop in marginal ratios from 64 percent (of GNP) in 1962–63 to 24 percent in 1965–66 was noted by Charles Wolf.[7] Falling marginal ratios mean that saving was to increase fastest at the beginning of the plan period when income was lowest.

Allocative efficiency among and within sectors is central to plan evaluation, but there is little evidence that can be used to assess efficiency. Planners could not apply project-appraisal techniques to evaluate the relative merits of different FFYP projects, because the necessary cost information was not available. Perhaps more important is the question of whether industrialization should have been emphasized in the FFYP. At issue here is the choice between agricultural and

6. Ibid., p. 31.
7. Charles Wolf, Jr., "Economic Planning in Korea."

industrial development or, since the question is more properly one of priority than of choice, whether agriculture should have received first priority. Agricultural output and productivity were little higher at the start of the FFYP than when "AID made a premature effort to industrialize Korea during the middle 1950s, before agricultural productivity was raised."[8]

One can argue, of course, that industrialization should have received priority if only to provide the chemical fertilizers and other manufactured inputs necessary to raise agricultural productivity, but the question of emphasis or priority is not likely to be resolved here. Nevertheless, it is clear that the apparent conflict between achieving self-sufficiency in food grains and building an industrial base was settled in favor of the latter. Between 1962 and 1966, while annual investment in agriculture was to increase only 28.3 billion *hwan* (10 hwan = 1 won). GNP originating in agriculture was to grow by 227.7 billion hwan. The implied incremental capital/output ratio (0.12:1) is unrealistically low. This is evidently one case where actual and ostensible goals differed.[9]

The years immediately preceding the FFYP were years of economic stagnation. Real GNP rose only 14 percent from 1956–59 to 1960–62; the annual increase in per capita GDP was less than 1 percent (see table 2.1). Agricultural output was no higher in 1960 than in 1958, investment rose little, and domestic saving was negligible. Output targets thus appeared to be overoptimistic, and the plan was criticized as too ambitious when it was released in early 1962.

Events during the first few years of the FFYP seemed to justify this criticism. Domestic saving, scheduled to rise from 3.1 percent of GNP in 1959–61 to 3.7 percent in 1962, was a miserable 0.8 percent. Government revenues also failed to increase as planned. Though foreign saving met plan targets, actual investment was less than two-thirds of the planned level in 1962 because of the short fall in total saving.[10]

8. Neil H. Jacoby, *U.S. Aid to Taiwan*, p. 160.

9. The implied ratio is well below the 1965 ratio for agriculture (1.5–2.0:1) derived from input–output data by Norton (see Roger D. Norton, "The South Korean Economy in the 1960's," p. 6).

10. Current-account deficits (foreign saving) that had averaged $230 million a year in 1959–61, were to rise to $307 million in 1962–64. The average of the deficits for 1962–64 was close to the target level, whereas actual aid imports totaled $593 million in these years. Therefore, it is incorrect to say that "a wide discrepancy occurred between the planned amount and the actual amount in the area of U.S. aid" (Nam Duck Woo, "Korea's Experience with Economic Planning," in Lee Sang-eun, ed., *Report of International Conference on the Problems of Modernization in Asia*, p. 521).

Poor harvests in 1962–63, an increasing rate of inflation, and the currency reform of mid-1962 compounded the difficulties encountered in meeting early FFYP targets. Harvest failures were responsible for a 250 percent rise in food imports from 1962 to 1963 and a large increase in the balance-of-payments deficit for 1963. Prices started to climb in 1960; led by grains, they advanced at an accelerated pace beginning in 1963. The currency reform required that all outstanding hwan be turned in for new won in order to bring out hoarded currency for development purposes, limit currency speculation, and end inflation. The immediate effect, however, was to reduce output because enterprises that depended upon loans from the unorganized money market were deprived of funds.[11]

Exogenous events such as crop failures may be impossible to incorporate in plans, but the inflation that had been a regular feature of economic life in Korea since the end of World War II was hardly an exogenous event. There are political and psychological reasons for omitting price increases from a plan, but this omission can—and did —distort saving, investment, and other major plan projections. The combination of economic difficulties, inflation-distorted projections, and increasing evidence that plan targets were unfeasible made it obvious by 1963 that the plan needed major revision.

An adjusted version of the plan (the Revised FFYP) was published in March 1964. Besides the difficulties cited above, reasons given for revision included defects of the FFYP such as failure to consider foreign-loan repayment obligations, insufficient attention to public finance, inadequacy of supply–demand scheduling and supporting measures, and neglect of intersectoral and interproject relationships. The FFYP was adjusted by converting 1961 to 1962 prices, replacing 1962 estimates with actual results, and scaling down 1964–66 projections.

Actual performance during 1962–66 exceeded expectations as GNP rose more than planned (table 8.1). Consumption grew more than anticipated and, because actual population growth (2.6 percent a year) equaled the Revised FFYP projection, the increase in living standards was greater than foreseen. Investment rose over two-and-a-half-fold during the FFYP period. This increase was also more than projected in either plan. The final total for 1962–66 (656 billion won) relative to

11. The reform has been described as "ill-conceived, ill-prepared, ill-timed, and therefore ill-fated," which seems apt (Kim Byong-kuk, *Central Banking Experience in a Developing Economy*, p. 45).

the actual increase in GNP from 1962 to 1966 (279 billion won) yields a marginal capital/output ratio of 2.4:1 rather than the 4.0:1 of the FFYP or the 4.5:1 of the Revised FFYP. Both plans were overly pessimistic about the amount of investment needed to increase GNP as well as the growth of GNP that might be expected.

Actual investment and output shares in 1962–66 for the major sectors were pretty much as planned, although agriculture's output share exceeded targets (despite a less than anticipated investment share) because of bumper crops in 1964 and 1966 (see tables 8.1 and A3). Domestic saving also increased rapidly. The main shortfall is found in the government-revenue ratio; the actual ratio was well below the planned level (table 8.1). Consequently, the government's share in total consumption and investment was considerably less than planned.[12] This was partly a result of deliberate attempts to reduce the inflationary impact of government deficits by holding down expenditures, but it was also due to the difficulty of raising revenues with a tax structure that was inelastic with respect to price change.

Reasons for discrepancies between plan targets and results and their consequences are of particular interest. The underestimate of the increase in agricultural output, for example, resulted when poor harvests in 1962–63 were followed by good ones in 1964 and 1966. Overestimate of manufacturing growth in the FFYP was due, at least in part, to the abandonment of plans to construct the integrated steel mill and expand machinery output; the underestimate of the Revised FFYP was caused by the unforeseen increase in manufactured exports. But the impact of the FFYP experience on SFYP policies is less apparent. Did the 1962–63 crop failures influence the decision to emphasize cash crops instead of grains in the SFYP? Did the dropping of major import-substitute projects lead to increased stress on export production? One consequence of FFYP experience is clear, however. Effects of unexpected change would have to be incorporated in the plans if the plans were to retain their relevance. The annual overall resource

12. Even if revenues from government enterprises and quasi-government corporations were included in the government-revenue ratios, as they should be, revenue ratios would not be much higher than those shown. Failure to increase the share of public expenditure may have been due to "a reduction in the number of public projects as a means of fostering the growth of free enterprise" (*Revised FFYP*, p. 13), or possibly a government decision that "the private sector will play a greater role in the development of the Korean economy" (*Revised FFYP*, p. 6). However, given the earlier formulation of "guided capitalism" in the FFYP, one may conclude that there was either a major change in economic philosophy between 1962 and 1964 or, more likely, that it was found necessary in the *Revised FFYP* to put the best possible face on evidence of inability to expand the public sector.

budgets (ORBs) later adopted during the SFYP were intended to handle this problem.

In spite of failure to raise the revenue ratio, the economic outlook was encouraging during the closing years of the FFYP. GNP rose more than 13 percent from 1965 to 1966; the investment ratio reached 20 percent in 1966; domestic saving doubled from 1964 to 1966, while rapid growth of commercial credit and large loan commitments from Japan offset declining grant assistance.[13] Exports, led by manufactures, were almost double the FFYP target for 1966. The First Plan appeared to be a success after the rice harvest in the fall of 1966; success was confirmed by mid-1967 as final figures for 1966 became available.

THE SECOND FIVE-YEAR PLAN

The SFYP for 1967–71 was released in mid-1966. There was more time to prepare it than had been available in drawing up the FFYP; in addition, input–output (I–O) tables for 1960 and 1963 had been constructed for use in planning. A sectoral model incorporating the I–O data was employed to check the balance of supply and demand in each sector and to set minimum investment levels. A growth model was also formulated to select an overall output target consistent with foreign and domestic-saving and foreign-exchange constraints. The I–O data revealed, however, that Korea's national-accounts estimates were not sufficiently accurate to provide the information needed for macroeconomic projection. Revision of the national accounts in 1967 permitted application of the growth model to the 1968 ORB, but it could not be used in setting SFYP targets. "It was [therefore] necessary . . . . to estimate most of the macroeconomic targets on a largely intuitive basis."[14] Despite reliance on intuition, the SFYP was a better constructed and more sophisticated document than the FFYP.[15]

"The basic objective of the Second Plan is 'to promote the moderniza-

---

13. The normalization treaty signed with Japan in late 1965 called for Korea to receive $200 million worth of "soft" loans and at least $300 million in commercial credits during the next decade.

14. Cole and Nam, "The Pattern and Significance of Economic Planning in Korea," p. 19. See also Irma Adelman, David C. Cole, Roger Norton, and Lee Kee Jung, "The Korean Sectoral Model," and Irma Adelman and Kim Mahn Je, "An Econometric Model of the Korean Economy (1956–66)," in Adelman, *Practical Approaches to Development Planning.* "The analytical framework of the model combines Gurley and Shaw's theory of finance with Chenery's 'two gap' approach" (Adelman and Kim, p. 78).

15. It is noteworthy that "consistency, not optimality, [was] the theme of the analytic work" (Roger D. Norton, "Planning with Facts: The Case of Korea," p. 63).

tion of the industrial structure and to build the foundations for a self-supporting economy.'" This was virtually the same as that of the FFYP. Major SFYP targets included "attainment of food self-sufficiency, investment in ... chemicals, machinery, and iron and steel [industries]," and "substantial increase in national income" with "special focus on increased farm productivity and income through diversification of farming." Rapid export expansion, increased capital mobilization, efficient manpower utilization, and continued financial stability were key strategies for achieving these targets. The projected annual GNP growth rate of 7.0 percent was below FFYP target and actual rates in 1962–66, but the planners expected SFYP investment to be more capital intensive than FFYP investment and believed that less excess capacity would be available.[16]

A number of FFYP projections are extrapolated in the SFYP. Population growth would continue to decline (at a steady 0.1 percent a year). Per capita income was expected to grow more rapidly than in the FFYP but below actual rates achieved in 1962–66. The unemployment rate would again drop (from 7.4 to 5 percent of the labor force) by the end of the Second Plan period. Continued decline in the proportion of GNP originating in agriculture was expected although agriculture's investment share was to rise (table 8.1). Investment was to grow less than in the FFYP or in 1962–66, and the aggregate capital coefficient of 2.9:1 was well below FFYP and Revised FFYP coefficients but above the actual 1962–66 level. This is consistent with the more capital-intensive nature of the projects to be undertaken in 1967–71.

Domestic saving ratios were above earlier plan levels and reliance on domestic (as opposed to foreign) saving was to increase, but the marginal ratio was below the terminal FFYP ratio. Initial-year saving and investment estimates (and ratios) shown in the plan are also less than actual 1966 levels because the plan was framed in 1965, before the full impact of the interest-rate reform was felt on economic aggregates.

The most important change embodied in the SFYP is the expansion of the public sector. The government's share in total investment would be higher than its actual 1962–66 or FFYP shares; government consumption was also scheduled to increase more rapidly than private consumption. The most ambitious targets, designed to reflect improvements in tax administration and expansion of the tax base, were those

16. Government of the ROK, *The Second Five-Year Economic Development Plan*, pp. 15, 33–34, 40.

for revenue ratios. SFYP revenue ratios rise sharply to 1968 and are well above earlier experience if not FFYP levels (table 8.1).[17]

One possible reason for expanding the public sector would be to increase investment in social overhead capital, which generally requires public rather than private outlays. However, with the exception of a statement that "health, education, housing, urban and regional planning, and the development of science and technology will be given greater emphasis," there is no indication that a higher proportion of investment in the SFYP was to be allocated to social overhead capital.[18] Another reason for expansion might have been that tax reform was expected to reduce private saving so that saving ratios would decline during the course of the SFYP unless government saving were substituted for private saving. However, there is no evidence of this; in fact, both saving ratios and private saving (as a proportion of GNP) show a steady increase during the SFYP plan period. A likelier reason for expanding the public sector was that policies required by the stabilization program had reduced the government's share of total expenditures below desired levels.

In the preface to the SFYP, the chief of the Economic Planning Board observed that "my fellow countryman criticize the Plan objectives as being too conservative. On the other hand, our friends from abroad observed that the Plan targets are too ambitious."[19] The chief's fellow countrymen were justified in their criticism. The actual overall growth rate during 1967–71 was well above the SFYP target rate. A combination of higher than expected output expansion and population growth roughly the same as that shown in the plan produced an increase in average per capita output of 47 percent from 1967 to 1971, much more than the 20 percent shown in the SFYP. Because the actual capital coefficient (2.8:1) was nearly equal to the plan coefficient for 1967–71, output increased more than planned because investment was greater than expected.[20] Investment ratios that were to average 19

17. Growth of the public sector is also seen in the savings estimates, where it is noted that "by far the most dramatic increase will occur in the government sector" (ibid., p. 43).

18. ROK, *The Second Five-Year Economic Development Plan*, p. 114.

19. Ibid., Preface.

20. Derivation of average GNP growth rates and capital coefficients is not explained in the plans. For instance, "an average annual growth rate of 7.1 percent [is] postulated for the plan period" (ROK, *Summary of the First Five-Year Economic Plan*, p. 28), but this proves to be an average increase from the reference year (1960) to 1966. Growth during the actual plan period (1962–66) was to average 7.5 percent. Similarly, the capital coefficient for the SFYP was evidently derived by relating investment during 1965–70 to the increase in GNP from 1966 to 1971. These same years were used here in calculating the actual capital coefficient for the SFYP period.

percent actually reached 31 percent in the SFYP period (table 8.1). According to the SFYP, "Korea's most serious problem is ... the degree to which domestic savings can be mobilized to finance a growing proportion of the nation's ... investment program."[21] In short, reliance on foreign resources would have to be reduced. Domestic saving rose to 15.6 percent of GNP during the SFYP after averaging only 7.4 percent in the FFYP period. Foreign saving ratios (GDCF − domestic saving/GNP) increased from 10 to 15 percent. Despite the rise in foreign saving levels and ratios, the *proportion* of capital formation financed domestically increased from 1962–66 to 1967–71. In this sense, reliance on foreign saving was diminished.

Planned and actual changes in economic structure during the SFYP period are shown in table 8.1. The share of agricultural output declined even more than planned, that originating in the service sector rose more. Agriculture's share of actual investment in 1967–71 was less than half its planned share. The absolute amount of investment in agriculture was also below the amount planned. This discrepancy was offset in the tertiary sector, where actual investment was more than twice the planned level. To the extent that investment is responsible for output growth, the relatively slow growth of agricultural output and the rapid increase in tertiary activity (which includes transport, construction, and utility output as well as trade and other service activities during the SFYP period) were due to the discrepancies between planned and actual investment. These discrepancies may also explain why the SFYP food self-sufficiency target had not been reached by 1971 and was, in fact, further from achievement than at the close of the FFYP (see p. 146).

Another deviation between planned and actual magnitudes is seen in the government sector. The SFYP called for a major increase in the government's investment share from earlier levels. Although government investment increased more quickly than private investment in the SFYP period, the government's share was little higher in 1971 than in 1966. Government consumption rose at the same rate as private consumption, so the public proportion of the total remained constant throughout this period. The overall expenditure shortfall undoubtedly resulted from a discrepancy between planned and actual revenues. Revenue ratios were to increase from an average of 11 percent (in

21. ROK, *The Second Five-Year Economic Development Plan*, p. 28.

1962–66) to 18 percent; however the actual average ratio during the SFYP period was only 13 percent (table 8.1).

Plan goals are usually set in absolute, not proportional terms, so that public sector targets might be met without an increase in the government's share of consumption and investment expenditure especially when, as in the SFYP period, GNP grew more than planned. Government expenditure in 1967–71 was actually very close to plan levels whereas revenues increased more and were higher by 1971 than shown in the plan. Nevertheless, demand for public services should increase with GNP, and a commonplace of economic growth has been that public revenue and expenditure rise more than proportionately with per capita income. This is why expenditure shares and revenue ratios have been employed here to show fiscal performance relative to output or demand for public services, and why the discrepancies between planned and actual expenditures and planned and actual revenue ratios may be interpreted as evidence of failure to achieve the SFYP target of expanding the public sector.

Some of the deviation between plan and result was undoubtedly due to the unexpectedly rapid GNP growth that occurred during the SFYP. For instance, investment in the tertiary sector was higher than planned —relatively as well as absolutely—because unanticipated output increase strained overhead facilities and required construction of additional power and transport capacity if the bottlenecks that threatened to strangle growth were to be broken (see pp. 169–71). Other deviations, however, such as the failure to meet agricultural targets or expand the public sector, were encountered earlier in First Plan shortfalls and were thus more likely to have resulted from long-term problems than from unexpected growth during the plan period.

The Second Plan, like the First, was seen to have surpassed expectations by the time data for the terminal year became available. This was recognized earlier in a series of upward revisions in plan goals as successive annual ORBs were released. Actual GNP growth was well above the target rate, total investment in 1967–71 was almost double the amount planned, exports reached almost twice the target level by 1971, and the increase in per capita GNP was more than double the increase anticipated. Employment rose by 1.19 million from 1965 to 1971, somewhat less than the 1.84 million shown in the SFYP. This was, nevertheless, a substantial increase given the relatively low labor-absorption rates of income growth observed in Korea and elsewhere (see pp. 118–19).

THE THIRD FIVE-YEAR PLAN AND NEW GOALS

"Rather than emphasizing 'economic growth,' the Third Five-Year Economic Development Plan can be characterized by its attempt to promote a 'balanced economy' by 'expanding regional development,' 'developing and improving life in rural areas,' and 'improving the quality of life of workers.'"[22] These goals are sufficiently vague to deserve quotation marks but suggest a shift in emphasis from building an industrial base (FFYP) and modernizing the industrial structure (SFYP) to rural development and redistributive programs. Prominent TFYP targets include achievement of self-sufficiency in food grains, raising of commodity exports to $3.5 billion by 1976, construction of heavy and chemical industries, and promotion of "balanced regional development." The annual increase in GNP is to average 8.6 percent during the plan period.

Decreased emphasis on rapid growth is evident in this growth rate, which is well below actual FFYP and SFYP levels. Planned investment ratios are less than actual 1967–71 ratios, and the time pattern of outlays (unlike the SFYP) yields ratios that drop over the plan period. Domestic saving ratios are to rise, as is the proportion of total investment to be financed from domestic resources. Reliance on foreign saving is to be reduced because exports are to triple from 1970 to 1976 while imports should only double. The relatively low TFYP growth rate is justified in terms of domestic and foreign savings gaps. That is, the planners felt that a growth rate higher than 8.6 percent would increase import demand and thus reliance on foreign saving, while the domestic saving needed to sustain a higher growth rate would be hard to obtain since "the projected marginal propensity to save is already high" (*TFYP*, p. 5).

Economic balance, regional development, and rural improvement should require absolute and relative increases in primary-sector investment and output. However, GNP originating in the primary sector (as a proportion of total GNP) continues to drop in the TFYP, while the investment share is less than that shown in the SFYP. Regional development may result from construction of industrial estates, and agricultural productivity can be raised by increasing fertilizer inputs, neither of which require investment in the primary sector, but the decline in the primary-sector investment share casts doubt on the feasibility of regional-balance and rural-development goals.

22. Government of the ROK, *The Third Five-Year Economic Development Plan*, p. vi.

As in the first two plans, TFYP expenditure estimates reveal an attempt to raise the government's share of consumption and investment outlays (table 8.1). This is especially significant because the TFYP emphasizes goals such as "improving life in rural areas" that usually require public rather than private expenditure. Public social expenditure (broadly defined) accounted for less than 20 percent of SFYP and TFYP outlays, however. Although investment in farm mechanization, marketing networks, and other projects that raise productivity and incomes also yields social benefits (as do current government welfare expenditures), such projects are not included in the plan's social-expenditure category. The extent of TFYP commitment and the need to expand the government's expenditure share may therefore be understated. On the other hand, when the president announced in early 1972 that major emphasis would be placed on farm community development (the "new village movement," *saemaul undong*), investment for this purpose had to be raised well above TFYP levels.

Outlays for community development may be too low in the TFYP or new stress on community development may call for more investment than planned; in either case, the public share of total expenditure will have to increase. Government expenditure growth is again likely to depend on success in raising revenue ratios. Average revenue ratios shown in the TFYP are 20 percent above SFYP levels and two-thirds above actual 1967–71 ratios (see table 8.1). This is perhaps the most ambitious aspect of the TFYP and, given past performance, the least likely to be achieved.

Self-sufficiency in staple food grains production is a major plan target as in the FFYP and SFYP but the target is modified, in effect, by plans to reduce consumption. "It is assumed that [average rice consumption of 140 kilograms per person in 1970] will not go up in the future since ... the pattern of food consumption will change due to increased income and the government's policy for an optimum rice price."[23] The increase in demand for grains was underestimated in the SFYP, while the expenditure elasticity of demand for rice has been unity or greater in recent years.[24] Like the revenue target, the self-sufficiency target seems unattainable by 1976.

23. Ibid., pp. 50–51. The TFYP goal for rice would actually require a 17 percent reduction in per capita consumption from 1973 to 1976, according to the minister of Agriculture and Forestry (*Korea Times*, 30 May 1973).

24. Pak Ki Hyuk and Han Kee Chun, *An Analysis of Food Consumption in the Republic of Korea*, tables 5.5–5.7.

Construction of heavy and chemical industries is another major TFYP goal that dates back to the FFYP. The integrated steel mill and a petrochemical complex were started during the SFYP and scheduled for completion during the TFYP period. The nonelectric machinery industry, a laggard industry in Korea, is also to be developed. These are primarily capital-intensive, import-substitute industries whose growth has been limited by competitive imports and the desire to prevent small-scale, high-cost domestic inputs from eroding the competitive position of Korea's export industries. Notwithstanding, the integrated steel mill was scheduled for expansion even before completion while some of the petrochemical plants appear to be below the minimum efficient size.[25] The drawbacks of import substitution were evidently outweighed in the TFYP by the need to right what was regarded as imbalance in the structure of manufacturing.

Planning strategy, particularly before the TFYP, was concerned largely with choices relating to the overall growth rate, industrial structure, and the composition of saving. Setting a target growth rate required that what appeared reasonable be reconciled with the maximum feasible rate; "there has been little disagreement over the desirability of striving for the highest practicable rates of growth."[26] "Reasonable" is usually interpreted as consistent with actual growth in the recent past, whereas "maximum feasible" rates stop short of overinvestment and its inflationary consequences and, where investment has been concentrated in a few sectors as in Korea, do not exacerbate income inequality. In fact, the feasible maximum was underestimated during the first two plans so that "bottlenecks in electric power, transportation and water supply retarded the rate of

25. A naptha cracking plant designed to produce 100,000 tons annually, for example, compares unfavorably with cracking plants in Japan and the United States that have average annual capacities of 200,000 and 320,000 tons, respectively (*Korea Times*, 11 Feb. 1972).

26. Cole and Nam, "The Pattern and Significance of Economic Planning in Korea," p. 23. This sidesteps a conflict in economic growth theory between long-run and short-run maximization. The growth path that maximizes output at some future date may require less rapid initial growth than alternative paths that yield higher initial but lower long-term growth (see John Hicks, *Capital and Growth*, chaps. 18, 19, and R. Dorfman, Paul Samuelson, and R. Solow, *Linear Programming and Economic Analysis*, chaps. 11, 12). However, this distinction fails to provide operational alternatives for planners, for the immediate problem is one of time sequence rather than of choice among alternatives. Fast initial growth increases available resources and allows more choice in subsequent years. Consequently, conceivable theoretical conflict between short- and long-run maximization may have no operational significance. See Wolfgang F. Stolper, *Planning Without Facts*, pp. 74–80.

increase in production."[27] Substantial plan revision was required to eliminate these bottlenecks.

The basic structural choices are clear in the first two plans. The choice between agriculture and manufacturing was settled in favor of manufacturing. Within manufacturing, emphasis was to be on light rather than on heavy industry, on labor-intensive rather than capital-intensive activities, and on "specialized" (export) rather than "integrated" (import substitute) products. The primary goal was to expand exports as rapidly as possible. Questions of whether demand for intermediate goods would increase sufficiently to permit construction of efficient import-substitute plants, or whether the benefits of access to imported equipment would offset the costs of a backward domestic machinery industry were deferred until the middle of the Second Plan period. These questions were taken up in framing the Third Plan, which unlike the first two plans, does not reflect clear structural emphasis.

Another major policy issue raised in each plan has been how much could domestic saving be increased and dependence on foreign saving reduced. It is related to the desire for self-sufficiency that lies behind attempts to raise revenue ratios and thus increase government saving and behind efforts to expand exports while holding down imports. The attempt to achieve self-sufficiency in food grain production is perhaps the most notable case in point. Food imports can be viewed as a charge against foreign exchange holdings that, unlike machinery or materials imports, does not contribute directly to output growth.

Domestic saving was relatively low by international standards before 1965 and reliance on external finance sufficiently high so that an increase in domestic saving ratios must have appeared necessary and desirable (see p. 78). Of the possible ways to achieve a more conventional balance between foreign and domestic saving, only an increase in domestic saving would normally be acceptable. Savings targets that call for an increased share of saving in total expenditure and require high marginal savings rates are common to most development planning, so the Korean plans are quite typical in this respect.[28] What is unusual,

---

27. *Overall Resources Budget: 1969*, pp. 1, 7–8.
28. Shares of gross national saving in gross national product given in the development plans of 19 countries in Africa, Asia, and Latin America are listed in the United Nations, *Journal of Development Planning*, p. 168. Sixteen of the 19 countries show rising shares during the course of the plan period, and in most cases the marginal saving rate is over 20 percent.

however, has been Korea's access to large-scale foreign aid and, more recently, to even larger inflows of foreign capital (pp. 77–78). These sources have been partly offset by rapid growth of government and private saving after the fiscal reform of 1963 and the interest-rate reform in 1965. Nevertheless, attempts to approach self-sufficiency have continued, probably because of increased concern for Korea's ability to handle rising debt-repayment obligations.

Major new goals introduced in the TFYP are likely to require new planning strategies. Like the FFYP and the SFYP, the TFYP embodies choices that relate to the overall growth rate, industrial structure, and the composition of saving, but the TFYP also calls for rural modernization, improvement of the agricultural distribution network, and other qualitative targets that demand institutional changes. These are very different from the quantitative targets associated with industrial expansion and modernization that were emphasized in the first two plans.

Achievement could be measured according to expansion of physical capacity or increased quantity and value of output in these plans, but the new TFYP goals should, logically, be evaluated in terms of reduction in regional or rural–urban income disparities. However, these indicators are incomplete. How, for example, is "improvement in the quality of life" to be measured? More important, the new targets require changes in marketing and other rural institutions. Unlike construction of factories or overhead capital projects, inputs as well as outputs for these institutional targets cannot always be specified. For instance, the TFYP shows investment of 41 billion won for agricultural mechanization distributed among 38,700 plow machines and other pieces of farm equipment; no distribution is shown of the 53 billion won allocated for "improvement of distribution channels and others."

The distinction here has several conceivable consequences. Inputs that cannot be specified may be underestimated. The cost in time and resources needed to improve rural institutions, for example, is likely to be enormous. Also, nominal rather than actual achievement may be stressed if output cannot be specified in quantitative terms. In short, the TFYP's qualitative targets may be difficult to achieve, and even if achieved, it may be difficult to demonstrate that they have been.

Despite inclusion of qualitative goals in the TFYP and the possible difficulties of making the institutional changes required to meet such goals, Korea's three plans represent both substantial achievement and the promise of further progress. The first two plans, especially the SFYP, established the ambitious saving, investment, and output increases needed to achieve rapid industrialization and export expansion. Accelerated growth during the second subperiod provided even larger increases in industrial output and exports than were foreseen in the plans. Except for agricultural and government-sector targets, plan goals were met and exceeded. Given Korea's economic endowment, such swift growth makes it difficult to demonstrate that planners' priorities were wrong, or even that the opportunity costs of the particular choices made were excessive.

Benefits of rapid growth were not costless, however; although major goals of the first two plans were repeated in the third, the new emphasis on regional development, rural improvement, and other targets associated with balance and equality- is significant because it points to problems that grew as the economy grew. "Balanced regional development," for example, would hardly be necessary if the economy were stagnant. Nor would raising farm income be a major target if concentration of output growth and increase in output per worker in the cities had not widened the rural–urban productivity gap during the late 1960s (p. 56).

The planners' choice, as Stolper once observed, is not so much a choice between alternatives as it is a choice of order among alternatives.[29] New emphasis on balance and qualitative goals in the TFYP suggests that Korea's economic alternatives were reordered in the early 1970s. Though "immediate emphasis [was] placed on export expansion," export expansion would have to be deemphasized if other goals were to be achieved during the TFYP period.[30] Whether there has in fact been a reordering is as yet unclear, but available evidence indicates that there has not been one. An evaluation report issued in mid-1974 calls for " 'stabilization first and growth next' in 1974."[31] Self-sufficiency in food production is seen as the most urgent short-run need; long-term goals include "gradual changes" to expand welfare measures and obtain a more equitable income distribution. However, most of the report is devoted to quantitative achievements, with little reference to progress in meeting qualitative targets.

29. Stolper, *Planning Without Facts*, pp. 75–76.
30. The quotation is from a government white paper setting forth economic policies for the decade of the 1970s (*Korea Times*, 18 March 1970).
31. Office of the Prime Minister, ROK, *Evaluation Report of the Second Year Program*, p. 135.

The evaluation report is essentially a short-range response to an Arab oil embargo and concurrent international economic disturbances. In this sense it is not a fair test of TFYP goal achievement. Also, the plan was less than half complete when the report was written. Nonetheless, failure to evaluate progress in meeting qualitative targets tends to confirm two points made above, namely, that the TFYP's new qualitative goals are likely to be difficult to achieve and difficult to evaluate. However, earlier goals have been repeated in later plans, and Korea's economic record during the FFYP and SFYP periods has been impressive. It seems reasonable to expect, therefore, that most Third Plan goals will eventually be reached—and exceeded—as were those set forth in the first two plans.

Statistical Appendix

Table A1. Total Population
(End of year unless otherwise indicated)

		Population (thousands)[a]	Average annual (compound) growth rate (%)
	1910	13,129	1910–15
	1911	13,832	4.0
	1912	14,576	
	1913	15,170	
	1914	15,621	
	1915	15,958	
	1916	16,309	1915–20
	1917	16,617	1.5
	1918	16,697	
	1919	16,784	
Oct. 1,	1920	17,264(C)	
	1921	17,059	1920–25
	1922	17,208	2.0
	1923	17,447	
	1924	17,619	
Oct. 1,	1925	19,020(C)	
	1926	18,615	1925–30
	1927	18,631	1.4
	1928	18,667	
	1929	18,784	
Oct. 1,	1930	20,438(C)	
	1931	19,710	1930–35
	1932	20,037	1.7
	1933	20,206	
	1934	20,513	

		Population (thousands)[a]	Average annual (compound) growth rate (%)
Oct. 1,	1935	22,208(C)	
	1936	22,374	1935–40
	1937	21,683	1.1
	1938	21,951	
	1939	22,100	
Oct. 1,	1940	23,547(C)	
	1941	23,913	1940–44
	1942	25,525	1.7
	1943	25,827	
May 1,	1944	25,120(C)	
		15,879(C)[b]	
	1945	—	1944–46
Aug. 25,	1946	19,369[c]	10.5
	1947	19,886[c]	1946–49
	1948	20,027[c]	1.4
May 1,	1949	20,189(C)	
	1950	—	
	1951	—	1949–53
Mar. 1,	1952	20,527[d]	1.6
Dec. 31,	1953	21,546[e]	
	1954	—	
Sept. 1,	1955[f]	21,526(C)[g]	1953–55
	1955	20,202	0.0
	1956	20,724	
	1957	21,321	
	1958	21,910	1955–60
	1959	22,974	3.1
Dec. 1,	1960	24,994(C)[g]	
	1961	24,926	
Dec. 1,	1962	26,278	1960–66
	1963	—	2.6
Dec. 1,	1964	28,181	
	1965	28,647	
Oct. 1,	1966	29,193(C)[g]	
	1967	29,854	1966–70
	1968	30,453	1.9
	1969	31,017	
Oct. 1,	1970	31,466(C)[g]	
	1971	32,130	
	1972	32,711	

Table A1. (continued)

Sources: Bank of Chosŏn, *Annual Economic Review of Korea, 1948*, pt. III-11 (excludes foreigners through 1944); Bank of Korea (BOK), *Economic Statistics Yearbooks*, various years.
a Includes both North and South Korea through 1944, South Korea only in later years. (C) indicates census data.
b South Korea only.
c Estimates of American Military Government.
d Estimates of Ministry of Home Affairs.
e Estimates of Bureau of Statistics.
f Year end (Dec. 31) population survey (excludes armed forces, foreigners, prisoners, and ship crews) from 1955 to 1961 except during census years.
g Census data: excludes foreigners.

Table A2. Expenditure on Gross National Product
(In billions of won at 1970 constant market prices)

	Private consumption	General government consumption	Gross domestic fixed capital formation	Increase in stocks	Exports of goods and services
1953	658.15	151.35	51.06	64.36	16.99
1954	710.10	147.52	65.04	26.51	10.25
1955	775.09	151.96	73.86	20.16	12.86
1956	809.52	159.25	78.58	−2.86	11.46
1957	840.36	159.18	91.08	44.18	15.56
1958	882.43	163.65	87.43	30.30	19.72
1959	924.72	162.50	93.27	−1.50	22.86
1960	942.62	164.52	97.01	−0.42	27.43
1961	950.65	163.39	104.45	16.90	38.20
1962	1,017.73	167.07	133.38	−13.50	42.96
1963	1,055.51	174.26	167.79	57.30	46.16
1964	1,124.20	172.15	155.12	33.06	57.06
1965	1,201.12	181.56	195.40	1.86	80.29
1966	1,282.37	200.30	294.28	23.21	122.28
1967	1,396.87	218.08	358.63	9.69	165.99
1968	1,545.55	240.62	498.30	10.75	235.03
1969	1,705.63	264.17	639.23	74.84	310.07
1970	1,884.25	281.81	650.20	54.46	381.23
1971	2,080.12	311.90	680.63	68.18	459.35
1972	2,226.03	325.55	659.14	8.79	643.34

	Less imports of goods and services	Statistical discrepancy	Expenditure on gross domestic product	Net factor income from the rest of the world	Expenditure on gross national product
1953	109.42	—	832.49	11.03	843.52
1954	78.09	—	881.33	8.85	890.18
1955	104.76	—	929.17	9.07	938.24
1956	122.38	—	933.57	8.64	942.21
1957	144.80	—	1,005.56	8.88	1,014.44
1958	125.27	—	1,058.26	8.89	1,067.15

Table A2. (continued)

	Less imports of goods and services	Statistical discrepancy	Expenditure on gross domestic product	Net factor income from the rest of the world	Expenditure on gross national product
1959	102.59	—	1,099.26	9.07	1,108.33
1960	117.53	7.46	1,121.09	8.63	1,129.72
1961	106.60	10.72	1,177.71	6.77	1,184.48
1962	141.23	7.00	1,213.41	7.57	1,220.98
1963	179.22	−1.44	1,320.36	7.95	1,328.31
1964	133.34	26.10	1,434.35	7.64	1,441.99
1965	149.55	10.08	1,520.76	8.94	1,529.70
1966	237.92	19.35	1,703.87	15.31	1,719.18
1967	320.73	−0.71	1,827.82	25.19	1,853.01
1968	468.04	−1.12	2,061.09	26.03	2,087.12
1969	583.77	−36.64	2,373.53	26.96	2,400.49
1970	642.44	−32.15	2,577.36	11.90	2,589.26
1971	773.55	2.21	2,828.84	−2.02	2,826.82
1972	801.23	−25.88	3,035.74	−12.11	3,023.63

Source: BOK, Economic Statistics Yearbook, 1973.

Table A3. Agricultural Production (Crops)
(In thousands of metric tons)

	Total	Rice	Barley	Naked barley	Vegetables	Potatoes	Pulses	Fruit	Others[a]
1956	5,655.8	2,437.6	691.5	399.7	1,166.3	271.0	172.8	117.0	399.9
1957	6,137.2	3,001.9	599.9	350.6	1,227.4	287.6	172.7	127.3	369.8
1958	6,489.1	3,160.9	712.1	470.9	1,111.9	304.3	175.0	151.3	402.7
1959	6,575.3	3,149.5	828.6	530.3	1,010.1	299.1	158.0	166.8	432.9
1960	6,557.9	3,046.5	852.2	517.8	1,088.1	326.0	150.4	166.4	410.5
1961	7,360.3	3,462.5	898.2	580.1	1,234.8	383.5	190.1	149.9	461.2
1962	6,951.8	3,014.9	767.7	610.5	1,299.5	439.3	181.6	195.3	443.0
1963	7,135.4	3,758.0	582.7	335.3	1,187.3	513.5	181.8	178.1	398.7
1964	8,761.8	3,954.5	895.5	619.1	1,436.4	936.0	190.6	228.7	501.0
1965	8,923.1	3,501.1	951.1	855.9	1,576.0	1,045.1	202.9	310.0	481.0
1966	9,654.7	3,919.3	975.3	1,042.9	1,717.2	971.6	195.0	331.1	502.3
1967	9,103.8	3,603.1	930.9	985.1	1,869.4	631.1	235.4	358.9	489.9
1968	9,466.3	3,195.3	840.9	1,242.8	2,150.2	758.7	287.7	392.4	598.3
1969	10,664.1	4,090.4	916.4	1,150.1	2,427.5	777.9	272.6	416.8	612.4
1970	10,491.9	3,939.3	819.0	1,154.9	2,520.3	783.2	276.8	423.3	575.1
1971	10,678.9	3,997.6	742.2	1,115.3	2,917.9	707.2	263.0	404.3	531.4
1972	10,479.2	3,957.2	751.1	1,213.4	2,716.8	673.7	261.0	488.9	417.1

Sources: EPB, Korea Statistical Yearbooks, various years; MAF, Yearbooks of Agriculture and Forestry Statistics.
Note: All grains shown are polished equivalents.
[a] Includes wheat, rye, other cereals (millet, corn, buckwheat, and sorghum), and industrial crops (cotton, hemp, ramie, black rush, sesame, wild sesame, and castor beans).

Bibliography

I. BOOKS AND THESES

Adelman, Irma; Cole, David C.; Norton, Roger; and Lee, Kee Jung. "The Korean Sectoral Model" (with an Appendix by Marshall Wood and David E. Labovitz). In *Practical Approaches to Development Planning: Korea's Second Five-Year Plan*, edited by Irma Adelman, pp. 109–43. Baltimore: Johns Hopkins University Press, 1969.

Adelman, Irma, and Kim, Mahn Je. "An Econometric Model of the Korean Economy (1956–1966)." In *Practical Approaches to Development Planning: Korea's Second Five-Year Plan*, edited by Irma Adelman, pp. 77–108. Baltimore: Johns Hopkins University Press, 1969.

Ahn, Seung Chul. "A Monetary Analysis of the Korean Economy, 1954–1966, on the Basis of Demand and Supply Functions of Money." Ph.D. dissertation, University of California, Berkeley, 1968.

Allen, Richard C. *Korea's Syngman Rhee: An Unauthorized Portrait.* Rutland, Vermont: Tuttle, 1960.

Balassa, Bela, and Hughes, Helen. "Statistical Indicators of Levels of Industrial Development." Working Paper no. 45. Washington: International Bank for Reconstruction and Development, May 1969. Mimeographed.

Ban, Sung-whan. "Growth Rates of Korean Agriculture, 1918–1968." Paper prepared for the Conference on Agricultural Growth in Japan, Korea, Taiwan, and the Philippines, February 1973. Seoul: Korea Development Institute, 1972.

Barclay, George W. *Colonial Development and Population in Taiwan.* Princeton: Princeton University Press, 1954.

Berger, Carl. *The Korea Knot: A Military-Political History.* Philadelphia: University of Pennsylvania Press, 1957.

Bix, Herbert P. "Regional Integration: Japan and South Korea in America's Asian Policy." In *Without Parallel: The American-Korean Relationship Since 1945*, edited by Frank Baldwin, pp. 179–232. New York: Pantheon, 1974.

Bloomfield, Arthur I., and Jensen, John P. *Banking Reform in South Korea.* New York: Federal Reserve Bank of New York, 1951.

Brandt, Vincent S. R. *A Korean Village Between Farm and Sea.* Cambridge: Harvard University Press, 1971.

Bronfenbrenner, Martin, and Holzman, Franklyn D. "A Survey of Inflation Theory." In American Economic Association—Royal Economic Society, *Surveys of Economic Theory.* Vol. 1, *Money, Interest, and Welfare,* pp. 46–107. London and New York: St. Martin's Press, Macmillan, 1967.

Brown, William Adams, Jr., and Opie, Redvers. *American Foreign Assistance.* Washington: Brookings Institution, 1953.

Caldwell, John C. *The Korea Story.* Chicago: Henry Regnery, 1952.

Campbell, Colin D. "The Velocity of Money and the Rate of Inflation: Recent Experiences in South Korea and Brazil." In *Varieties of Monetary Experience,* edited by David Meiselman, pp. 341–88. Chicago: University of Chicago Press, 1970.

Chenery, Hollis; Ahluwalia, Montek S.; Bell, C. L. G.; Duloy, John H.; and Jolly, Richard. *Redistribution with Growth.* Joint Study by the World Bank's Development Research Center and the Institute of Development Studies, University of Sussex. London: Oxford University Press, 1974.

Cho, Soon Sung. *Korea in World Politics: 1940–1950.* Berkeley and Los Angeles: University of California Press, 1967.

Cho, Yong Sam. *"Disguised Unemployment" in Underdeveloped Areas with Special Reference to South Korean Agriculture.* Berkeley and Los Angeles: University of California Press, 1963.

Choe, Ehn-hyun. *Population Distribution and Internal Migration in Korea.* 1960 Census Monograph Series. Seoul: Bureau of Statistics, Economic Planning Board, 1966.

Choo, Hakchung. "Review of Income Distribution Studies, Data Availability, and Associated Problems for Korea, the Philippines, and Taiwan." Paper presented at Brookings–Princeton Income Distribution Conference, September 1974. Seoul: Korea Development Institute, 1974.

———. "Some Sources of Relative Equity in Korean Income Distribution: A Historical Perspective." Paper presented for the Japan Economic Research Center—Center for Applied Manpower Studies Seminar on Income Distribution, Employment, and Economic Development in Southeast and East Asia. Tokyo: December 1974.

Chung-Ang University (The Institute of Social Science). *Income Distribution and Consumption Structure in Korea.* Seoul: Chung-Ang University Press, 1966.

Cohen, Benjamin I., and Ranis, Gustav. "The Second Postwar Restructuring." In *Government and Economic Development,* edited by Gustav Ranis, pp. 431–71. New Haven: Yale University Press, 1971.

Cole, David C., and Lyman, Princeton N. *Korean Development: The Interplay of Politics and Economics.* Cambridge: Harvard University Press, 1971.

Cole, David C., and Nam, Young Woo. "The Pattern and Significance of Economic Planning in Korea." In *Practical Approaches to Development Planning: Korea's Second Five-Year Plan,* edited by Irma Adelman, pp. 11–37. Baltimore: Johns Hopkins University Press, 1969.

Conroy, Hilary. *The Japanese Seizure of Korea: 1868–1910.* Philadelphia: University of Pennsylvania Press, 1960.

Dallet, Charles. *Traditional Korea.* Behavior Science Translations. New Haven: Human Relations Area Files, 1954. Originally published as the *Introduction to Histoire de l'Eglise de Coree*, Paris: Victor Palme, 1874.

Dorfman, Robert; Samuelson, Paul; and Solow, Robert. *Linear Programming and Economic Analysis.* International Student Edition. New York and Tokyo: McGraw-Hill, Kogakusha, 1958.

Eckstein, Alexander. *Communist China's Economic Growth and Foreign Trade: Implications for U.S. Policy.* New York: McGraw-Hill, 1966.

Emery, Robert F. "The Korean Interest Rate Reform of September 1965." Washington, D.C.: Board of Governors of the Federal Reserve System, 1966. Mimeographed.

Faculty Members of Seoul National University. *Analysis of Korea's Import Substitution Industries.* Seoul: Seoul National University, 1967.

Fehrenbach, T. R. *This Kind of War: A Study in Unpreparedness.* New York: Macmillan, 1963.

Friedman, Milton, and Schwartz, Anna. *A Monetary History of the United States: 1867–1960.* A National Bureau of Economic Research Study. Princeton: Princeton University Press, 1963.

Galenson, W., and Pyatt, G. *The Quality of Labour and Economic Development in Certain Countries.* Geneva: International Labour Office, 1964.

Gilbert, Milton, and Kravis, Irving B. *An International Comparison of National Products and the Purchasing Power of Currencies.* Paris: Organization for European Economic Cooperation, 1954.

Grajdanzev, Andrew J. *Modern Korea.* Institute of Pacific Relations. New York: John Day, 1944.

Gurley, John G.; Patrick, Hugh T.; and Shaw, E. S. *The Financial Structure of Korea.* Reprint. Seoul: Bank of Korea, 1965.

Han, Kee Chun. *Estimates of Korean Capital and Inventory Coefficients in 1968.* Seoul: Yonsei University, 1970.

Han, Woo-keun. *The History of Korea.* Seoul: Eul-yoo Publishing Company, 1970.

Harbison, Frederick, and Myers, Charles A. *Education, Manpower and Economic Growth.* New York: McGraw-Hill, 1964.

Hatada, Takashi. *A History of Korea.* Translated and edited by Warren W. Smith, Jr. and Benjamin H. Hazard. Santa Barbara, California: American Bibliographical Center, Clio Press, 1969.

Hayami, Yujiro. "Green Revolution in Historical Perspective: The Experience of Japan, Taiwan, and Korea." Minneapolis: University of Minnesota (Department of Agricultural Economics), November 1969. Dittographed.

Henderson, Gregory. *Korea: The Politics of the Vortex.* Cambridge: Harvard University Press, 1968.

Henthorn, William E. *A History of Korea.* New York: Free Press, 1971.

Hicks, John. *Capital and Growth.* New York and Oxford, England: Oxford University Press, 1965.

Hulbert, Homer B. *The Passing of Korea.* New York: Doubleday, Page and Company, 1906.

Im, Tae-bin. *The Korean Labor Force and School Population.* 1960 Census Monograph Series. Seoul: Bureau of Statistics, Economic Planning Board, 1965.

International Labour Office. *Towards Full Employment.* A programme for

Columbia, prepared by an Interagency team organized by the International Labour Office. Geneva: International Labor Office, 1970

Jacoby, Neil H. *U.S. Aid to Taiwan: A Study of Foreign Aid, Self-Help, and Development*. New York: Praeger, 1966.

Jain, Shail, and Tiemann, Arthur E. *Size Distribution of Income: Compilation of Data*. Development Research Center, Discussion Paper no. 4. Washington: International Bank for Reconstruction and Development, August 1973.

Johnston, B. F. *Japanese Food Management in World War II*. One of a group of studies on Food, Agriculture, and World War II. Stanford: Stanford University Press, 1953.

Jones, Homer. "*Korean Financial Problems*." Reprint. Seoul: Bank of Korea, June 1968. Mimeographed.

Kahn, Ely J., Jr. *The Peculiar War: Impressions of a Reporter in Korea*. New York: Random House, 1951.

Kanesa-Thasan, S. "Stabilizing an Economy: The Korean Experience." In *Practical Approaches to Development Planning: Korea's Second Five-Year Plan*, edited by Irma Adelman, pp. 257–76. Baltimore: Johns Hopkins University Press, 1969.

Keynes, John Maynard. *The General Theory of Employment, Interest and Money*. New York: Harcourt, Brace, 1936.

Kim, Byong-kuk. *Central Banking Experiment in a Developing Economy: Case Study of Korea*. Korean Studies Series no. 12. Seoul: The Korean Research Center, 1965.

Kim, Chong Ik Eugene, and Kim, Han Kyo. *Korea and the Politics of Imperialism, 1876–1910*. Berkeley: University of California Press, 1968.

Kim, Kwang Suk. "An Appraisal of the High Interest Rate Strategy of Korea." Course paper for Economics 510, Center for Development Studies, Williams College. Williamstown, Massachusetts, May 1968. Dittographed.

Kim, Mahn Je, and Nam, Duck Woo. "A Statistical Model for Monetary Management: The Case of Korea, 1956–1967." A Paper presented before the Third Far Eastern Meeting of the Econometric Society, June 27–29, 1968. Seoul: United States Operations Mission to Korea, 1968. Mimeographed.

Kim, Young Chin, and Kwon, Jene K. *Capital Utilization in Korean Manufacturing, 1962–1971: Its Level, Trend and Structure*. Seoul: Korean Industrial Development Research Institute, May 1973.

The Korea Annual. Seoul: Hapdong News Agency.

Korea Federation of Education Associations. *Korean Education Yearbook, 1965*. Seoul: Korea Federation of Education Associations, 1965. In Korean.

Korea Land Economics Research Center. *A Study of Land Tenure System in Korea*. Seoul: Korea Land Economics Research Center, 1966.

Korean Development Association. *Effective Protective Rates of Korean Industries*. Seoul: Korean Development Association, June 1967.

Kuznets, Paul W. "Korea's Five-Year Plans." In *Practical Approaches to Development Planning: Korea's Second Five-Year Plan*, edited by Irma Adelman, pp. 39–73. Baltimore: Johns Hopkins University Press, 1969.

————. "Labor Absorption in Korea Since 1963." (Working Paper no. 16). Bloomington: Indiana University, International Development Research Center, September 1972.

Kuznets, Simon. *Economic Growth and Structure: Selected Essays.* New York: W. W. Norton, 1965.

————. *Modern Economic Growth: Rate Structure and Spread.* New Haven: Yale University Press, 1966.

————. *Six Lectures on Economic Growth.* New York: Free Press of Glencoe, 1959.

Kwon, E. Hyock; Kim, Tae Ryong; Cha, Chul Hwan; Yun, Dork Ro; Ko, Ung Ring; and Park, Hyung Jong. *A Study in Urban Slum Population.* Seoul: College of Medicine and School of Public Health, Seoul National University, July 1967.

Leckie, Robert. *Conflict: The History of the Korean War, 1950–1953.* New York: Putnam, 1962.

Lee, Hoon, K. *Land Utilization and Rural Economy in Korea.* Shanghai and Hong Kong: Kelly and Walsh Ltd., 1936.

Lee, Kie Wook. "Efficiency of Resource Allocation in Traditional Agriculture: A Case Study of South Korea." Ph. D. dissertation, Vanderbilt University, 1968.

Lewis, John P. *Reconstruction and Development in South Korea.* Planning Pamphlet no. 94. Washington, D. C.: National Planning Association, 1955.

Lim, Youngil. "Factor Contents of Foreign Trade in South Korea." Technology and Development Institute, East–West Center. Honolulu: University of Hawaii, no date. Mimeographed, 17 pp.

————. "Price Formation Process and Stabilization Policy in Korea: A Quantitative Analysis." No place, August 1968. Mimeographed.

McCune, George M. *Korea Today.* Cambridge: Harvard University Press, 1950.

McKinnon, Ronald I. *Money and Capital in Economic Development.* Washington, D. C.: Brookings Institution, 1973.

Marshall, Samuel L. A. *The River and the Gauntlet.* New York: William Morrow, 1953.

Meade, E. Grant. *American Military Government in Korea.* New York: Columbia University, King's Crown Press, 1951.

Merhav, Meir. *Technological Dependence, Monopoly, and Growth.* New York and London: Pergamon, 1969.

Mills, John E., ed. *Ethno-Sociological Report on Four Korean Villages.* Seoul: United States Operations Mission to Korea, 1960.

Musgrave, Richard A. "Revenue Policy for Korea's Economic Development." Prepared for the Nathan Economic Advisory Group. Seoul: United States Operations Mission to Korea, September 1965. Mimeographed.

Myrdal, Gunnar. *An Approach to the Asian Drama: Methodological and Theoretical.* New York: Random House, 1970.

Nam, Duck Woo. "Korea's Experience with Economic Planning." In *Report of International Conference on the Problems of Modernization in Asia,* edited by Lee Sang-eun, pp. 517–29. Conference held June 28–July 7, 1965. Seoul: Asiatic Research Center of Korea University, 1966.

————. Lee, Seung Yun; and Kim, Byong Kuk. *Determinants of Money Supply and the Scope of Monetary Policy: 1954–1964.* Seoul: Research Institute for Economics and Business, Sogang College, August 1968.

Nelson, M. Frederick. *Korea and the Old Orders in Eastern Asia.* Baton Rouge: Louisiana State University Press, 1945.

Norton, Roger D. "The South Korean Economy in the 1960s." Paper presented before the annual meeting of the Association for Asian Studies. Washington, D. C.: International Bank for Reconstruction and Development, March 1971. Mimeographed.

————, and Lee, Kee Jung. "The Korean Input–Output Planning Model." Paper presented before the Second Far Eastern Meeting of the Econometric Society, Tokyo, June 29–July 1, 1967. Seoul: United States Operations Mission to Korea, 1967. Mimeographed.

Pak, Ki Hyuk, and Han, Kee Chun. *An Analysis of Food Consumption in the Republic of Korea.* Seoul: Yonsei University, 1969.

Ranis, Gustav, and Fei, John C. H. "Agrarianism, Dualism, and Economic Development." In *The Theory and Design of Economic Development,* edited by Irma Adelman and Eric Thorbecke, pp. 3–41. Baltimore: Johns Hopkins University Press, 1966.

Reeve, W. D. *The Republic of Korea: A Political and Economic Study.* London: Oxford University Press, 1963.

Renaud, Bertrand. *Economic Growth and Income Inequality in Korea.* Paper prepared for the ACLS–SSRC and Seoul National University, Population and Development Studies Center, Conference on Population and Development in Korea. Seoul, January 1975.

Rosovsky, Henry, ed. *Industrialization in Two Systems: Essays in Honor of Alexander Gerschenkron.* New York: John Wiley, 1966.

Schumpeter, E. B., ed. *The Industrialization of Japan and Manchukuo, 1939–1940: Population, Raw Materials, Industry.* New York: Macmillan, 1940.

Snodgrass, Donald R. *Ceylon: An Export Economy in Transition.* Economic Growth Center, Yale University. Homewood, Ill.: Richard D. Irwin, 1966.

Sohn, Pow-key; Kim, Chol-choon; and Hong, Yi-sup. *The History of Korea.* Seoul: Korean National Commission for UNESCO, 1970.

Southworth, Herman, ed. *Farm Mechanization in East Asia.* Proceedings of the Second East Asian Regional Workshop on Economic and Social Aspects of Farm Mechanization, Tokyo, 1971. New York: Agricultural Development Council, 1972.

Stolper, Wolfgang F. *Planning Without Facts: Lessons in Resource Allocation from Nigeria's Development.* Cambridge: Harvard University Press, 1966.

Stone, Isidor F. *The Hidden History of the Korean War.* New York: Monthly Review Press, 1952.

Suh, Sang-Chul. "Growth and Structural Changes in the Korean Economy Since 1910." Ph. D. dissertation, Harvard University, 1966.

Turnham, David (assisted by Ingelies Jaeger). *The Employment Problem in Less Developed Countries: A Review of the Evidence.* Development Centre Studies, Employment Series no. 1. Paris: Organization for Economic Cooperation and Development, 1971.

Westphal, Larry E., and Adelman, Irma. "Reflections on the Political Economy of Planning: The Case of Korea." In *Basic Documents and Selected Papers of Korea's Third Five-Year Economic Development Plan,* edited by Sung-Hwan Jo and Seong-Yawng Park, pp. 13–31. Seoul: Sogang University,

1972.

Wideman, Bernie. "The Plight of the South Korean Peasant." In *Without Parallel: The American–Korean Relationship Since 1945*, edited by Frank Baldwin, pp. 271–317. New York: Pantheon, 1974.

II. ARTICLES

Adekunle, Joseph O. "The Demand for Money: Evidence from Developed and Less Developed Economies." *IMF Staff Papers* 15, no. 2 (July 1968): 220–64.

Ahluwalia, Montek S. "Income Inequality: Some Dimensions of the Problem." *Finance and Development* 11, no. 3 (September 1974): 2–8.

Ahrensdorf, Joachim, and Kanesathasan, S. "Variations in the Money Multiplier and their Implications for Central Banking." *IMF Staff Papers* 8, no. 1 (November 1960): 126–49.

Argy, Victor. "Structural Inflation in Developing Countries." *Oxford Economic Papers*. New series, vol. 22, no. 1 (March 1970): 73–85.

Baer, Werner, and Hervé, Michel E. A. "Employment and Industrialization in Developing Countries." *Quarterly Journal of Economics* 80, no. 1 (February 1966): 88–107.

Balassa, Bela. "Industrial Policies in Taiwan and Korea." *Weltwirtschaftliches Archiv* 106, no. 1 (1971): 55–76.

Bottomley, Anthony. "The Cost of Administering Private Loans in Underdeveloped Rural Areas." *Oxford Economic Papers*. New series, vol. 15, no. 2 (July 1963): 154–63.

Bruton, Henry J. "Economic Development and Labor Use: A Review." *Research Memorandum Number 56*. Center for Development Economics, Williams Collage, June 1973, 90 pp.

Byun, Hyung-yoon. "Industrial Structure in Korea: With Reference to Secondary Industry." *Seoul National University Economic Review* 1, no. 1 (December 1967): 33–69.

Campbell, Colin, and Ahn, Chang-Shick. "*Kyes* and *Mujins*—Financial Intermediaries in South Korea." *Economic Development and Cultural Change* 11, no. 1 (October 1962): 55–68.

Chenery, Hollis B., and Strout, Alan M. "Foreign Assistance and Economic Development." *American Economic Review* 56, no. 4, pt. 1 (September 1966): 679–733.

Chenery, Hollis B., and Taylor, Lance. "Development Patterns: Among Countries and Over Time." *Review of Economics and Statistics* 50, no. 4 (November 1968): 391–416.

Choi, Hochin. "The Process of Industrial Modernization in Korea: The Latter Part of the Chosen Dynasty Through 1960's." *Journal of Social Sciences and Humanities* 26 (June 1967): 1–33.

Chu, Suk-Kyun. "Impact of U.S. Surplus Agricultural Products on Korean Agriculture." *Korean Affairs* 2, no. 2 (1963): 222–33.

Clague, Christopher K. "Capital–Labor Substitution in Manufacturing in Underdeveloped Countries." *Econometrica* 37, no 3 (July 1969): 528–37.

Dick, G. William. "Authoritarian versus Nonauthoritarian Approaches to

Economic Development." *Journal of Political Economy* 82, no. 4 (July–August 1974): 817–27.

Engebretson, T. O. "Agriculture and Land Reform in Korea." U.S. Department of Agriculture, *Foreign Agriculture* 14 (October 1950): 231–35.

Ezekiel, Hannan, and Adekunle, Joseph O. "The Secular Behavior of Income Velocity: An International Cross-Section Study." *IMF Staff Papers* 16, no. 2 (July 1969): 224–37.

Fisher, J. Earnest. "Korea Today." *Far Eastern Quarterly* 3, no. 3 (May 1946): 261–71.

Goode, Richard, and Thorn, Richard S. "Variable Reserve Requirements against Commercial Bank Reserves." *IMF Staff Papers* 7, no. 1 (April, 1959): 9–45.

Griffin, K. B., and Enos, J. L. "Foreign Assistance: Objectives and Consequences." *Economic Development and Cultural Change* 18, no. 3 (April 1970): 313–27.

Griliches, Zvi. "Research Costs and Social Returns: Hybrid Corn and Related Innovations." *Journal of Political Economy* 66, no. 5 (October 1958): 419–31.

Healey, Derek T. "Development Policy: New Thinking About an Interpretation." *Journal of Economic Literature* 10, no. 3 (September 1972): 757–97.

Ho, Samuel P. S. "Agricultural Transformation Under Colonialism: The Case of Taiwan." *Journal of Economic History* 28, no. 3 (September 1968): 313–40.

Hong, Young-Pyo. "Agricultural Overpopulation in Korea." *Journal of Population Studies* no. 2 (1966): 3–23. In Korean.

Johnson, D. W., and Chieu, J. S. Y. "The Savings-Income Relation in Underdeveloped and Developed Countries." *Economic Journal* 78 no. 310 (June 1968): 321–33.

Johnston, Bruce F., and Mellor, John W. "The Role of Agriculture in Economic Development." *American Economic Review* 51, no. 4 (Spetember 1961): 566–93.

Kaneda, Hiromitsu. "The Sources and Rates of Productivity Gains in Japanese Agriculture, as Compared with the U.S. Experience." *Journal of Farm Economics* 49, no. 5 (December 1967): 1443–51.

Kaukonen, J. L. "The South Korean Wage Earner Since Liberation." Bureau of Labor Statistics, U.S. Department of Labor. *Monthly Labor Review* 68, no: 4 (April 1949): 401–06.

Keesing, Donald. "Outward Looking Policies and Economic Development." *Economic Journal* 77, no. 306 (June 1967): 303–20.

Krishna, Raj. "Unemployment in India." *Development Processes and Planning* (March 1974), no page nos. (Agricultural Development Council Teaching Forum, no. 38).

Lauterbach, Richard E. "Hodge's Korea." *Virginia Quarterly Review* 23 (1947): 349–68.

Lotz, Jorgen R., and Morss, Elliott R. "Measuring 'Tax Effort' in Developing Countries." *IMF Staff Papers* 14, no. 3 (November 1967): 478–99.

McCune, George M. "Korea: The First Year of Liberation." *Pacific Affairs* 20, no. 1 (March 1947): 3–17.

Macario, Santiago. "Protectionism and Industrialization in Latin America."

Economic Bulletin for Latin America 9, no. 1 (March 1965): 78–81.

Melitz, Jacques, and Correa, Hector. "International Differences in Income Velocity." *Review of Economics and Statistics* 52, no. 1 (February 1970): 12–17.

Myers, Ramon H., and Ching, Adrienne. "Agricultural Development in Taiwan Under Japanese Colonial Rule." *Journal of Asian Studies* 23, no. 4 (August 1964): 555–70.

Norton, Roger D. "Planning with Facts: The Case of Korea." *American Economic Review* 60, no. 2 (May 1970): 59–64.

Oshima, Harry T. "Income Inequality and Economic Growth: The Postwar Experience of Asian Countries." *Malayan Economic Review* 15, no. 2 (October 1970): 7–41.

———. "Labor Absorption in East and Southeast Asia: A Summary with Interpretation of Post-War Experience." *Malayan Economic Review* 16, no. 2 (October 1971): 55–77.

———. "Labor-Force 'Explosion' and the Labor Intensive Sector in Asian Growth." *Economic Development and Cultural Change* 19, no. 2 (January 1971): 161–83.

Papanek, Gustav F. "Aid, Foreign Private Investment, Savings and Growth in Less Developed Countries." *Journal of Political Economy* 81, no. 1 (January–February 1973): 120–30.

Park, Yung Chul. "The Role of Money in Stabilization Policy in Developing Countries." *IMF Staff Papers* 20, no. 2 (July 1973): 379–418.

Polak, J. J. "Monetary Analysis of Income Formation and Payments Problems." *IMF Staff Papers* 6, no. 1 (November 1957): 1–50.

Power, John H. "Import Substitution as an Industrialization Strategy." *Philippine Economic Journal* 5, no. 2 (Second semester, 1966): 167–204.

Ranis, Gustav. "The Financing of Japanese Economic Development." *Economic History Review*. 2nd Series, vol. 11, no. 3 (April 1959): 440–54.

———. "Industrial Sector Labor Absorption." *Economic Development and Cultural Change* 21, no. 3 (April 1973): 387–408.

Renaud, Bertrand S. "Conflicts Between National Growth and Regional Income Equality in a Rapidly Growing Economy: The Case of Korea." *Economic Development and Cultural Change* 21, no. 3 (April 1973): 429–45.

Reynolds, Lloyd G. "Wages and Employment in a Labor-Surplus Economy." *American Economic Review* 55, no. 1 (March 1965): 19–39.

Rosenberg, Nathan. "Capital Goods, Technology, and Economic Growth." *Oxford Economic Papers* New series, vol. 15, no. 3 (November 1963): 217–27.

Sarafan, Bertram D. "Military Government: Korea." *Far Eastern Survey* 15, no. 23 (November 20, 1946): 349–52.

Spey, J. M. "The Peasants of Korea." *Asiatic Review* 47, no. 170 (April 1951): 168–78.

Stentzel, James. "Seoul's Second Bonanza." *Far Eastern Economic Review* (July 30, 1973): 43–44.

Stewart, Frances, and Streeten, Paul. "Conflicts Between Output and Employment Objectives in Developing Countries." *Oxford Economic Papers* 23, no. 2 (July 1971): 145–68.

Taeuber, Irene B. "The Population Potential of Postwar Korea." *Far Eastern*

Quarterly 5, no. 3 (May 1946): 289–307.

Takahashi, Kamekichi. "Protracted War and the Stability of the Japanese Economy." *Central Review* (Chuo Koron). 53, no. 3 (March 1938); translated and reproduced in Institute of Pacific Relations, *Industrial Japan.* New York: Institute of Pacific Relations, 1938.

Tang, Anthony M. "Discussion: U.S. Endeavors to Assist Low-Income Countries [to] Improve Economic Capabilities of Their People." *Journal of Farm Economics* 43, no. 5 (December 1961): 1079–80.

Thorn, Richard S. "Per Capita Income as a Measure of Economic Development." *Zeitschrift fur Nationalokonomie* 28, no. 2 (October 1968): 206–16.

Voivodas, Constantin. "Exports, Foreign Capital Inflow, and South Korean Economic Growth." *Economic Development and Cultural Change* 22, no. 3 (April 1974): 480–84.

Watanabe, Susumu. "Exports and Employment: The Case of the Republic of Korea." *International Labour Review* 106, no. 6 (December 1972): 495–526.

Weeks, John. "A Brief Note on the Unemployment Crisis in Poor Countries." *Manpower and Unemployment Research in Africa* 7, no. 1 (April 1974): 32–33. Newsletter published by the Centre for Developing-Area Studies of McGill University, Montreal.

Wilbur, Martin. "Japan and the Korean Farmers." *Asia* 35, no. 7 (July 1935): 394–97.

Williamson, Jeffrey G. "Capital Accumulation, Labor-Saving, and Labor Absorption Once More." *Quarterly Journal of Economics* 85, no. 1 (February 1971): 40–65.

Wolf, Charles, Jr. "Economic Planning in Korea." *Asian Survey* 2, no. 10 (December 1972): 22–28.

III. OFFICIAL PUBLICATIONS

A. Korean Government

Bank of Korea. *Annual Economic Review, 1948.* (Author varies: Bank of Choson; 1948, 1949; Bank of Korea, 1955 on. Title varies: *Economic Review* or *Annual Economic Review*, 1948–49 and 1955–59). From 1960. annual publication divided into *Economic Statistics Yearbooks* and *Review of Korean Economy.* Seoul: Bank of Korea, 1948 on.

———. *Annual Report.* Seoul.

———. *The Banking System in Korea.* Seoul, 1969.

———. *Economic Statistics Yearbook.* Seoul, 1960 on.

———. *Financial Development Since Interest Rate Refrom.* Seoul, 1970.

———. *Interindustry Relations Tables for 1966.* Seoul, 1968.

———. *Monthly Economic Statistics.* Seoul, April 1969 on.

———. *Monthly Statistical Review.* Seoul, through March 1969.

———. *National Income Statistics Yearbooks.* Seoul.

Economic Planning Board. *Annual Report on the Economically Active Population.* Seoul.

———. *Annual Report on the Current Industrial Production Survey.* Seoul.

———. *Annual Report on the Family Income and Expenditure Survey.* Seoul.

———. *First Five-Year Economic Development Plan (1962–1966): Adjusted*

Version. Seoul, March 1964 (English version).
———. *Korea Statistical Yearbook.* Seoul.
———. *Overall Resources Budget: Second Five-Year Economic Development Plan, 1967–1971.* Seoul, annual since 1967.
Government of the Republic of Korea. *The Second Five-Year Economic Development Plan: 1967–1971.* Seoul, July 1966 (English version).
———. *The Third Five-Year Economic Development Plan: 1972–1976.* Seoul, July 1971 (English version).
Medium Industry Bank. *An Introduction to Small Industries in Korea.* Seoul, 1966.
Ministry of Agriculture and Forestry. *Report on the Results of Farm Household Economy Survey and Production Cost Survey of Agricultural Products.* Seoul.
———. *Yearbook of Agriculture and Forestry Statistics.* Seoul.
Ministry of Transport. "Korea Transportation Survey: Draft Report." 2 vols. Prepared by a World Bank consultative group including the Bureau Central d'Etudes pour les Equipments d'Outre-mer, Societe Francaise d'Etudes et de Realisations Ferroviaires, Netherlands Engineering Consultants, and Netherlands Economic Institute. Seoul, June 1966. Mimeographed.
National Agricultural Cooperative Federation. *Agriculture Yearbooks.* Seoul.
———. *Problems and Means of Improvement of Agricultural Credit in Korea.* Seoul, 1965.
———. *Rural Credit Survey in Korea.* Seoul, 1965.
Office of the Prime Minister. *Evaluation Report of the Second Year Program: The Third Five-Year Economic Development Plan.* Seoul, 1974.
Republic of Korea. *Summary of the First Five-Year Economic Plan: 1962–1966.* Seoul, 1962. English version.

B. Other Government and International Organizations

Agricultural Economics Research Institute (Ministry of Agriculture and Forestry), and Department of Agricultural Economics, Michigan State University. *Korean Agricultural Sector Analysis and Recommended Development Strategies, 1971–1985.* Seoul: United States Agency for International Development/Korea, 1972.
Asian Development Bank. *Changing Trade Patterns and Opportunities in Industrial Exports.* Occasional Paper no. 3. Manila: October 1970.
Bank of Japan. *Hundred-Year Statistics of the Japanese Economy.* Tokyo: Bank of Japan, 1966.
Organization for Economic Cooperation and Development. *National Accounts of Less Developed Countries.* Paris, July 1968.
United Nations. *Demographic Yearbook,* New York.
———. *Journal of Development Planning,* no. 1. New York, 1969.
———. *Monthly Statistical Bulletin.* New York.
———. *A Study of Industrial Growth.* New York, 1963.
———. *Yearbook of National Accounts Statistics.* New York.
United Nations, Economic Commission for Asia and the Far East. *Economic Survey of Asia and the Far East, 1966.* Bangkok, 1967.
———, ———. *The Planning and Financing of Social Development in the*

ECAFE Region. Revised version of the fourth *Review of the Social Situation in the ECAFE Region*, E/CN.11/1.288, ECAFE Social Development series no. 1. No place, 1969.

United Nations, Economic Commission for Asia and the Far East, and Bureau of Technical Assistance Operations. *The Role and Application of Electric Power in the Industrialization of Asia and the Far East*. Bangkok, 1965.

United Nations, Food and Agriculture Organization. *The Response of Rice to Fertilizer*. FAO Agricultural Studies no. 70, by J. J. Doyle. Rome, 1966.

————. *The State of Food and Agriculture*. Rome. Annual.

United Nations, Korean Reconstruction Agency. *An Economic Programme for Korean Reconstruction*. New York: United Nations Korean Reconstruction Agency, 1954.

United Nations, Korean Reconstruction Agency, and Food and Agricultural Organization. *Rehabilitation and Development of Agriculture, Forestry, and Fisheries in South Korea*. New York: Columbia University Press, 1954.

United States, Department of Agriculture. Economic Research Service. *Changing Food Consumption Patterns in the Republic of Korea*. ERS Foreign no. 306. Washington, D.C., December 1970.

United States, Operations Mission to Korea (USOM/K). "Growth Prospects in Manufacturing." Seoul, November 1965. Mimeographed.

————. "Revised Foodgrain Production and Consumption for 1962–1964, and Projections to 1971." Seoul, December 1965. Mimeographed.

————. "Rural Development Program Evaluation Report: Korea, 1967." Seoul. Mimeographed.

————, and the University of Wisconsin. "Study of Agricultural Cooperatives in Korea: National Agricultural Cooperative Federation." Seoul: U.S. Operations Mission, March 1966.

Index

Agency for International Development (AID), 139

Agriculture: cadastral survey, 15–16; capital inputs, 134; comparison with Formosa (Taiwan), 18, 47; compulsory grain collection, 30; credit, 136, 140–42; crops, 14, 130; cultivated area, 14, 21, 133; domestic product share of, 56, 80, 87, 128; domestic supply, 146; East Asian production increases compared, 129; education for, 143; effects of imports on, 138, 143–45; elasticities of demand for food, 61, 145–46; employment, 13, 52; farm parity index, 136; fertilizer inputs, 30, 134–35; food imports, 71, 146–47; food prices, 129; food shortages, 30; government policies, 135–36; grain-fertilizer exchange program, 139; impact of war on, 27; investment share, 68; irrigation, 133–34; labor absorption in, 120–21; labor-force share, 56; labor inputs, 131–33; mechanization, 138–39; physical setting, 130; postliberation history, 129–30; production, 47, 129; productivity, 13–16 passim, 30; research and extension, 136–37, 142–43; rice exports, 14, 22; Rice Production Increase Plans, 15; self-sufficiency in, 146–48, 199, 206, 208, 210–11; utilization ratios, 16, 133. *See also* Aid, from United States; Land ownership; Private consumption

Aid, from United States: Civilian Relief in Korea (CRIK) program, 38; Economic Cooperation Administration (ECA) Korean program, 32, 35–36; Government Relief in Occupied Areas (GAROIA), 31; military support, 105, 109; omission of military component from national accounts, 65; U.S. Public Law 480 (PL 480) imports, 77, 103, 138, 144–45; U.S. share of Korean imports, 73–74; wheat shipments' effect on labor costs, 103. *See also* American Military Government

Allen, Horace, 6

American Military Government (AMG): aid under ECA, 32, 35–36; economic and political problems for, 28–34, 89–90; education role, 33; emergency relief, 31; grain collection program, 30; land distribution, 30–31; vested property disposal, 31–32, 35. *See also* Aid, from United States

Asian Development Bank (ADB), 162

Balance of payments: components of, 71; crises and import restrictions in the early *1960*s, 151; debt servicing and, 74–75; deficits during the early *1970*s, 99–101, 104; foreign savings offset trade deficits, 77; growing food imports and, 146–47; harvest failures and, 203; negative trade balance, 59, 74; plan targets for, 201; within Yen Bloc, 12–13

Ban, Sung-whan, 16

Bank of Korea (BOK), 48, 78, 141, 158, 181–93 passim

Capital formation: accelerated growth and high rates of, 67; aggregate plan

Economic Growth Center Book Publications

Werner Baer, *Industrialization and Economic Development in Brazil* (1965).

Werner Baer and Isaac Kerstenetzky, eds., *Inflation and Growth in Latin America* (1964).

Bela A. Balassa, *Trade Prospects for Developing Countries* (1964). Out of print.

Albert Berry and Miguel Urrutia, *Income Distribution in Columbia* (1976).

Thomas B. Birnberg and Stephen A. Resnick, *Colonial Development: An Econometric Study* (1975).

Benjamin I. Cohen, *Multinational Firms and Asian Exports* (1975).

Carlos F. Díaz Alejandro, *Essays on the Economic History of the Argentine Republic* (1970).

Robert Evenson and Yoav Kislev, *Agricultural Research and Productivity* (1975).

John C. H. Fei and Gustav Ranis, *Development of Labor Surplus Economy: Theory and Policy* (1964).

Gerald K. Helleiner, *Peasant Agriculture, Government, and Economic Growth in Nigeria* (1966).

Lawrence R. Klein and Kazushi Ohkawa, eds., *Economic Growth: The Japanese Experience since the Meiji Era* (1968).

Paul W. Kuznets, *Economic Growth and Structure in the Republic of Korea* (1977).

A. Lamfalussy, *The United Kingdom and the Six* (1963). Out of print.

Markos J. Mamalakis, *The Growth and Structure of the Chilean Economy: From Independence to Allende* (1976).

Markos J. Mamalakis and Clark W. Reynolds, *Essays on the Chilean Economy* (1965).

Donald C. Mead, *Growth and Structural Change in the Egyptian Economy* (1967).

Richard Moorsteen and Raymond P. Powell, *The Soviet Capital Stock* (1966).

Douglas S. Paauw and John C. H. Fei, *The Transition in Open Dualistic Economies: Theory and Southeast Asian Experience* (1973).

Howard Pack, *Structural Change and Economic Policy in Israel* (1971).

Frederick L. Pryor, *Public Expenditures in Communist and Capitalist Nations* (1968).

Gustav Ranis, ed., *Government and Economic Development* (1971).

Clark W. Reynolds, *The Mexican Economy: Twentieth-Century Structure and Growth* (1970).

Lloyd G. Reynolds, ed., *Agriculture in Development Theory* (1975).

Lloyd G. Reynolds and Peter Gregory, *Wages, Productivity, and Industrialization in Puerto Rico* (1965).

Donald R. Snodgrass, *Ceylon: An Export Economy in Transition* (1966).